The American Social Experience Series
GENERAL EDITOR: JAMES KIRBY MARTIN
EDITORS: PAULA S. FASS,
STEVEN H. MINTZ, CARL PRINCE,
JAMES W. REED & PETER N. STEARNS

*1. The March to the Sea and Beyond:
Sherman's Troops in the Savannah
and Carolinas Campaigns*
JOSEPH T. GLATTHAAR

*2. Childbearing in American Society:
1650–1850*
CATHERINE M. SCHOLTEN

*3. The Origins of Behaviorism: American
Psychology, 1870–1920*
JOHN M. O'DONNELL

4. New York City Cartmen, 1667–1850
GRAHAM RUSSELL HODGES

*5. From Equal Suffrage to Equal Rights:
Alice Paul and the National Woman's
Party, 1910–1928*
CHRISTINE A. LUNARDINI

*6. Mr. Jefferson's Army:
Political and Social Reform of the
Military Establishment, 1801–1809*
THEODORE J. CRACKEL

MR. JEFFERSON'S ARMY

*Political and Social Reform of
the Military Establishment, 1801–1809*

THEODORE J. CRACKEL

NEW YORK UNIVERSITY PRESS
NEW YORK AND LONDON
1987

Copyright © 1987 by New York University
All rights reserved
Manufactured in the United States of America

Library of Congress Cataloging-in-Publication Data

Crackel, Theodore J.
Mr. Jefferson's army.

(The American social experience series ; 6)
Bibliography: p.
Includes index.
1. United States. Army—History—19th century.
2. Civil-military relations—United States—History—
19th century. 3. Jefferson, Thomas, 1743–1826—Contri-
butions in civil-military relations. 4. United States—
History—1801–1809. I. Title. II. Title: Mister
Jefferson's army. III. Series.
UA25.C73 1987 335'.033573'0924 87-10721
ISBN 0-8147-1407-2

Book design by Ken Venezio

To my sons

Contents

List of Illustrations, Maps, Tables, and Figures   ix

Preface   xi

Introduction   1

1. Mr. Hamilton's Army, 1798–1800   17

2. A Chaste Reformation   36

3. The Founding of West Point   54

4. A More Republican Establishment   74

5. The Army in the Field   98

6. General Wilkinson's Army   123

7. Mr. Jefferson's Army   158

Conclusion   180

Notes   185

Bibliography   225

Index   245

List of Illustrations, Maps, Tables, and Figures

Illustrations

Alexander Hamilton by John Trumbull   20
Thomas Jefferson by Cornelius Tiebout   37
Henry Dearborn by Charles Willson Peale   41
Barracks at West Point, artist unknown   63
Jonathan Williams by Thomas Sully   67
William A. Barron, artist unknown   68
Thomas Jefferson by Thomas Sully   72
Henry Dearborn by Saint-Memin   75
Fort Washington, on the Site of Cincinnati   89
Raising the Flag at New Orleans by T. de Thulstrup   105
Thomas Butler by Jose de Salazar   117
Colonel Keldermaster in his Coffin by Felix Darley   119
James Wilkinson by Charles Willson Peale   127
Aaron Burr by John Vanderlyn   132
Samuel Smith by Gilbert Stuart   140
John Randolph by John Wesley Jarvis   165
James Wilkinson by John Wesley Jarvis   167

Maps

U. S. Military Posts, 1798–1809   99
Western Military Posts   125

Tables

Table 2.1 Discharges in the Reduction, June 1, 1802   50
Table 7.1 Jeffersonian Appointments in the Army   176

Figures

Figure 7.1 Officer Strength, 1801–9   174
Figure 7.2 Political Distribution of Officers, 1801–9   175

Preface

In the course of conceiving, researching, and writing this work, I have incurred more debts of gratitude than I can immediately repay. In its conceptual phase, the theme of this book first came together in a paper delivered at the 1977 Missouri Valley Historical Conference in Omaha, Nebraska. That concept matured in papers, articles, a dissertation, and finally this book—but always with the encouragement of Richard H. Kohn, a scholar and friend, whose enthusiasm for this project provided repeated encouragement.

The initial research necessary for this work was made possible by Brigadier General Thomas E. Griess (USA, Retired), then Chairman and Head of the Department of History, United States Military Academy at West Point, who allowed me a year on the Dean's Research Faculty and helped obtain support from the academy's Faculty Development and Research Fund. My debt to General Griess, however, extends beyond his professional interest in my work and includes the many personal kindnesses shown me by this fine soldier, scholar, and gentleman.

In the end, however, I am most indebted to a patient teacher—a scholar whose interests are truly catholic—and firm friend, Rudolph M. Bell of Rutgers, who furnished encouragement and exhortation as each proved necessary over the years.

I also owe thanks to John W. Chambers and Thomas P. Slaughter whose penetrating and challenging critiques helped shape this work. In addition, I am indebted to other scholars who shared their own work with me and invited my criticism. Exchanges with Lawrence D. Cress, and with James Kirby Martin and Mark E. Lender, materially helped me sharpen the focus of my own work.

At West Point, Robert Schnare, Director of Special Collections, U. S. Military Academy Library, was both good-natured and resourceful in supporting my unending resarch needs. At a more advanced stage, Colonel Donald Shaw, Director of the U. S. Army Military History Institute at Carlisle Barracks, made the resources of that institution available to me. To both of them, and to their able and kind staffs, particularly Marie Capps of West Point, and John Slonaker, Dennis Vetuck and Louise Arnold of Carlisle, I am greatly indebted.

I am also grateful for the help and consideration of the staffs of the other libraries and depositories visited: the Manuscripts Division, Clements Library of the University of Michigan, Ann Arbor; the Manuscripts Collection, Lilly Library of Indiana University, Bloomington; the Indiana Historical Society Library, Indianapolis; the Joseph Regenstein Library of the University of Chicago; the Research Collections of the Chicago Historical Society; the Newberry Library, Chicago; the Archives Division of the State Historical Society of Wisconsin, Madison; the Library and Archives of the Missouri Historical Society, St. Louis; the St. Louis Mercantile Library Association; the Archives of the Filson Club, Louisville, Kentucky; the Kentucky State Library and the Library of the Kentucky Historical Society, Frankfort; Special Collections of the University of Kentucky Library, Lexington; the Tennessee State Library and Archives, and the Tennessee Historical Society, Nashville; the Archives-Manuscript Division of the Ohio Historical Society, Colombus; the Cincinnati Historical Society; the Darlington Memorial Library of the University of Pittsburgh; the Archives of the Historical Society of Western Pennsylvania, Pittsburgh; the Historical Society of Berks County, Reading, Pennsylvania; the Manuscripts Department of the Historical Society of Pennsylvania, Philadelphia; the Library Company of Philadelphia; the Library of the American Philosophical Society, Philadelphia; the Library of the Maine Historical Society, Portland; the Archives of the New Hampshire Historical Society, Concord; Special Collections of

Norwich University, Northfield, Vermont; the Library of the Vermont Historical Society, Montpelier; the Department of Rare Books and Manuscripts of the Boston Public Library; the Library of the Massachusetts Historical Society, Boston; the Library of the American Antiquarian Society, Worchester, Massachusetts; Sterling Memorial Library of Yale University, New Haven; the Library of the Sleepy Hollow Restorations, Tarrytown, New York; Special Collections of the New York Public Library; the Archives of the New-York Historical Society; the Manuscripts Department, Alderman Library of the University of Virginia, Charlottesville; the Archives and Records Division of the Virginia State Library, Richmond; the Library of the Virginia Historical Society, Richmond; the Manuscript Department, Perkins Library of Duke University, Durham, North Carolina; and the Southern Historical Collection, Wilson Library of the University of North Carolina at Chapel Hill. This list would not be complete without special mention of particular help given by the staffs of the various manuscripts divisions of the National Archives and Library of Congress.

Thanks also to the staffs of those libraries which I could not visit, but who nonetheless made the effort to search their collections for materials I might use: the Huntington Library, San Marino; the University of Georgia Library, Athens; the University of Missouri Library, Columbia; and the Western Reserve Historical Society, Cleveland, Ohio.

Chapters two and three contain material that was earlier presented in a paper and two articles, the product of a research year at West Point. A portion of chapter two was first given as a paper in 1979 at the annual conference of the Society of Historians of the Early American Republic at Annapolis, and later appeared as "Jefferson, Politics, and the Army: An Examination of the Military Peace Establishment Act of 1802," in the *Journal of the Early Republic* (April 1982). A portion of chapter three appeared as an article, "The Founding of West Point: Jefferson and the Politics of Security," in *Armed Forces and Society* (Summer 1981). My thanks to the editors of those journals for allowing me to borrow portions of those pieces for use here.

The errors or omissions herein are entirely my responsibility, as are the central themes that define this work. In all else, I share with many others any credit which may accrue.

Introduction

"On the surface, Thomas Jefferson seems all sunlight and clarity," wrote the modern scholar, Henry F. May. "But," he added, "those who have tried to get far beyond this glowing surface have found themselves in a difficult tangle of contradictions and complexities."[1] Historians' renderings of Jefferson's relationship with the military establishment are a case in point. On the surface the construct is simple: Jefferson, out of fear of a standing army and with a republican regard for economy, reduced the regular force, and then consigned it to a distant frontier while trusting the defense of the nation to the militia he had always preferred.[2] "I am," he wrote in 1799, "for relying, for internal defense, on our militia solely, till actual invasion . . . and not for a standing army in time of peace."[3]

But beneath the surface lay paradox and contradiction. His creation of a military school at West Point—the quintessence of that regular army which he supposedly detested—cannot be made to fit this mold. It was a "Hamiltonian institution created by Jefferson"; it was "a curious turn of the wheel"—"ironical"—that Jefferson should create such a school, wrote historians.[4] Neither can that construct account for his dramatic expansion of the army in 1808 (for a conflict that he fully intended to avoid) or for the Republican failure to oppose it. When the Federalists had expanded the army in 1798–99, ostensibly to meet a similar foreign threat, their action had attracted the full weight of

Republican fury and opposition. Few raised the cry against standing armies in 1808—and "the Republican party," as Henry Adams noted, "found itself poorer by the loss of one more traditional principle."[5]

The old paradigm—defined by a Republican fear of a standing army, a preference for militia, and concerns for economy—cannot explain Jefferson's superintendence of the military. Mary P. Adams's study of Jefferson's frontier military policy clearly established Jefferson's close attention to these affairs. She "confounded the conventional wisdom on the subject," wrote Marshall Smelser, "by troubling to read military archives instead of drawing deductions from Jefferson's reputation for military idiocy."[6]

This study argues that his attention to the affairs of the military establishment was not only extensive, but structured and purposeful—not paradoxical. In Jefferson's reasoned universe, his management of the military establishment—including the creation of a military academy and the rapid enlargement of the army—would have conformed to a conscious, rational design. This study sketches out a new, more adequate paradigm in which to consider his actions.

I

In the process of researching and writing this story of Thomas Jefferson's relations with the army, it became obvious that my findings were inconsistent with long-held views of Republican attitudes. That not only forced me to reconsider the evidence, but to reexamine the premises on which many earlier interpretations were based.

Upon examination it became clear that the findings of a number of modern historians have fallen well outside the traditional interpretive framework. The old view had at its core the conviction that Jefferson and his Republican followers subscribed rather uniformly and faithfully to a clutch of Whiglike, antiarmy sentiments. Evidence is mounting that calls this view into question. Detailed studies of the years leading up to the Revolution have detected little evidence of the Whiggish antimilitarism so often portrayed. Republicanism, one scholar concluded, was "too complex a body of thought" to be described merely in negative terms—particularly in matters concerning the military.[7] Though, in the years immediately following the Revolution, there was opposition to the formation of a regular establishment—as there was to enlarging the regular force a few years later—that opposition was not as pervasive as often portrayed. Republican diversity of mind on the issue was sometimes masked by the temporary necessity for unity in the face of Federalist hostility, but after Jefferson took office in 1801, party members seldom evidenced the prejudices so often said to characterize them. A small but vocal minority led by John Randolph of Roanoke did continue to repeat old antiarmy lines, but they increasingly stood alone—on this issue and others.[8]

Recent works on the colonial experience have raised considerable doubt about the extent of any deep-seated anxieties concerning standing armies. There was little evidence, these studies found, of any broad concern among the colonists regarding the British regulars who were stationed among them until those troops were sent to Boston to still trouble that had begun before their arrival there. On the frontier— even in New York City—there had been little concern.[9] Troops and warfare had been an accepted, though usually temporary, way of life. "Enlightenment concepts attacking war did not strike a responsive cord" in the colonies, argues John E. Ferling. "Americans," he asserts, "lived in an environment of considerable violence" which "perhaps rendered [them] psychologically eager for conflict."[10] That is not to say that in late eighteenth-century America there was no opposition to things military. There were repeated and sometimes vocal charges that standing armies were a threat to civil liberties. But, as Lawrence Cress has shown, these protests "do not represent a fundamental antimilitaristic strain in American culture." The linkage between standing armies and the destruction of liberties in Republican ideology, Cress points out, lay not in any inherent evil in armies, but in ministerial conspiracy, moral corruption, and political oppression. It was not armies *per se* that Republicans feared, but an army loyal to incorrect political principles—an army of lower-class ragamuffins led by upper-class Federalists.[11]

Much has been made of the reluctance of the Confederation congresses to create a regular force, but that situation changed so rapidly under the new governmental forms of 1789 that the earlier years appear an anomaly. Under the provisions of the new Constitution, the Congress brought the existing force of about 800 men under its control, as a regular establishment. Early the next year that force was expanded to over 1,200. A year later the force was again enlarged—to over 2,100. Not since the proposals of Washington and Hamilton in 1783 had such numbers of regular troops been seriously contemplated. Only a few years earlier such expansion would have been impossible.

With the end of hostilities in 1783 came the necessity of creating new peacetime institutions and forms—military as well as civil. Some believed that the time had come to disestablish the army. It was, they said, inherently dangerous to republican institutions. Locally organized militiamen, they argued, would be better able to resist the ambitions of a central political authority. In the years between 1783 and 1788, a handful of men—a few doctrinaire republicans like Elbridge Gerry, but most more guided by parochial interests—successfully resisted the creation of a viable military force under the Confederation.

Those who opposed the army were a distinct minority—but, the rules of voting under the Articles of Confederation favored them, allowing even a small minority to impede progress on vital issues.[12] A majority of delegates and delegations regularly voted to retain some regular establishment. They were defeated at each turn by a minority in opposition that included New York—whose concerns stemmed not from ideology but from contested claims to western lands—and (for a time) Massachusetts and New Hampshire where opposition was rooted in different, but equally parochial matters.[13] Of course, the group did include a small number of doctrinaire republicans, led by Elbridge Gerry, who opposed on principle any attempt to give the new federal government the authority to raise a military force. This eclectic group, though always in the minority, blocked all movement toward a permanent regular force under the Confederation.[14]

The majority, however, recognized the necessity of garrisoning at least the distant western posts with a regular force. Some, like Jefferson, accepted the necessity of a small regular force, but would have preferred some constitutional means of limiting its size. When it proved impracticable, they took comfort in "the idea that a republic would be secure from [the] abusive potential of standing armies as long as the decision to raise troops remained the prerogative of the representative branch of government."[15] Though the majority conceded the principle of using regulars—on the frontiers in particular—there was still concern about the mischief an army could be put to if allowed to exceed the number for which there was some explicit utility. Such an army could become the instrument of an ambitious national government. Still, rather than oppose all regular forces, they by and large looked to a free press and the local militia as counterweights. "Even a standing army . . . as numerous as the abilities of any nation could maintain, would not be equal to the purpose of despotism over an enlightened people."[16]

Central to any understanding of early American attitudes toward the military is an appreciation of the faith many seemed to place in the militia. There is more than a little irony here—or seemingly so—for this reverence for the militia developed in the face of considerable evidence of its inadequacies.

This glorification of the militia—the myth of the citizen-soldier—is a central theme of Charles Royster's *A Revolutionary People at War*.[17] In the beginning, Royster argues, there was a *rage militaire*—the standard of 1775: "Every breast had felt military ardor and every lip had spoken words of self-sacrifice.'" This implied a rejection of regulars, and suggested more explicitly that native courage could obviate discipline; that a willingness to die for liberty could insure it; that traditional American skills—the sure aim of the frontier riflemen—could overcome trained regulars; that a haphazard conjoining of citizen soldiers in an "Army of Israel" could impose their will on the British; and that Americans everywhere were ready to sacrifice for the struggle.[18]

Time and experience revealed the distance between ideal and reality. In their ideology, the regular army was "only ancillary to the revolution." The reality was quite different; a regular force had been essential to victory. Their experience was at odds with their vision.[19]

In Royster's view, accommodating that dilemma required the rejection of the regular force as a legitimate legacy of the war: the denial and disbandment of the army at war's end; and the abrogation of promised pay and pensions. To acknowledge that Americans could not have maintained their independence "in the absence of a trained and regulated army would have conceded the collapse of public virtue." Few had lived up to the demands of the *rage militaire* of 1775, yet in victory they fabricated a myth that would "enable a whole generation to claim that their strength had been proven" and allow them "to bequeath the standard and example to posterity."[20]

But, Royster's construct works better as a rhetorical than as a motive device. It helps us understand how the glorification of the militia was rationalized, but not what prompted it. This was hardly the first generation to experience a "collapse of public virtue"—nor would it be the last. For most, in fact, this was the steady state of affairs. This factious self-interest or lack of public virtue was a natural human frailty. James Madison thought it one of "the diseases most incident to republican government."[21] Yet, in *The Federalist, No. 10*, he portrayed it as a stabilizing feature—self-interested factions would balance self-interested factions; none would be able to achieve a majority or overwhelm the whole. To Madison, the new Constitution provided a republican remedy that assumed inadequate public virtue and took advantage of it. In his lexicon there was no need to accommodate the failure to live up to the *rage militaire*. Royster's argument is unpersuasive in this context.

Still, in seeking a motive for the rejection of the experience of the revolution—the rejection of the regular army—Royster's work is helpful. "In the eyes of critics," he writes, "the [regular army] officers' worst crime was . . . their claim to social distinction based on superior revolutionary merit."[22] Fearing that the former officers sought position and power through such pretensions, the critics attacked both the commutation of officers' pensions and the officers' creation of the exclusive Society of Cincinnati. Those who had not served had no intention of conceding any special merit or place to those who had, for that might translate into political leverage.

The evidence strongly suggests that the citizen-soldier and militia myth—implicitly denying any special distinction to the officers of the regular army—arose from a fear (in those without service in the long-suffering Continental Line) that such honor might confer unnatural social and political advantages. Those outside the military coterie could only assure their status if they could insure themselves as much "revolutionary merit" as the former officers—and deny any special recognition to the latter. Men outside the military bonds, who suddenly saw their political placement jeopardized, argued that the revolution had been begun in order to supplant one class of privileged placement; they had no intention now of creating another. The former military men, they feared, aimed to "divide among themselves and their friends, every place of Honour and of profit."[23]

The Revolution had brought a new order. Political mobility had been achieved through rebellion and the boundaries surrounding office holding had become more flexible. Those that had benefited sought to preserve their gains.[24] Men who had begun life in humble circumstances had bettered themselves in the civil (not military) arena had no intention of seeing barriers erected or preferments offered which might exclude them.[25]

Jefferson reviewed objections to the Cincinnati for fellow Virginian, George Washington. It degraded the republican emphasis on talent and merit, he argued, and replaced them with connection and favor; it honored only one class of the citizens, the former officers. "A distinction is kept up," he pointed out, "between the civil and military, which it is for the happiness of both to obliterate." In his investigation, he reported, he was able to find only one nonmilitary member of the Congress who did not oppose it.[26]

The civilian leaders—who might, when compared with the former Continental officers, have appeared less valorous, less patriotic, or even less capable—solved their problem simply "by claiming that they had actually been there all along, all evidence to the contrary notwithstanding."[27] Though a blatantly political maneuver, it worked because it had broad, popular appeal. It redefined the experience for the vast majority, who had served (at best) in ancillary ways. It made their contribution seem as heroic as it ought to have been. They thus insured that there would be no superior claims, against which their own political gains might be sacrificed.

Revealingly, despite the apparent concern, the issue was resolved almost as soon as it was raised. The former officers, it turned out, evidenced no desire for any exclusive hold on the political process. The membership of the Cincinnati, for example, readily agreed that the visible marks of service—the eagle badge and ribbon—would be worn in public only at their own conventions and at funerals. These symbols of superior service would not become fixtures in the new nation's political contests. With that, opposition largely abated.[28] At the same time—and possibly because the "political" issue was resolved—controversy over commutation disappeared from public debate. Says Royster, "they just quit talking about it."[29] If former service was not to be a political asset, it was not to be an issue.

What survived was the myth of the citizen-soldier militia, for once propounded it had a popular appeal that was regularly refreshed by the loquacious patriot orators. Moreover, it was to have continued political utility. It complemented the historic Whig opposition to standing armies and, thereby, the prejudices of the more radical republicans. Still, most of the political leaders of the age understood it for what it was: a myth with substantial powers of persuasion, but a myth nonetheless. "Our Leaders flatter the People by declaiming against standing Armies, and pretending to believe that the Militia is the best Security of a Nation" wrote Charles Nisbet, president of Dickinson College in Carlisle, Pennsylvania, "but they are not in earnest, and their own Experience may convince them of the futility of this Notion."[30]

One did not have to be a senior officer of the Continental Line to appreciate the limitations of the popular militia. Jefferson, for example, had had ample opportunity to assess their qualities while governor of Virginia. He found them unreliable. Moreover, they could neither be sent a long distance from their homes, nor kept in armies any significant period of time.[31] For such service he preferred regular troops. Regulars, he told the Virginia legislature, might be burdensome, but "no possible mode . . . can be so expensive to the public and so distressing and disgusting to the individuals as by militia."[32]

By 1790 the militia had lost its status as a viable military institution, but it had retained its symbolic role as the guarantor of republican liberties. Few Americans now rejected the right of the civil government to raise regular forces for extended hostilities; and most accepted the idea that the nation was secured against the potential abuse of standing armies so long as the power to raise (and disestablish) troops lay with the representative branch of government. Some, like Elbridge Gerry, clung to the view that the military clauses of the Constitution were but a first step toward the end of republican institutions, and predicted the inevitable rise of tyrannical government behind the strength of a standing army. Most, however, rejected that view. Even among those who would soon coalesce as the new Republican party, only a small fraction shared Gerry's apocalyptic vision.[33]

II

For a more than a decade after the Revolution, Alexander Hamilton and others had argued that the only way to avoid war was through military strength and preparedness. These views were refined in the debates over the proposed federal Constitution in 1788, and were reflected in that document. Its adoption represented a victory for the majority, who were convinced that some regular army, levied by the central government, was essential. Nonetheless, though the new forms they adopted sanctioned this army, there was much less agreement on its proper extent.

The defeats in the West of Josiah Harmar's forces in 1790 and of Arthur St. Clair the next year demonstrated the inadequacy of a policy that kept the number of regulars small and forced reliance on inexperienced conscripts and militia. Henry Knox, the Secretary of War, and Washington concluded that the performance of the militia and levies in 1790 and 1791 showed the necessity for more regular troops. Jefferson's first reaction to St. Clair's defeat was to blame the regulars and to hope that the affair would force the government to "confide more in Militia operations." However, after learning that the militia had broken and run, he raised no further objection to the administration's plan for a stronger force of regulars.[34]

The administration concluded that they must now attack the northwestern tribes and establish more forts to protect the progress of settlement. In January 1792, Washington sent a request to Congress for four new regiments of regular infantry, a regiment of riflemen, and a battalion each of artillery and cavalry. The total, over 5,000 men costing more than one million dollars annually, was substantially greater in size and cost than any previous establishment since the Revolution. After a two-week, secret debate, the House voted 29–19 to create the new force. The bill passed the Senate in similarly short order. What opposition there had been centered on administration policy and the western war, not on the issue of a larger regular force; the division was sectional—the middle and southern states versus those of the northeast.

In many respects the first four months of 1792 marked the inception of a regular, national military establishment in the United States. During this period Congress endorsed an administration decision to fight the Indian war with regulars and moved to enlarge that force. At the same time the administration reorganized the force into a legionary system and replaced St. Clair with Anthony Wayne.[35]

Also, at this watershed, the nation effectively—and rather heedlessly—disposed of the militia system, though quite the opposite seemed to be the case. The Uniform Militia Act of 1792 created a massive militia force—requiring all able-bodied white male citizens from eighteen through forty-five to enroll and arm themselves. Yet, nothing in the law insured either adequate training, or uniformity of structure or equipment. Nor were provisions made (or would there ever be) for enforcing any national guidelines.

The militia act clearly illustrates the two different levels on which the myth of the citizen-soldier worked. On the one hand there was the *rhetoric*—the oft-repeated preference for a militia and fear of a standing army. On the other there was the *reality*—the unwillingness to create an effective militia and the repeated reliance on regular or volunteer forces. Even at the state level, where concerns over the power of central government should have been no hindrance, the militias were not perfected, or even improved. Washington did find some utility for this body in western Pennsylvania against the Whiskey rebels, but there too they proved unable even to march without undisciplined incident. Federalist and Republican administrations alike discovered that they had to find a more reliable source of military manpower. Volunteer units provided that alternative and became the traditional adjunct to America's regular military establishment.

In February 1793, Great Britain, Holland, and Spain joined the struggle against the French Revolution. The conflict inevitably impinged on American trading interests in Europe and the West Indies. In April, President Washington proclaimed neutrality, but the British ignored that act and authorized the seizure and preemptive purchase of American cargoes bound for ports in France or French colonies. British naval officers acted with dispatch and seized some 300 American vessels, mostly in the West Indies—virtually paralyzing American shipping. This, coming on the heels of frontier incidents which had been actively encouraged by the British Governor-General in Canada, brought an outraged cry in America for war.

In 1793 and 1794, Washington and his administration reacted with warlike preparations—and in the process, helped define the growing rift between political factions.[36] Coastal fortifications and harbor defenses were begun, a corps of engineers and artillerists was created to man them. Naval vessels were planned, and new arsenals and armories were created for the manufacture and storage of weapons and equipment. In the emerging Republican faction, however, there were those who were suspicious of Federalist motives in these preparations. This could be, James Monroe wrote, "the commencement of a military establishment"—something more than an army only to garrison and protect the nation's several frontiers. This establishment, he feared, could be one modeled on "the Engl[is]h standard"—a standing army whose loyalty was to the Crown not the people.[37]

In the midst of all this, western Pennsylvania farmers began to chafe at the excise that had been placed on whiskey (in part, to pay for the enlarged establishment) and broke into near rebellion in July 1794. After some delay, Washington called out a militia force of some 12,000 men and marched them westward.[38] Resistance melted in the face of this massive army. While a few chafed at the administration's use of force, most (including Republicans) supported the President's moves. There was little to object to. The press of both parties had generally opposed the rebels, and Republicans had competed with Federalists for places on the militia rolls.

When the threat of war with Great Britain diminished—and after Wayne's victory at Fallen Timbers in August 1794—Republicans began to argue for reductions in the army. By 1796, Henry Dearborn's study of frontier requirements and Albert Gallatin's report on finances had given Republicans the facts they needed to argue persuasively for reductions—though these were arguments based on utility and expense, not ideology.[39] Debates over the future of the army ebbed and flowed, but the net result was a force adequate only for essential frontier duty and coastal defense.

The last years of the eighteenth century produced one of the most decisive crises in the new nation's experience—a crisis that had a pro-

found effect on Jefferson's later management of the military establishment. Precipitated by troubled relations with France—and marked by
the XYZ affair, the Alien and Sedition Acts, and the Quasi-war—
events of the period convinced each of the newly forming political
parties that the other was diverging from the true legacy of the Revolution, and therefore becoming a dangerous and illegitimate opposition.[40]

During the decade of the 1790s temporary political alliances began
to give way to more highly disciplined and organized parties. However, this first party system differed from later systems in a quite
fundamental sense—neither new party recognized the legitimacy of
the other's opposition.[41] The catalyst for much of this domestic turmoil was the Revolution in France, the Jacobin excesses that accompanied it, and the larger European conflict it provoked. Attitudes toward
the new French regime mobilized parochial and partisan prejudices in
America to a point where civil strife threatened and where the Union
seemed endangered.

In the spring of 1798, talk of a French-influenced conspiracy at
home and the possibility of United States involvement in the war
abroad raced through Philadelphia and the nation. This worked to the
advantage of the incumbent Federalists. Pressures for Federalist pro-
grams, including a larger regular military establishment, became almost irresistible. Still, Republicans feared the ultimate result of this.
The true motive, they believed, was to crush domestic opposition.
Their fears seemed confirmed when, in June and July, the Federalists
pushed through a series of Alien and Sedition Acts aimed quite explicitly at silencing the political opposition.[42] "To remove our danger," one Federalist orator told his audience, "we must remove divisions, jealousies, and suspicions . . . , we must silence slanderers,
and set our faces against them."[43] When it became clear that the newly
enlarged army was to be an explicitly partisan force—an arm of the
Federalist terror—Republican fears and objections were exacerbated.
Lacking legitimacy, opposition seemingly invited attack.

This crisis in American politics ended with the election of Jefferson
in 1800, but even this did not signal any new understanding of, or
sympathy for the concept of a "loyal" opposition. In his inaugural
address Jefferson called for tolerance, but tolerance that would allow

Republican reason to prevail over wrongminded opposition. Still, implicit in his address was the idea that there could be only one right-minded, loyal view—"brethren of the same principle."

Taking the reins of a government so recently in the hands of his opponents presented Jefferson with a number of unique problems. His was not to be a government cut from whole cloth; Jefferson inherited an ongoing establishment. These were men (and institutions) who considered him a part of an illegitimate opposition—and whom he in turn had counted illegitimate. The fact of the election and transfer of power did not eradicate that. Upon entering the presidency, Jefferson began immediately to address the implication of this. Carl Prince's study of his removal of Federalists in the civil service, and Richard Ellis's examination of the courts, documented his efforts in those areas.[44]

The army was equally as much a partisan stronghold as any civil branch of government. When Jefferson took office in 1801 he inherited an army filled with Federalist officers—by Hamilton in 1798–99, and again by Adams in the last days of his presidency in 1801. It was an army that had been set loose on the people in 1799 and, though reduced in 1800, an army which many Republicans had feared would be used against them to deny them the fruits of their victory at the polls. Dealing with the opposition in this element of government was just as vital as cleansing the civil service and courts. In its essence, this study addresses his management of the problem of the opposition in the army.

The episodes of 1798–1800 are vital to understanding Thomas Jefferson's subsequent relationship with the army, and are fully addressed below. Events convinced him that the existing army would constitute an illegitimate opposition to his regime. He inherited a government and army openly hostile to Republican political aims, if not to republican values themselves. Regulars he knew were essential, but he also knew that they must be loyal. Republican rhetoric held that standing armies were a threat to republican liberties. But that was rhetoric. For Jefferson and the more moderate Republicans, the events of 1798–1800 demonstrated not the necessity of dissolving the army, but the necessity of creating a Republican army—a military appendage loyal to the new regime. This study begins with a detailed review the events of those three years, examines their influence on Republican thinking, and demonstrates how they shaped the actions of the new administration.

III

It is the thesis of this work that President Thomas Jefferson, far from ignoring or shunning the regular military establishment, undertook a social and political reformation of it in an effort to insure its loyalty to the new regime. Jefferson had ample reason for concern about the regulars he had inherited in 1801—the Federalist regulars, remnants of the army Hamilton and Adams had created. Some of these officers had opposed him vociferously and a few had not ceased their vocal opposition. Still, he gave no thought to disbanding them. Rather, Jefferson moved to mold an army that would threaten neither the new Republican regime, nor the republic itself. This he sought to do by Republicanizing the force—by introducing Republicans into the officer ranks at every opportunity; by winning over moderate Federalists—often by stratagems that would divide the opposition against itself; and ultimately by expanding the force and appointing new Republican officers at every level.

Jefferson was well aware of the difficulty he would encounter in his effort to find qualified Republicans. His immediate solution was the creation of a military academy in which to train otherwise poorly prepared (but politically acceptable) sons of the Republican faithful.

Efforts to gain control over the senior elements of the force led the administration into a series of (sometimes poorly) calculated schemes: the retention of General Wilkinson in preference to the more staunchly Federalist officers who followed him in line of seniority; the continuing efforts to dilute the general's power by encouraging the anti-Wilkinson elements of the army; and ultimately the threefold expansion of the force that allowed Republicans to be appointed directly into senior positions, including two new brigadier generals made coequal to Wilkinson.

This new view, which attributes Jefferson's actions to his effort to Republicanize the army and insure its loyalty, resolves the paradoxes inherent in the old paradigm centered on some supposed antiarmy bias. Now, Jefferson's relations with his army assume a rational character. The new paradigm—constructed around a reformation of the military establishment—explains West Point, Wilkinson's retention, and the "reduction" of 1802. It sheds new light on the President's actions during the Burr affair—and on Wilkinson's role. And, it explains the expansion of the army in 1808.

of the army, but the real reins rested in the hands of Alexander Hamilton who had augered his way into the position of inspector general.

Republican concerns were further deepened when they found themselves systematically excluded from the ranks. The Federalist press boasted, "The Federal Officers have it in charge not to inlist [sic] any man into the service of the United States, who, within a certain period of time, has had the audacity to mount the French cockade." This was to be a blatantly political army.[3] Washington warned that Republicans might seek commissions in order "to divide and contaminate the army by artful and seditious discourses and perhaps at a critical moment bring on confusion."[4] Federalist leaders took few chances. They screened officer applications personally. The slightest hint of Republican sympathies drew the telling note, "won't do."[5] "We were very attentive to the importance of appointing friends of the Govern[ment] to military stations," wrote Hamilton.[6]

Volunteer units had a similar—even deeper—political tint. Recruiters invited only men of correct political persuasion to join the ranks. "Federalists of the County of Berks," read a typical advertisement, were invited "to join a Volunteer Troop of Light Horse" that was to be raised "for the support of [the] Government."[7] These units were further screened before being accepted into federal service. McHenry, the Secretary of War, was quite clear on the issue, commenting, "it was, and is deemed important not to accept . . . companies composed of disaffected persons who may from improper motives, be desirous to intrude themselves into the army."[8]

Federalists, of course, saw the army as an essential bulwark for a nation threatened from both without and within by a Jacobin influence. This army could be used to defend the nation from external assault and internal subversion. Over the years Federalists had become suspicious that Republicans were little more than tools of the French—"French apostles of sedition," Harrison Gray Otis called them. An army capable of dealing with such illegitimate opposition was as much a part of the Federalist response as any of the alien or sedition laws.[9]

Republican suspicions ran just as deep in the opposite direction. The Federalists planned "to arm one half of the people, for the purpose of keeping the other in awe," observed one Republican.[10] The

Alexander Hamilton by John Trumbull.
NATIONAL PORTRAIT GALLERY, SMITHSONIAN INSTITUTION, WASHINGTON, D.C.

It was the use of regular troops of Hamilton's *New Army* against the people of Pennsylvania that triggered the most vociferous Republican opposition to things military. Washington had once told Hamilton that if regulars were used in that way, the people would raise a cry against the army. Hamilton paid too little heed to that prophetic warning.

prospect that this army might be used to enforce the statutes on sedition—in effect to silence political opposition—frightened and appalled Republicans, but it also propelled them to action. The Kentucky and Virginia Resolves penned by Jefferson and James Madison, respectively, were a frontal assault on Federalist policies and drew the desired response. Petitions flooded Congress opposing standing armies and urging repeal of the offending laws.[11]

"What, My Dear Sir, are you going to do with Virginia?" Hamilton asked Theodore Sedgwick. The resolves, he argued, were "full evidence . . . of a regular conspiracy to overturn the government." The government had to move aggressively to counter its enemies. Continue to raise the army, he counseled, and "when a clever force has been collected let them be drawn towards Virginia for which there is an obvious pretext—and then let measures be taken to act upon the laws and put Virginia to the test of resistance."[12]

II

It was in Pennsylvania, however, not Virginia, that opposition broke into the open; and the Federalist response fixed the course of all future debate. Both parties believed that their worst fears had been realized.

Discontent over the Federalist program was particularly manifested against the direct tax on land and houses that was levied by Congress in 1798 to pay for the expansion of the army. Jefferson followed the progress of discontent in Pennsylvania with particular interest. "This state is coming forward with a boldness not yet seen," he observed. "Petitions with 4,000 signers demonstrate against the Alien and Sedition laws, standing armies, and discretionary powers in the President."[13]

Among the petitions was one drawn up in Bucks County, and among the drafters was a militia captain—a veteran of the Revolution and of the Whiskey Insurrection expedition—by the name of John Fries. Fries and his men, many of whom had until quite recently been staunch Federalists, put on the red, white, and blue cockade of opposition and proceeded to eject the tax collectors. Opposition in Milford township of Bucks County, Fries's home, was so staunch that assessors could make virtually no progress in their work. At public meetings they were shouted down each time they tried to explain the laws. Assessors who made any effort to levy the tax were routed by Fries and his men. "They damned the house tax and the Stamp Act, and called me a stamper," reported one tax official.

> They damned the Alien and Sedition laws and finally all the laws. . . . They damned the Constitution also. . . . They damned the Congress, and damned the President, and all the friends to government because they were all Tories. . . . They said they would not have the government, nor the President, and they would not live under such a damned government; "We will have Washington"; others said no, "No, we will have Jefferson, he is a better man than Adams; hazzah for Jefferson."[14]

This resistance took an even more ominous turn when, in adjacent Northampton County, a similar demonstration against the tax ended in the arrest and jailing of eighteen tax resisters. Fries organized some 140 armed followers and rode to the rescue. Not a shot was fired, but the Northampton men were released, a circumstance that owed more to the prudence of the federal marshall than it did to Fries. Fries meanwhile became a local hero.

From Monticello, where he had recently returned, Jefferson took a philosophical view of events. "The spirit of 1776 is not dead," Jefferson wrote, "it has only been slumbering." Now it had awakened.[15] In Philadelphia, however, the Federalist administration denounced Fries's act as the beginning of a long predicted French-inspired uprising. "We have got an insurrection in Northampton County and adjoining parts," McHenry wrote Alexander Hamilton.[16] It was treason, McHenry informed Adams. He urged the President to issue a proclamation that would condemn the actions as "overt acts of levying war against the United States" and call forth "military force in order to suppress the combinations."[17]

Adams signed the proclamation on March 12 and departed for Quincy, leaving the situation in the McHenry's hands. Adams had authorized the use of the federal Volunteers—a force sure to be politically loyal. The Secretary, however, soon decided that the operations of the volunteers "would be facilitated, and made more certain, by the presence of a body of regulars." On March 15 he ordered an infantry company from Frederick Town, and artillery companies from Philadelphia, Carlisle, New York City, and West Point to rendezvous at Reading and Newtown in Pennsylvania.[18] Hamilton warned him only to "beware . . . of magnifying a riot into an insurrection, by employing . . . an inadequate force." "Tis better far," said Hamilton, "to err on the other side."[19]

It is this that makes Fries's rebellion—an otherwise rather trivial affair—important to our story. The use of regular federal troops instead of militia, was both unique and the fulfillment of Republican prophecy. The Federalists indeed did intend to use the New Army against the people. Earlier episodes of tax resistance—the Shays's and Whiskey Rebellions—have captured more attention from historians.[20] But it was Fries's Rebellion, or more precisely the use and performance of the army in suppressing the affair, that crystallized Republican concerns about a military establishment in a way that those earlier episodes had never done. John Adams later recalled that in this instance, "the army was as unpopular as if it had been a ferocious wild beast let loose upon the nation to devour it. In newspapers, in pamphlets and in common conversation they were called cannibals. A thousand anecdotes, true or false, of their licentiousness were propagated and believed."[21]

In Philadelphia, the government prepared for action. William Macpherson, a brigadier general in the Pennsylvania militia, was appointed to the same rank in the United States Army and designated to lead the forces against the insurgents. In addition to the regulars (about 500 strong) who were already on their way to Reading and Newtown, nine troops of volunteer cavalry from Philadelphia, Bucks, Chester, Lancaster, and Montgomery Counties were ordered to be ready to march. The regulars began to arrive in late March and the volunteers started to move to their rendezvous shortly thereafter.[22]

Early in April the units fanned out into Bucks, Berks, and Northampton Counties scouring the countryside for insurgents, but their zeal for the work soon became a cause célèbre. A letter from Quakerstown in Bucks County, just a couple of days after taking the field, described "the system of terror" they imposed. "Conceive your home entered at the dead of night by a body of armed men," wrote one critic, "and yourself dragged from your wife and screaming children."[23]

From other cities came further reports of outrages. "Seven [were] detained in irons," noted one account, and among them were "some old men, whose wrists were raw to the bone with the hand-cuffs." A second report the next day indicated that "the number of persons confined in heavy irons" had increased and again charged that "some old men" were suffering "from their fetters." Such accounts became fodder for local Republican papers and were widely reprinted throughout the country.[24]

The *Readinger Adler*, a German-language paper, accused the troops from Lancaster of intimidating innocent men, women, and children. They "abused the good wife of [Innkeeper Isaac] Feather," the editor charged. "They raged about with drawn sabers and threatened to do unspeakable things to her."[25] In the English language edition on the same date the troops were mocked for their courage in cutting down "liberty trees." They came to restore "Peace and good Order," the readers were told, but, by their conduct, were "more apt to excite the people to insurrection."[26]

The Lancaster volunteers operated extensively in and about Reading and became a special target of Jacob Schnider, the publisher of the staunchly Republican *Adler* (and *Eagle*). He had scourged them regularly for their treatment of the local citizens, but when he labeled them "Banditti," they took their revenge.[27] Storming into his office, they grabbed him, ripped off his clothes, and dragged him into the street. Their commanding officer, a Captain Montgomery, then ordered Schnider taken to the public market house and given twenty-five lashes. Before that sentence could be fully carried out troops of another company arrived and intervened. But the damage had been done.[28]

The story of the attack on Schnider was bannered in the Republican press across the country. The Newark *Centinel of Freedom* called it "striking evidence of the danger which a free state is exposed to from an army under the control of a single individual."[29] William Duane of Philadelphia wrote in the *Aurora* that the people "may see from this what they have to expect from a military force under the orders of the administration."[30] In Georgetown it was said that troops were called to "suppress insurrection" but that it was evident from this that they "would rather create one."[31] "There never was a greater outrage committed, thundered the *Virginia Argus* in Richmond, while in

Frankfort, Kentucky *The Paladium* warned that, "it was hardly to be expected that any republican printer or editor should be exempt from similar violence."[32] Even Reading's Federalist paper, the *Weekly Advertiser*, admitted that the affair "was of a very serious nature." The young "gentlemen" of the troop, that editor said, were "blinded by prejudice and by party spirit" and had not yet learned "to abstain from vili[f]ying every man and set of men whose politics run counter to their own."[33] Such Federalist sympathy, however, was localized and brief.

Unlike the events of 1794, when papers of both parties had urged against rebellion, the Fries affair drew sympathy from Republican and independent papers across the nation—and general condemnation from the Federalist press. Adams complained about the lack of united opposition to this affair: "The sordid spirit which produced this as well as the former insurrection in Pennsylvania, and which has given so much trouble to the government, anxiety to the nation, and burden on the treasury, ought to excite more general indignation than it has done."[34]

The military expedition, so far as its object had been to arrest the leaders of the insurrection, was entirely successful, though a great number of the offenders had simply given themselves up. Fries was captured early in the operation, and like the others, jailed in Philadelphia. There he was convicted of treason, then retired, convicted again, and sentenced to death. Ultimately, however, Adams pardoned him.

In a larger and more important sense, however, the operation was a disaster. The affair eroded popular support of the administration, hastened the split in Federalist ranks, and solidified the Republican opposition. Troops wearing the black Federalist cockade had swaggered about the countryside with little more to do than hew down the liberty poles. Many who observed them came to agree with Jefferson: "Should they really raise the whole army . . . and a great body of volunteer militia . . . it will leave me without doubt that force on the constitution is intended."[35]

When Macpherson dismissed the volunteers by expressing his gratitude for their efforts, Republican papers charged him with sanctioning and condoning their misdeeds. "The gen[eral] publicly thanks

Captain Montgomery and his troop," complained Charles Holt of *The Bee*, "for dragging an unaccused and unconvicted citizen from his dwelling, tearing his clothes from his back, and whipping him in a public market place!!"[36] But the Reading publisher was not the only member of the press to be roughly handled by the solidiery.

Shortly after their return to Philadelphia, several officers and men of a local volunteer troop—also Macpherson's men—attacked William Duane, publisher of the Republican *Aurora*. Duane, like Schnider, was dragged from his shop and beaten while his workers were held at pistol point. These "friends of good order and regular government" were, in Republican eyes, nothing more than "ruffians" and "assassins."[37] At this last outrage, the Republican press around the country focused with a vengeance on the danger and misdeeds of the Federalist army.[38] In Philadelphia, a short-lived journal entitled *Cannibal's Progress* chronicled the offenses of Federal troops remaining in the region.[39]

The volunteers were discharged in May and most of the regulars were ordered back to their normal duty stations. A few of the latter, however, were retained in the disaffected counties. McHenry had suggested the possibility of such a move soon after he had decided to bring regular units into the operation. Duane, at the *Aurora*, had caught wind of the plans in mid-April and reacted strongly. The aim, he claimed, was to influence the upcoming gubernatorial election. "It was this kind of election influence," he argued, that prompted the English to prohibit "men in military array from coming within a certain number of miles" of the polls.[40] Hamilton, too, had opposed the idea, though for different reasons, but McHenry overruled him.

The bulk of this force was left at Reading under Major John Adlum. Hamilton, who by now was understandably concerned about friction between the soldiers and the populace, instructed Adlum to be especially attentive to the discipline of the troops "and to prevent injury or insult to the Inhabitants."[41]

Adlum, however, failed to impress the importance of Hamilton's message on his young officers. On June 24 three of them, Lieutenants Zebulon Montgomery Pike, Lewis Howard, and a third unidentified officer became involved in still another altercation with a member of the Republican press. Like the Lancaster troops before them, the regulars had been the targets for barbs thrown by Jacob Schnider in his Reading papers. One day, at Wood's Tavern in Reading, Lieutenant Howard accosted one of Schnider's employees who was said to be responsible for many of the items about the army. Howard threw a glass of water on the young man, and then, when it was learned that the youth had taken out a warrant against him, the officers sought him out and proceeded with some vigor to administer a whipping. The young printer had to be rescued from this trio by Joseph Heister, a Republican congressman, and his son. Again the opposition press flayed the army.[42]

The events sparked by Fries's Rebellion had caused a cascade of criticism of the army's behavior in the Republican press—criticism that soon grew to disapprobation of all things martial. In earlier years scattered items opposing standing armies had appeared in the press, but the number was small when compared to the deluge which began with Fries's Rebellion in April 1799 and only ended twelve months later with the disbanding of the New and Provisional Armies. Abuse of the army took on a new tenor with the Fries affair. From that time on, any incident that could be construed to bring discredit to the army was seized upon by Republican editors.[43]

Among the most persistent critics was Charles Holt, editor of New London's *Bee*, whose efforts on this behalf drew a conviction for sedition. Holt's offense was in discouraging recruiting. "Where are these recruits for a stand'ng army to be found?" he had asked. Certainly not from among the "enterprising young farmers, who by industry and economy may grow rich." These men would "never give their bare backs to be smitten under Prussian military discipline, or devote their valor to promote the views of ambition or to oppress their country." These youth, he said would "never spend their best days in arms and vice."[44]

As usual editors borrowed articles from each other. In May, Duane reprinted a long denunciation of the Federalist army out of the Boston *Independent Chronicle*. It was an insult, the piece contended, to any nation with a well-armed militia "to suppose a STANDING ARMY in time of PEACE, would be necessary to defend it." The "first fruits of our military institutions," the writer pointed out, are "an excise law, stamp act, and a land tax." Ultimately, the article contended, that army would be used to destroy the nation's republican institutions and impose "an indolent and oppressive aristocracy."[45]

The misadventures of officers and soldiers were a frequent subject in the stories attacking the army. "If the people cannot see," wrote Holt, "in the outrages committed in the various parts of these states by persons holding military authority under the United States, the danger to which public liberties are exposed, they deserve to be dragooned into military subjection."[46] Holt continued his attack on recruiting by reporting the abuse of a recent recruit who had been absent from a roll call. He was put into a small box, referred to as an "oven," and removed a few hours later in convulsions. Holt suggested that, "there were many military men . . . who would undoubtedly be much mended by such . . . *roasting*."[47]

Jefferson, in Monticello, followed events through the newspapers and correspondence. Reports of the army's activities in Pennsylvania and news from Boston that Adams had decided to raise a substantial portion of the Provisional Army caused him concern. "Can such an army under Hamilton be disbanded?" he wondered. "I doubt it," he mused. His only refuge was the hope that the administration would be unable to recruit any for the force but officers.[48]

III

In early December 1799 the new Sixth Congress took their seats and Republicans prepared for an organized attack on the military establishment. Jefferson had included "the disbanding of the army" on his list of major issues that should be addressed by the Congress, but warned that they must do nothing that would "look or lead to force, and give any pretext for keeping up the army."[49]

The Republican assault began on New Year's Day 1800 when John Nicholas of Virginia introduced a motion to repeal the laws that had authorized the New Army.[50] Debate began a week later and occupied the House for four days.[51] Nicholas spoke for the Republicans and focused first on the expense of maintaining such a force, and then on its utility. "I cannot conceive for what they are wanted." Invasion was "the only ground upon which their necessity could be founded," and that, he argued, was "absolutely impossible."[52]

Delaware Federalist James A. Bayard answered Nicholas's attack the next day. The country, he insisted, not only could, but must afford the force so long as the French threatened. Negotiations with the French were under way, he acknowledged, but to disband the army before they were successfully concluded would undercut that process. "If after having raised an army against them" we should disband it "without any change on their part" they would see it as weakness; that could harm the diplomatic efforts.[53]

On the third day of debate the young freshman congressman from Roanoke, Virginia, John Randolph, spoke. His maiden speech delighted his Republican colleagues; they interrupted it, Jefferson wrote, with "infinite applause."[54] The speech was generally temperate in tone, but on occasion he warmed considerably to the subject. The raising of the New Army, Randolph observed, had had a "deleterious effect upon the public temper." It "excites the gall of our citizens," he asserted with a vigor accentuated by his shrill voice. They are justly indignant "at the sight of loungers" living "upon the public," and consuming "the fruits of their honest industry, under the pretext of protecting them from some foreign yoke." The people, he concluded, "put no confidence . . . in the protection of a handful of Ragamuffins."[55]

The next day Randolph referred to his "ragamuffins" remark, saying he would like to exchange the term. "He took it back of his own accord handsomely," said Jefferson. Others, however, might have found the retraction equally as bitter a pill as the original.[56] The remark, Randolph said, had been "extorted" from him by the "character and appearance of the recruits" he had seen. They were "the most abject and worthless" men in the community. It is "to their protection . . . we are told to confide our Liberties and Independence." "We revolt," he said, "from the idea."[57] Not unexpectedly, the motion to disband the new regiments failed by a wide margin.

The debate, Randolph's ragamuffin remark, and even Randolph himself, took on a special significance in the light of a rather remarkable sequel—one played out at the theater that night. There, young

Randolph became the focal point of taunts and insults delivered by a small group of military officers. By chance (or design) three marine officers, Captains James McKnight and George Taylor, and Lieutenant Michael Reynolds, were seated in a box adjoining that of Randolph and a company of other congressmen. The farce on the stage, *Blue Beard*, ideally suited the officers' purpose. Each time the villain's pantalooned retainers marched about, the marines commented loudly, "they were well-looking mercenaries," or "these ragamuffins march badly; they want drilling."

When Randolph ignored his tormentors, they became more direct. Two of them—McKnight and Reynolds—moved into the box with Randolph and company, and began again. "I think our ragamuffins would make a better appearance than those men," said McKnight, almost in Randolph's ear. When that prompted no response, Reynolds rudely wedged himself in beside the congressman. Again there was no response. When the crowd rose to their feet to get a better look at the stage (possibly to view the corpses of the blue bearded rogue's several former wives) McKnight stepped upon Randolph's seat and, when the latter again sat down, complained loudly, "Sir, you are sitting on my feet." The Virginian now fuming, rose slightly to allow his tormentor to step down, but held his tongue.

About that time, Lieutenant Campbell Smith arrived at the box and inquired quietly about what had transpired. Smith, an army officer and one of the few Republicans on the rolls, had been in another part of the theater but had heard whispers that a confrontation was planned, and moved to prevent it. He spoke briefly, but with some apparent effect, to McKnight and Reynolds, and then left.

The balance of the performance was completed without incident, but as Randolph left the box someone pulled at his coattails. "Who was that that jerked my coat?" he demanded. There was no answer. He asked again, adding that the person who had done it "was a damned puppy, let him be who he might." The marines said nothing, but as the parties left the theater they engaged in a last bout of pushing and crowding on the stairs and sidewalk.[58]

Randolph was justly irate, and his friends convinced him to address the president and demand the dismissal of "those rash youths."[59] Adams, instead, returned his letter to the House and told them that if they thought there had been a breach of privilege or insult to the Congress that they should investigate it themselves. In the eyes of Republicans, this affair was simply a further embodiment of their fears of a Federalist military force. Even congressmen in the nation's capital—Republican congressmen, at least—were not immune to insult, and by extension, to intimidation by such a force.[60]

His first adventures in Congress not only reflected his youthful expectations of political life, they exemplified what always continued to be at the heart of his public life: the literal seriousness with which he understood issues to be most accurately dramatized in and by himself. His attempt to focus in one personal incident opposition to standing armies, to Federalist plans for the army, and to the Adams administration, was typical.[61]

A few years later Randolph would seize on (or create) a personal conflict with General James Wilkinson, who commanded the army, as a means to internalize and dramatize his opposition to the regular establishment. This habit of internalizing and personalizing issues made him vindictive, yet he cultivated the practice. Though this ultimately isolated him from his friends and foes alike, it also made him a source of fascination.

The events at the theater that night made a lasting impression on Randolph. They confirmed in his mind what he had only suspected before about the danger of a vagrant military establishment. It was a lesson he would not forget—a lesson that made it difficult if not impossible for him to reconcile himself to a later Republican army. And, as we will see, his one effort at such a reconciliation—a single instance of support for the regular establishment—was turned on him and made him even more vengeful.

Republicans were not surprised at their failure to effect a disbanding of the army, but did not anticipate the support they were about to get on this issue from disgruntled Adams Federalists. "Another motion will be tried today, to stop recruiting," wrote Jefferson, on January 13, "but I see no reason to expect it to succeed."[62] But, surprisingly, Harrison Gray Otis, a leading Adams man and chairman of the House committee on defense, introduced a similar measure. The Adams faction was beginning to share Republican concerns about Hamilton's force. Adams had never favored the full Hamiltonian program, but his appointment of Washington to head the army robbed him of the ability to control events fully.[63] Washington's death, in December 1799, had freed him to act.

Encouraged by this unexpected shift in events, Republicans reached further. They proposed to consolidate the troops already recruited into as many regiments as they would fill and then to discharge any excess officers. The Adams men would not go that far, but Otis's bill, which effectively stopped recruiting, won handily.[64] The bill was approved by the Senate without change on February 17 and signed into law three days later.

Over the next several months Republicans (and sometimes Adams Federalists) pursued a legislative program that was designed to miti-gate the power of Hamilton's military establishment. Their success was limited but they did manage to block creation of the military academy he sought. Such a school, the *Aurora* argued, would only enhance the army's ability "to suppress whatever [the] government may please to call a spirit of discord, and to keep in awe those who venture to express doubts of the wisdom and patriotism of their mea-sures."[65]

All Federalist military power was suspect. With the presidential election approaching—and with the apparent failure of efforts to dis-band the additional regiments—Republicans tried, but failed to re-strict the use of troops at or near polling places, and thereby to pre-vent their interference with elections. They were more successful against Federalist-proposed militia reform, which, like the academy bill, was postponed to the next session. "Their new militia bill," raged Georgia Republican Abraham Baldwin, "is . . . part of the same system which gave to the President the power of appointing the officers of the vol-unteer militia, directly in the face of the Constitution."[66] The events of the year before had quite convincingly demonstrated that regulars were not the only forces the administration could apply to political ends. The volunteers in Pennsylvania had proved at least as dangerous to republican liberties as had the regulars. That lesson had not been lost on Republicans. Jefferson, in an assessment that drew a parallel with Napoleon's recent rise to power, noted the potential danger. "Beware," he wrote, "of a military force, even of citizens."[67]

Republican success in their effort to blunt the Federalist weapons owed as much to internal dissession within their opponent's camp as to their own wiles. Adams, aware that Hamiltonians were scheming to displace him from the presidency, finally rallied his forces and struck out. He replaced his cabinet, a major agency of Hamilton's influence, and began to dismantle the military apparatus he had allowed them to construct. A surprising Republican victory in the New York election at the end of April only widened the breach in the Federalists' ranks and brought their conflict more into the open.[68]

In some sense the disbanding of the army was serendipitous. In late April the Senate voted to suspend all further officer appointments to the new regiments. (The promotion and appointment of officers had continued despite the cessation of enlistments.) The House amended that bill to authorize the disbanding of the additional army as soon as Franco-American relations would permit. The Senate then set June 15 as the date for the disestablishment of the New Army and the House immediately concurred. Adams signed the bill within hours and ordered the Secretary of War to begin the stand down immediately.

Though, in the end, the Republicans had played little more than the spectator, they were jubilant. The disbanding of the army was celebrated around the country as a major partisan victory. Bells, cannons and toasts saluted the event wherever the Republican faithful gathered—by some accounts, quite as adequately as if commemorating the nation's independence.[69]

The standing army had been disbanded. The Old Army—the first four regiments of infantry, and the two regiments of artillerists and engineers—was retained, but Republicans, excepting a small number of the ilk of John Randolph, had never intended otherwise. Certainly, the greatest threat—Hamilton and his New Army—had been removed. The remaining force was safely employed guarding the maritime and western frontiers. Their numbers were within limits that raised no alarm. Besides, experience indicated that recruiting problems would make even this small force difficult to maintain.

These concerns now took a back seat to the upcoming election. Political rhetoric recalled the dangers of times recently past when Hamilton and his "hired regulars, and party, and monarchic volunteers" had conducted a reign of terror in the Pennsylvania countryside.[70] But, election rhetoric was the province of a select group of publicists; the principal contenders were required by circumstances (not the least of which were sedition statutes still on the book) to remain above this rather vulgar fray.

With the election fairly won (and finally conceded) Jefferson moved quickly to organize his administration, including the military establishment. On February 18, 1801, the day after the House (on the twenty-third ballot) elected him President, he wrote Henry Dearborn, offering him the post of Secretary of War. Dearborn was a veteran of the Revolution, but more important he had given yeoman service to Republicans as a member of military committees of the House in the mid-1790s. Moreover, he had, in his days in the House, exhibited a position on the army that paralleled Jefferson's, favoring a force wholly adequate to protect the nation's various frontiers—but, no larger.[71]

Within a week the President had decided to take an army officer, Meriwether Lewis, as his private secretary. He chose him, he said, for what he could "contribute to the mass of information which it is interesting for the administration to acquire." In particular he enumerated Lewis's knowledge of the west and "of the army and all its interests and relations."[72] Rumors abounded concerning alterations he planned, reflecting the consideration such issues were receiving.[73]

It took little reflection to remind Jefferson that the army he was about to inherit remained essentially Federalist; the product of the years 1798 to 1800 remained to be undone. The new administration would soon turn itself to this task. Many officers had been vocal in their opposition to Jefferson and the Republicans, and a few allowed their political sentiments to overawe good judgment. In Pittsburgh, John Smur, a Republican tavern keeper, became an unwitting figure in one such vignette. It began when officers obstructed his efforts to collect the tabs due him by the troops who frequented his establishment. Credit was an integral part of army life—the more so in the west where the paymaster's rounds were irregular at best. Smur had granted it liberally. When he was denied permission to enter the post and collect his debts as the paymaster settled accounts with the men— a commonly accepted practice—he protested that it was his political views that caused his difficulty. The officers may have concluded that without Smur's credit their troops would spend less time in that alien political environment. In any case, when the editor of the local Republican paper joined Smur in the protest the officers relented.[74]

The events of 1798, 1799, and 1800 had given a political character to the military establishment—and a Federalist, even Hamiltonian character at that. The army's loyalty to Jefferson and to his new administration was an open question. Tavern owner Smur had received satisfaction. Still, the partisan attitude revealed by such an affair suggested a problem with which Jefferson would ultimately have to deal.

CHAPTER 2

A Chaste Reformation

By the end of the highly charged campaign of 1800 Jefferson was convinced that the ultimate success of the Republican cause required a careful redirection of the nation's course. "So long," he wrote Robert Livingston,

has the vessel run on this [the Federalist] way and been trimmed to it, that to put her on her republican tack will require . . . the new establishment of republicanism: I say, for its new establishment: for hitherto we have only seen its travesty.[1]

To Jefferson this new tack implied two rather incongruous goals. The first was a reconciliation of the political differences that had made the years leading up to the campaign of 1800 so rancorous. In his inaugural address, he outlined a public policy of moderation and conciliation that he hoped would begin the process of reconciling the opposition to Republican views. The second goal was a new Republican dominance in positions of authority and power in all areas where the President had cognizance. This second task required more discretion.

The problem of the military establishment in the context of Republican dominance received careful consideration. Jefferson never doubted the need for some regular forces. He had long believed that regulars were essential on the nation's far-flung frontiers, and conceded their utility where skills such as those of artillerists and engineers were required.[2] But how loyal were the officers and corps of the current

Thomas Jefferson by Cornelius Tiebout (after Rembrandt Peale).
NATIONAL PORTRAIT GALLERY, SMITHSONIAN INSTITUTION, WASHINGTON, D.C.

Jefferson had long conceded the need for regulars, but was concerned about the loyalty of the force he inherited from his Federalist predecessors. He lost little time in instituting a *chaste reformation*—political and social—of that establishment.

army? Jefferson could hardly be certain. After all, only a small fraction of the officers were identified with the Republican cause and more than a few—some in positions of great responsibility—were "most violently [opposed] to the administration and still active in its vilification."[3] The army that he had inherited might be unreliable in the event of factional conflict, and some warned of just such a possibility. "I think your attention," wrote Elbridge Gerry,

should extend to the security of fortresses, magazines, and arsenals; by placing them under the protection of faithful officers and corps, and preventing by proper defenses their seizure or destruction. This precaution seems necessary even if the country was not infested by a desperate faction.[4]

Jefferson, he seemed to warn, might have to use the army to secure the Union against a monarchist element that still seemed a threat.

To achieve Republican dominance in the army—an organization with such real power (and more than latent antagonism)—required delicate maneuvering. Still, the aim was to bring the army into accord with the political philosophy of the new administration, and Jefferson lost no time in getting started. "The Army," he reported to Nathaniel Macon just two months after his inauguration, "is undergoing a chaste reformation."[5]

Though they would have to move with caution, all vestiges of monarchical Federalism were to go. The army was to be Republicanized. The architects of that reformation were Jefferson and Henry Dearborn, his Secretary of War. Their principal instrument was to be the Military Peace Establishment Act of 1802. The mechanisms were carefully conceived and written into that bill—the first and the most comprehensive of the Jeffersonian enactments on the subject.

I

In speculating on policy under Jefferson, Major Thomas H. Cushing, the adjutant and inspector, reported grimly, "We shall most probably go to the right about."[6] Barely a week after the new administration had taken office he reported to James Wilkinson, the commanding general, "It is understood on all sides that an entire new administration is to be formed and that many other alterations are to take place."

He urged the general to leave the field and return to Washington "as immediately as possible"—suggesting that this would be the best hope of protecting the army's interests.[7]

Cushing's surmise was close to the mark. Hardly a month had passed before word began to spread that changes were imminent.[8] In that time the President and Dearborn had begun to sketch out the shape of the new Republican military establishment and to examine the means by which this could be accomplished. Jefferson worked closely with Dearborn to develop the administration's policy concerning the army, and seldom sought (or seriously entertained) other council.[9] General Wilkinson, for example, was not consulted; he, in fact, was dispatched to treat with the Indians while the key decisions were made and implemented.

These decisions took shape quickly. In early April came the announcement to insiders that the President had decided to establish a military school at West Point.[10] In May, promotion was regularized and new rules of administration were put into effect—relieving the chaos that had characterized the last months of the Adams administration.[11] By June, Dearborn had worked his way through the paymaster's division and had issued instructions to reorganize this operation with an eye toward speeding the flow of money to the troops.[12] Bit by bit the new Secretary of War proceeded through the whole military structure—studying, questioning, and revising—though the more comprehensive framework of reform was revealed to only a few.

By July, rumors were circulating widely within the service concerning cuts being considered. "We talk much here of a part of the Army being disbanded at the next Session of Congress," wrote one officer from the field.[13] This speculation was well founded. Dearborn, it would seem, had already begun to fill in the outlines of one major element in the administration's plan—a carefully constructed "reduction" of the army.

Dearborn's plan, its essence a tightly guarded secret, was a consolidation of units that would reduce (and change) the requirement for officers while minimizing any actual reduction in overall strength. The beauty of the plan was that it would allow the discharge of many senior Federalist officers (and incompetents of all stripes), and still provide openings into which to appoint young Republicans. All this was to be done quite surreptitiously, and all under a fitting Republican banner that proclaimed both reduction and economy.

Plans were drawn and legislative proposals were in readiness by fall. In late November, Jefferson wrote his daughter, Martha Jefferson Randolph, that "we are now within 10 days of Congress, when our campaign will begin and will probably continue till April."[14] Early the next month, Major Jonathan Williams visited Dearborn and was told of the administration's plans. "I found the Secretary of War fully occupied with his plan for a Peace Establishment," he wrote Wilkinson later. "His whole plan was read to me by himself, in private, and I was ordered not to reveal a word to anyone."[15]

The bill lay before Congress for several months, but was often overshadowed by attention given the administration's simultaneous assault on the judiciary. Still, Dearborn worked patiently behind the scenes to achieve both the public and private goals of the administration.

The State of the Union message, which Jefferson sent to the Congress in early December 1801, set the tone. He pointed out that the number of men actually needed by the army was "considerably short of the present military establishment." "For the surplus," he added, "no particular use can be pointed."[16] Dearborn followed up by sending to Congress a report on the specific requirements for the posts and stations where garrisons were necessary.[17]

The administration was promising a reduction, and their legislative proposal was cast in that light. Dearborn communicated the administration's quite comprehensive plan (the one he had read to Williams) privately to Joseph B. Varnum, a Massachusetts Republican, who chaired the House committee charged with reporting a bill to reduce the army. Varnum and the committee, after giving it legal form, presented it to the House on January 11.[18]

On the surface there was nothing remarkable about the bill, and it seemed responsive to the promise of a reduction. The strength of the new establishment was to be just under 3,300—barely 60 percent of the old authorization. In place of the current four infantry regiments there were to be only two, and in place of the two regiments of artillerists and engineers there was to be a single corps of artillery and a

Henry Dearborn by Charles Willson Peale.
INDEPENDENCE NATIONAL HISTORICAL PARK COLLECTION.

Henry Dearborn, the nation's longest serving Secretary of War, had Jefferson's full confidence. Dearborn's influence in military affairs was paramount in the cabinet, and he and the President worked closely to reform the military establishment.

tiny separate engineer element. The House sent only two days debating the bill in the committee of the whole, and made no substantive changes to the original draft.[19]

When the bill reached the House floor, however, James Bayard, a Maryland Federalist, led the opposition with an assault first on the office of the brigadier general. One Federalist newspaper reported the issue this way.

These men who, under the former administration were most vociferous in condemning what they termed the lavish expenditure of the public money, are now seen the foremost in contending the sinecures and frivolous employments. On the bill fixing the peace establishment . . . Mr. Bayard and the Federal members generally, were for abolishing certain offices, whose pay is immense, and their service nominal. Messrs. Giles, Smith, Randolph, etc. were strenuous in favor of retaining these expensive supernumeraries. Such is the consistency of these men.[20]

The Republicans, however, were well aware that the elimination of the position of brigadier general would mean the dismissal of the essentially apolitical James Wilkinson. Should that happen command would devolve to a man (or set of men) more inclined to Federalism. It was no secret, in and out of the army, that Wilkinson was the only senior officer "friendly to the politics of the now reigning party."[21] The Republicans were having no part of Bayard's masquerade. Samuel Smith settled the question by reminding the Federalists that just a few years before (in a force little larger than the one now proposed) they had authorized both a brigadier general and a major general for the army.

The Republicans prevailed on this issue, but Bayard was not done. He next opposed the reintroduction of the rank of colonel which the administration now proposed reviving after years of disuse. Though only three colonels were anticipated—the commanders of the two infantry regiments and of the Artillery Corps would be made colonels rather than lieutenant colonels—there was a purpose served by the scheme. The three senior officers promoted would gain prestige and formal recognition from the administration. Both would instill a degree of independence from the general nominally above them. The administration design tended to decentralize control. Having installed

Wilkinson, the administration was, at the same time, consciously creating a system that would diminish his authority.

Administration supporters, and the measure's floor managers, defended it effectively against each attack, and in the end many Federalists joined in support. The bill passed the House seventy-seven to twelve, and was sent to the Senate.

Debate in the Senate began on February 24, and continued for three days, though no really substantive changes were made. Senate amendments: delayed the effective date of the new establishment by a month—from May 1 to June 1, 1802; provided extra rations for post commanders, who regularly entertained guests and travelers as a part of their function of command; and authorized rations for the hospital matrons and nurses, and women who washed for the troops.[22] Senate action also amended several items dealing with military jurisprudence. The most important of these was the striking of a provision making the 1776 "Rules and Articles of War"—under which the army still operated—applicable only so far as they were "compatible with the Constitution." The loss of this clarification prompted the administration to propose new "articles of war" (introduced in 1804, and approved in 1806).

The only issue that generated real debate in the Senate was the amount of separation pay allowed those officers who were to be discharged. The House version (from the administration's draft) provided a flat rate of three months' pay. The Senate argued for a somewhat more liberal arrangement—one months' pay for each year of service, or a minimum of three months' pay. The Senate prevailed.[23]

In substance, the bill passed as it had been submitted by the administration. As Jonathan Williams later reported to Wilkinson, the version he heard from Dearborn in early December "has not been otherwise altered than [to put it into] the mere legal form required."[24]

II

When examined in detail, the substance of the act reveals an intricate program of reform, one the administration would use to shape the army into an instrument responsive to Republican direction—an army

Jefferson could live with. It was, in effect, the plan for a comprehensive reformation of the army.

The Military Peace Establishment Act of 1802 has been customarily portrayed as a manifestation of both a Republican tendency toward economy and the Republican abhorrence of standing armies. Jefferson's aim, it has been widely asserted, was to reduce the army, and in the process, cut expenditures. The administration capitalized on the perception that some major economy had been achieved. In fact, they fostered such a view. The reduction would achieve "a savings of nearly $500,000 annually, according to a report and estimate of the Secretary of War," wrote one congressman to his constituents. The army had been reduced by one-third, it was commonly said. This apparent assault on the standing army—and the resultant economies claimed—matched the rhetoric of Republican ideology. Few looked closely at the facts.[25]

A detailed examination reveals, however, that the bill resulted in little real reduction in size or associated savings. Despite recruiters' efforts the army had steadily dwindled in size. The Federalists had found that the New Army of 1798 had been impossible to fill, and even the smaller force of 1800 had proved difficult to maintain. In the last year of the Adams administration the army's strength had steadily receded from the 5,438 officers and men authorized. Under the new Republican administration, the downward drift was allowed to continue. By early 1802 the force numbered less than 3,600 and was continuing to decline. In all, the ceiling of 3,289 mandated by the new Peace Establishment Act in March required a reduction of less than 300.[26]

It was the dismissal of officers that seemed to portend a significant reduction; fully one-third were eliminated. In reality, however, it was only these ranks which needed to be reduced. President Adams had filled the commissioned ranks just before leaving office; between February 16 and March 3, 1801, more than eighty appointments had been made. Even Jefferson's administration had filled these vacancies as they occured. As a result the army had a disproportionately large component of officers. Dismissals were required to restore the balance and to bring officer strength into line with the actual strength levels which had been formalized by the new law. In the end, eighty-eight of some

230 officers were removed. (Twenty new positions were created at the same time and filled, leaving a net reduction of 68 officers.) Any actual monetary savings that resulted from force reductions came largely as a result of the change in the number of officers. These savings, however, totaled only about $35,000 per year—a far cry from the half million claimed by, and often credited to, the administration.[27] While Jefferson did, for a time, reduce military expenditures, he did so by cutting in areas other than personnel.

Despite its rhetoric, the administration brought about neither substantial force reductions nor sizable monetary savings. This fact was not lost on everyone. The irony in that appealed to Hamilton, who noted that though they were hardly reducing the army, Republicans still insisted on "tickling our ears with the trite but favorite maxim, that 'a standing army ought not to be kept up in time of peace.' "[28] As he may have guessed, the real aim of the administration's carefully drawn act lay concealed behind a screen of old-line Republican rhetoric.

The Military Peace Establishment Act of 1802 was not intended to reduce the army; rather, it provided the administration with a means to accomplish a political catharsis of the military establishment. As we shall see, it offered four vehicles of reform: it provided a means of eliminating Federalist domination of the army's internal hierarchy; it offered a way to remove many of the most persistent political opponents; it provided some immediate *entrée* for loyal Republicans; and it established a source of Republican officers for the future.

III

The first step in this Republicanization was to sever Federalist control of the army's internal administration. To a large degree that dominance was exercised through the small army staff. There had been a staff in the Revolutionary Army but none in the early post-war years. In 1790, however, two inspectors were authorized and with subsequent enlargements of the army, the staff also grew. With the addition of the second regiment of infantry in 1791, a quartermaster and chaplain were authorized; an adjutant, deputy quartermaster, and paymaster were added the next year. In 1795 the term General Staff was introduced and the titles correspondingly became inspector general, quartermaster general, and adjutant general. A surgeon general was added the same year, and the paymaster became a paymaster general the next. When Jefferson took office the army was headed by a brigadier general with a staff that consisted of a quartermaster general, a civilian paymaster general, and an adjutant general who also served as inspector general. In addition there were two deputy inspectors, and a deputy quartermaster. Of these, only the quartermaster general and paymaster general were separately authorized, the balance being drawn from among the officers of the line, though their staff duties occupied them full time.

The quartermaster general, John Wilkins, and his assistant, were the focal point of army supply activities. They consolidated requests, forwarded them to the appropriate agencies and, when the items were made available, delivered them to the field. Items in stock at a Federal arsenal were issued by the superintendent of military stores in charge of that site. If a purchase or contract was necessary, the requisition was sent to the purveyor of supplies who procured clothing, shoes, camp utensils, military stores, equipage, medicines, and hospital supplies. Routine actions were handled without reference to the Secretary of War, but larger transactions needed his approval. Rations were provided by contracts executed by the Secretary of War and were delivered by the contractor to the posts.

Personnel actions were the responsibility of the adjutant general, Major Thomas Cushing, who issued the orders that transferred, promoted, or discharged the officers and men of the army. He also served as a clearing house for information to and from the field, and as a repository for routine reports. In his added role as inspector general, he was responsible for insuring that individuals and units compiled with the various directives issued. His purview as inspector included almost the whole of the army's day-to-day routine: recordkeeping, material accountability, and the condition of stocks—arms, powder, and equipment—at the scattered posts. It also included the conduct of training—the latter prescribed by a drill and "discipline" laid out years earlier by Baron Frederick von Steuben. The burden of his duties as adjutant, however, left Cushing little time to pursue his additional responsibilities. The inspections fell largely to his deputies.

Though small, the staff controlled the day-to-day operation and maintenance of the army, and that staff was dominated by Federalists. Aside from General Wilkinson, who was something of a political chameleon, the five military officers assigned to the staff were ardent and vociferous Federalists. Wilkins, Cushing, Captain Bartholomew Schaumburg, the deputy quartermaster, and the two deputy inspectors, Major Isaac Guion and Captain Edward D. Turner, were all identified as political opponents "most violently" opposed to Jefferson's new administration and "active in its vilification."[29] Their staff positions gave them an inordinate opportunity to influence the army and thereby made them dangerous. Federalists—particularly of that hue—could not be left unfettered.

Dismissal was a partial solution. Three of the men, Wilkins, Guion, and Schaumburg, were discharged and a fourth, Turner, was removed from the staff. Removal alone, however, left the administration with another problem. Who would replace them? The majority of Republican officers were too junior for such an assignment. The one field grade officer of correct—that is to say, Republican—politics, Major John H. Buell, was judged inadequate to handle such responsibilities.[30] The system of promotion by seniority to fill vacancies essentially precluded the appointment of new Republican officers except to the lowest grades. Thwarting that process risked alienating the entire officer corps and, as the administration later learned, was impracticable.

The ultimate solution was to do away with as many of the staff positions as possible, or to convert them into civilian positions that could be filled by trustworthy Republicans without raising the ire of the officer corps. Four of the six positions were thus eliminated. The quartermaster's duties were split between the Secretary of War and three new civilian military agents. The functions of the deputy inspectors were simply eliminated.

Cushing, the adjutant general, and Calab Swan, the civilian paymaster and a more moderate Federalist, were retained. The role of the adjutant general—the focal point of communications to and from the field—could not be dispensed with, and Cushing's knowledge and experience made him invaluable to the new administration. The activities of both, however, received the early and continued close attention of Dearborn.

This reorganization of the staff and the discharges it occasioned had the desired effect; an important apparatus of Federalist domination of the military was dismantled. The influence these staunch Federalist officers had exerted through their staff positions was demolished. The result was greater control by the Secretary of War—and the President.

The second step in the administration's reformation of the army was the actual removal of the more obstreperous Federalists from throughout the officer corps. Removals had played an important role in the Republicanization of all offices of the executive and were, likewise, an essential step in Jefferson's reform of the army. Removals in the army, however, required particular discretion. As the President explained, army officers, like judges, were "not removable but by established process."[31] The parallel he drew with the judicial arm is instructive. For, as in the judiciary, this process of removal entailed the elimination of offices.[32] The administration discovered that it could fulfill the expectations of Republican followers—who called on them to reduce the army and cut expenditures—and at the same time accelerate the process of Republicanization. There was a happy conjunction between pledges of frugality and the necessity of creating a more Republican army. The bill that promised cuts and savings in reality brought reforms that altered the political and social structure of the army.

That process was aided by some restructuring of the force—some organizational sleight of hand—which allowed the administration to maximize the elimination of Federalist officers. For example, in the artillery, by creating fewer but larger companies and by putting all of these larger companies under a single corps (eliminating the the two regimental headquarters), they reduced the number of officers required while retaining most of the enlisted strength—fewer commands and fewer headquarters meant fewer officers.[33] The same was generally true of the infantry. The consolidation of the four regiments into two allowed the elimination of a number of officers while almost all the enlisted men were retained.

In addition, while making cuts in many areas, the administration's new law actually provided some appointment opportunities. The number of officers in the infantry companies was increased by adding an ensign—a new rank, subordinate to existing lieutenants, to which officers being discharged were unlikely to consent to be reduced. This new position, therefore, meant immediate appointment opportunities which naturally went to young Republicans.

Jefferson made as much of the opportunity to remove selected officers as he reasonably could and a majority of the most persistent opponents of the administration were dismissed. A roster of officers found in Jefferson's papers (annotated by his private secretary, Captain Meriwether Lewis, to indicate both the officer's military qualifications and political sentiments) suggests that Jefferson monitored closely Dearborn's efforts to decide which men were to be kept and which were to be discharged.[34]

In line with administration policy elsewhere, those found wanting in skill were the most certain to be removed—of forty-one identified as "unworthy" of their commissions, thirty-five (85 percent) were dismissed. Better officers were much more likely to be retained. Of the best (1st Class) only seven of fifty-eight (12 percent) were discharged. (See Table 2.1). "The business of selection is extremely unpleasant," wrote Dearborn to General Wilkinson,

but after availing myself of such information as time and circumstances will admit I shall endeavor to do it without favor or affection. Having a single eye on the good of the service, it will be my object to retain such as merit alone, shall point out as entitled to a preference.[35]

Still, "merit alone" does not seem to have been the whole basis for selection, unless, as Dearborn's biographer Richard Alton Erney put it, " 'merit alone' included correct political sentiments."[36] The dismissal of Lieutenant Colonel Lewis Tousard made that point; "the enjoyment of the esteem and confidence of Washington," complained one Federalist, "is too strong a proof of merit to be suffered to remain in office."[37] In the case of Tousard, however, it was the "esteem and confidence" of Hamilton and other High Federalists that had earned him his dismissal. The careful notation of the political affiliation of officers in the president's roster (particularly of those who appeared otherwise qualified) lends weight to the supposition that an officer's party affiliation weighed in retention decisions. A careful analysis of

TABLE 2.1: *Discharges in the Reduction June 1, 1802*
Percentage Discharged by Military Qualifications and Political Affiliation
$(n = 230)$[a]

	Military Merit					
Politics	1st Class (1)[b] +	2nd Class (2) =	Total Qualified (1&2) +	Un- worthy Men (3) +	Quality Unknown (11) =	Row Total
Republicans (4)[b]	17% [d]1/6[c]	0% 0/4	10% [d]1/10	100% 1/1	— 0/0	18% 2/11
Moderate Federalists (5&6)	6% 1/18	40% 4/10	18% 5/28	57% 4/7	0% 0/4	23% 9/39
Strong Federalists (7)	0% 0/2	67% 2/3	40% 2/5	100% 2/2	50% 1/2	56% 5/9
No Political Creed (8)	0% 0/4	20% 1/5	11% 1/9	— 0/0	33% 1/3	17% 2/12
Political Apathy (9)	0% 0/4	40% 6/15	32% 6/19	100% 1/1	— 0/0	35% 7/20
Politics not Identified (10&11)	21% 5/24	32% 6/19	26% 11/43	90% 27/30	38% 25/66	45% 63/139
Column Total	12% 7/58	34% 19/56	23% 26/114	85% 35/41	36% 27/75	38% 88/230

Sources: "Annotated list" (see chapter 2, note 3). Francis B. Heitman, *Historical Register of the United States Army* (Washington: Government Printing Office, 1903).

[a] Number on active duty as of May 31, 1802.

[b] The numbers in parentheses are keyed to the categories described in the "annotated list." (see n. 3.)

[c] Fraction indicates the number in each category discharged and the total number in each category.

[d] Individual requested to be discharged.

the reduction using that annotated list demonstrates that politics did indeed play an important role.

When politics and military qualification are both considered, the pattern of dismissals evidenced is quite consistent with the administration's practice in the civil areas.[38] Officers considered "unworthy" were forced out with little reference to other measures, but, among those who were dismissed despite being found militarily qualified, political affiliation was clearly an important factor. Of the strong Federalists said to be qualified (1st or 2nd class) 40 percent were discharged. Among similarly qualified Republicans only one in ten was dismissed—and that officer asked to be removed.[39] Analysis reveals that officers who were unlikely to be influenced by Republican political appeals (strong Federalists and the politically apathetic) were eliminated at rates significantly greater than those who might have been more susceptible to the Jeffersonian persuasion (Republicans and those whose political loyalties were not yet fixed).[40] Likewise, moderate Federalists were discharged at a rate less than half that of their more doctrinaire political comrades—a practice consistent with Jefferson's actions in other departments. Here was another group that he hoped to win over to the Republican cause.

The reorganization and reduction had allowed the administration to remove many of its most vociferous opponents, but just as important was the effort to convert the more moderate Federalists—the Republican Federalists, as Jefferson referred to them—and those who, as yet, had no political creed. Both groups fared well during the reduction, and became the targets of a special suasion conducted by the President and Dearborn. Joseph Swift, the first graduate of West Point—but an Adams appointee, noted that his political views had become the subject of conversation when he dined with the President, and again later with the Secretary.

Mr. Jefferson jocosely asked me, "To which of the political creeds to you adhere?" My reply was, that as yet I had done no political act, but that my family were Federalists. Mr. Jefferson rejoined "There are many men of high talent and integrity in that party, but it is not the rising power"; a hint that was lost on me, though General Dearborn reminded me of it in a short period thereafter.[41]

The administration's efforts were not always so direct. The new Peace Establishment Act was consciously designed to extend the hand of conciliation, but in subtle ways. The reorganization and reduction that eliminated so many, produced promotions (and sometimes pay raises) for those senior officers retained. Such a windfall could hardly have been a coincidence coming from an administration that made so much of economy and an egalitarianism that seemed the antithesis of

rank and privilege. The Republicans had reintroduced the rank of
colonel and bestowed it on the commanders of the newly reorganized
infantry regiments and of the new Corps of Artillery. Their senior
subordinates also benefited. Dismissals were managed in such a way
as to insure the promotion, to lieutenant colonel, of the officer placed
second-in-command in every new regiment or corps.[42] To officers whose
upward mobility had been stymied even under the Federalist regime,
and who expected little, if anything, from the Republicans, these promotions must have been both a welcome surprise and evidence of the
new administration's charitable disposition. Nine of the ten highest
ranking army officers were made beneficiaries of Republican largess—
a result that could hardly work to the new administration's disadvantage.[43] Thomas Cushing, the one strong Federalist retained in a key
staff position, was the beneficiary of an even more special generosity.
Republican reforms had worked in such a way as to place him second
in command of his line regiment, though he would continue to serve
as adjutant general. His elevation within his regiment earned him both
a promotion and a pay raise, but there was more. The administration
also restored the additional compensation staff positions had earlier
paid. Over and above the ten dollars per month the promotion brought,
he would now receive an additional thirty-eight dollars for his service
as adjutant. The act not only brought a promotion, but virtually doubled his pay. Certainly, Cushing was an effective, proud officer whose
loyalty could not be bought, but as one who had earlier expected
affairs to "go to the right about," this turn of events must have been
welcomed.

Jefferson signed the act into law on March 16, 1802, and Dearborn
began immediately to notify those officers that were to be dismissed.
With that formality out of the way the administration moved on to
the task of organizing its own new military establishment.

The chaste reformation of the army that Jefferson had promised
Nathaniel Macon was fully voiced in the administration-sponsored
Military Peace Establishment Act of 1802. It was, however, cleverly
scored, and harmonized so well with the Republican idiom that its
full impact and importance was apparent to only a few. Portrayed,
and usually viewed, as little more than an economy measure, the re-

duction and reorganization provided a means of ridding the army staff of Federalist domination, and of removing many of the most obnoxious Federalist officers. It also furnished an immediate entrée for a number of Republicans, and hastened the day when Jefferson's appointees would constitute a majority in the army. It was the foundation upon which the administration would rebuild the army—an army that would come to reflect the republican society from which it was drawn, and an army whose loyalty to republican principles would be assured.

CHAPTER 3

The Founding of West Point

"It is contemplated to establish a Military School at West Point," the Secretary of War, Henry Dearborn, wrote to the commanding officer of that post barely a month after the new administration had taken office.[1] Within as short a time as another month plans had taken firm shape: a Superintendent had been selected; curriculum considerations were addressed; measures had been taken to engage a qualified faculty; and facilities were ordered ready.[2]

Dearborn and Jefferson moved with a purpose and alacrity that suggests they saw the new academy as part of some broader scheme. In fact, the school was *formally* established by the same Peace Establishment Act of 1802 that Jefferson would use to reform the military establishment as a whole. As the story will reveal, the institution at West Point provided one more means to further Jefferson's reformation and Republicanization of the army.

I

As early as 1776 there had been talk of a military academy. Little of substance was done, however, to create one until 1798, when Hamilton, nominal head of the New Army, began actively to promote the idea. In July Hamilton asked General Louis Le Begue Du Portail, former Chief of Engineers of the Revolutionary Army, to draft a plan for such a school. "This," Hamilton wrote him, "is an object I have extremely at heart."[3] Du Portail's plan reached Hamilton late in the year and was submitted to the War Department.[4]

Though nothing came of the effort in the spring or summer of 1799, Hamilton again turned his mind to the subject that fall.[5] "A regular Military Academy appears to me indispensable," he wrote James Wilkinson, and he promised that in the upcoming session of Congress this issue would command his "best exertions."[6]

In November, Hamilton submitted another plan which was forwarded to Congress, where it lay in committee until McHenry personally interceded with Harrison Gray Otis, the Chairman.[7] "I consider the measure of the last [greatest] importance," he said, "as it respects character, efficiency, utility and economy in every part and portion of our system of defense. . . . I ask for it your protection."[8] Under normal circumstances the bill might have been in good hands, but affairs were seemingly traumatized by the upcoming transfer of the seat of government from Philadelphia to the new capital of Washington. Moreover, Republican attacks against the Federalist military establishment were gaining breadth and vigor, and the Adams faction was beginning to lend support to the opposition. The Military Academy bill was attacked on its first reading, and again it languished. Otis, who had been charged by McHenry with the issue's protection, departed Philadelphia in late March and did not return to his seat until Congress met in the new term in Washington.[9] Lacking his support, and without the votes he might have been able to deliver, the bill died.[10]

Bleak as prospects for an academy appeared when congress adjourned, they did take a turn for the better in the summer of 1800 when the new Secretary of War, Samuel Dexter, began considering ways or circumventing congressional foot dragging and opposition. Hamilton too continued to press the issue. The school, he wrote Dexter, was "an object of primary importance" which should "be zealously pursued."[11] Dexter, however, needed no prodding; the basis of a plan was in hand. Cadets of Artillery and Engineer (presumably to have been groomed in their units to fill vacancies in the junior officer ranks) had been authorized in 1794. And, Congress had recently given the President power to appoint "teachers of the arts and sciences" for each of the regiments who could instruct them.[12]

Dexter's plan envisioned using existing authority to appoint cadets and instructors, and assembling them at West Point for training. That would require no congressional approval. West Point was chosen because facilities remained from a short-lived Revolutionary War era school, and because several companies of artillerists and engineers were already stationed there. President Adams was enthusiastic. "I am very ready," he promised, "to appoint both cadets and teachers," and he then launched into a catalogue of specific instructions. Dexter was to "take the earliest measures" to obtain the books, instruments, and apparatus that would be necessary and that were provided for by law. He was also to make inquiries "for proper characters" for teachers. The Secretary had recommended that they begin modestly with two teachers and an engineer. Adams concurred and suggested Captain William A. Barron, a former teacher of mathematics who had recently been commissioned in the Second Regiment of Artillerists and Engineers. Dexter, in reply, proposed as head mathematician a foreign engineer, Jean Xavier Bureaux de Pusy, but Adams rejected him. "I have an invincible aversion to the appointment of foreigners, if it can be avoided. It mortifies the honest pride of our officers, and damps their ardor and ambition."[13] While Dexter continued his efforts to identify other American candidates, he submitted the name of Jean Foncin, an associate of de Pusy's.[14] Adams tentatively agreed to appoint Foncin, but only if no other qualified American could be found. Even then, Foncin was not to be placed ahead of Barron. "If you can find another American mathematician better than Barron, it is well," wrote Adams, "if not, we will appoint him first teacher."[15] He suggested, nevertheless, that they should continue to inquire about young American instructors.

The upcoming fall election soon diverted Adams's attention, but Dexter continued his search for acceptable faculty. In August, he began to make inquiries about Jonathan Williams. Williams was not a teacher, but was well read in mathematics, the sciences, and natural philosophy. Neither was he a soldier—despite short service with the

Pennsylvania militia and volunteers during both the Whiskey and Fries's Rebellions—but his translation of two French texts on artillery and fortifications suggested more familiarity with these subjects than most active officers could boast. In September, Dexter offered Williams a commission as a major and hinted at his plans for a military academy, but made no promise to Williams of a position there. The latter declined in hopes of obtaining a civil appointment, but did agree to have his works on artillery and fortifications published for use by the War Department.[16]

However, in November events once again seemed to conspire against plans for the academy. The election was lost and a fire gutted the War Department offices, where work on all matters simply ground to a halt. "All the papers in my office [have] been destroyed," wrote Dexter, as he began the slow process of restoring some measure of order to the day-to-day routine.[17] But, coming as near the end of Adams's administration as it did, many projects were simply abandoned. For the President, personal tragedy further dampened any ardor he might have had for such tasks. Thus again, plans for a military academy languished.

In the early months of 1801, however, Dexter once more began to promote his plan, though he must have realized that little could be brought to fruition before the administration left office. He renewed the offer of a commission to Williams and this time was somewhat more direct about the role he might play. "Since the hint you gave me," Williams replied, in accepting, "I have been indefatigable in brushing up all my former mathematical knowledge and adding to the stock." In addition, Williams wrote, he had begun to gather a personal library on military engineering and had started work on a program of lectures on subjects he thought essential to the young men he soon hoped to be instructing.[18]

On his last full day in office, Adams filled the vacancies in the cadet ranks, and in doing so returned one last time to the project that he had embraced so warmly the summer before. But this effort, in the midst of an orgy of appointments made in the last days of the administration, was more an act of political opportunism than a compliment to those earlier plans.[19]

II

Adams departed Washington March 4, 1801, only hours before the inauguration, and left the fate of the military school in the hands of a new administration which, past actions being the guide, seemed likely to dismantle any progress that had been made. By all indices proponents of the school should have expected little. While in Washington's cabinet, for example, Jefferson argued that proposals to create a military school were unconstitutional.[20] More recently, in 1800, an Academy bill had been roundly attacked by the same Republicans who were now in control. For any who might have given thought to the issue on inauguration day the future of such a school must have seemed bleak.

Yet, the fact of the matter was that the new administration moved ahead quickly, and with an energy and facility that had escaped Adams, McHenry, and Dexter. Within a month the decision had been made to establish a military academy. In April, Dearborn selected Jonathan Williams to head the new school and offered the position of teacher of mathematics to George Baron, an Englishman who was at the time residing in New York, indicating that "West Point on the Hudson, will probably be the position for the school."[21] (Baron, who had taught at the Royal Military Academy at Woolwich, is not to be confused with the American, Captain William Amhurst Barron, whom Adams had favored, and who in 1802, was ordered to West Point, by the new administration, to teach mathematics.) Shortly thereafter, Dearborn notified the commander at West Point of the plans "to establish a military school" there.[22]

In May, the facilities at West Point were formally surveyed and plans made to prepare the buildings for use once again as a school. Lieutenant Colonel Lewis Tousard reported that $1,500 would suffice to prepare a mathematics room, a drawing room, quarters for the cadets, two mess rooms, and quarters for the officers, teachers, and surgeon, and their families.[23] Dearborn ordered work to proceed immediately—but did not ignore Republican concerns for economy. "No expense must be incurred," he instructed, "that shall not be actually necessary to render the . . . buildings comfortable."[24] Mayor John

Lillie, who took command of the post in June, supervised the repairs. His young daughter, Mary Ann, was amused when he had the seats painted green. But green paint was what was at hand, and economy dictated its use.[25] On July 2, less than four months after the administration had taken office, Dearborn ordered the cadets to West Point.[26]

One might ask how Jefferson and Dearborn were able to move so much more effectively in establishing such a school than the previous administration. In part, of course, they built on the foundation created by Adams and Dexter. But the real answer is bound up in the object that impelled them to do so at all.[27]

When obliged to account for their motive most modern writers have relied on a couple of related theses. They intended to create: either, a national academy that emphasized science instead of the classics; or a school that would provide trained engineers (military and civil) for the new nation; or both. "[Jefferson] was eager," writes Stephen E. Ambros, "to found a national institution that would eliminate the classics, add the sciences, and produce graduates who would use their knowledge for the benefit of society. Within this framework Jefferson realized that a military academy had the best chance of success."[28] Dumas Malone suggests that Jefferson was "little concerned about the professional training of army officers in time of peace, [but that] he fully recognized the usefulness of engineers in peace or war and valued the infant Academy chiefly for its potential scientific contribution.[29] Some authors have emphasized the military side of the school.[30] Most, however, have stressed the more pacific benefits it produced—particularly the engineers it trained.[31] But none have proceeded far beyond the limits of the two basic themes—science and engineering—and, under close scrutiny these efforts to explain Jefferson's founding of the military academy proved unpersuasive.

To take the first point, the extent of scientific training conducted at the military academy in its early years is very easy to exaggerate. As a matter of fact the administration even resisted efforts to increase the school's emphasis on science. When the first superintendent, Jonathan Williams, requested new books on science he was put off with the excuse that scientific thought was changing so fast that they would soon be useless.[32] The faculty would have been better characterized

as laymen with interests in science and mathematics than as professional scientists and scholars such as were beginning to appear on the
faculties at the better colleges.[33]

The curriculum at West Point clearly showed the very limited extent of either scientific or engineering instruction. In 1802 and for
several years thereafter, while many other schools were offering higher
mathematics, astronomy, natural philosophy, and chemistry as basic
fare, the military academy offered only the rudiments of mathematics
and military fortification.[34] The mathematics text—C. H. Hutton's
Mathematics— was basic enough to be used in primary schools. The
curriculum was in many ways more like that of a secondary or even
elementary school than that of a college—and for good reason. Some
cadets, upon arrival, could neither read nor write; a larger number
had little skill with either basic arithmetic or grammar.[35] Conse-
quently, instruction was designed to impart only the most basic, practical knowledge needed by army officers of that day—sufficient mathematics and practical skills to lay artillery, to construct simple
fortifications, and to make rudimentary maps—and even that limited
goal proved difficult to attain. After six years of effort, Williams conceded, "that mere mathematics would not make either an artillerist or
an engineer." French and drawing had been added but the administration resisted efforts to alter the basic nature of the school.[36]

If Jefferson *had* intended West Point to be an important element of
a national scientific school, then he would have made markedly different choices in terms of student body, faculty, and curriculum. But,
in fact the President's efforts to create a school that *would* promote
science were focused, and were always focused, on Virginia. Toward
that end, he indicated in 1803 that he was still "endeavoring to procure material for a good plan."[37] Similarly, his perfunctory call for a
national university another three years later contained no suggestion
that his school at West Point should be linked to it in any way. But
then, the military school he had created on the Hudson made no pre-
tense of being an institution of higher learning.

Moreover, turning to the second point, formal engineering training
was neither the sole nor the primary goal, nor was it even attempted
until nearly a decade after Jefferson left office. It was not until after
Sylvanus Thayer became superintendent in 1817 that the school be-

gan to produce truly qualified engineers. At "the elementary school at West Point," reported a graduate of 1806, cadets "so fortunate as to render themselves serviceable either in the artillery or engineers" must have done so by "their own industry, and not in the education received by them at West Point, which was barely sufficient to excite a desire for military inquiries and of military pursuits."[38]

The wording of the 1802 enactment formally creating the school—"The Corps of Engineers shall constitute a Military Academy"—has suggested to some that the school was intended to produce only engineers, but that fiction is easily dispensed with. Examine the facts. The law authorized the new Corps of Engineers up to sixteen officers—in a combined total of twenty officers and cadets. In the beginning there were to be ten cadets, but as the engineer officer ranks were gradually filled (to the total of sixteen) the number of engineer cadets would decline to four—maintaining the authorized combined total of twenty. Dearborn had indicated from the beginning that the academy would have from twenty to thirty cadets; he obviously envisioned it as something more than a mere school of engineers.[39]

In point of fact, the cadets appointed by Jefferson were almost uniformly given artillery rather than engineer warrants. A few, from among the best of these, were later chosen to be engineers. In 1808, both Jefferson and Williams called attention to the training in both artillery and engineering that the academy offered.[40] Though Jefferson usually referred to West Point simply as a school of instruction for artillery, noting that even the instruction in fortification was "for the artillery,"[41] the fact is that the school graduated men into all the branches. The newly commissioned graduates were assigned where they were needed. Of the fifty commissioned during Jefferson's two terms, fourteen were made engineers, twenty-seven were sent to the artillery, eight to the infantry, and one to the dragoons. (One additional cadet was graduated, but not offered a commission.)

Efforts to explain Jefferson's founding of the military academy at West Point as a manifestation of his Enlightenment interest in science or engineering simply cannot be made to square with the evidence. Rather, the founding of the military academy needs to be seen as part of a more comprehensive Jeffersonian plan for the military establishment as a whole. It was no coincidence that the formal sanction he sought for the academy was contained in the first broad program of military reform. The army had to be made compatible with the views of the new administration. The creation of the military academy is no paradox when viewed as part of a broader context: the necessity to create and safeguard a new, Republican regime.

Jefferson's announcement to Nathaniel Macon of a "chaste reformation" of the military establishment came just two days after the first formal report contemplating the establishment of the military academy.[42] That juxtaposition was hardly coincidental. The academy was to be an integral part of Jefferson's effort to Republicanize the army. The President's new school would prepare loyal young Republicans for commissioned service in his reformed army.

At West Point, where the first handful of cadets had been Adams appointees, the change was immediately noticeable. Cadet Joseph Gardner Swift, one of the Adams cadets, reported that after the new administration had come into power, "appointments to military office were made from families of prominent Democrats and of less Educated Persons than had been heretofore appointed."[43] Drawn from Republican families and trained under officers carefully selected for the task, these young men, it was hoped, would form an officer corps that would be thoroughly attached to the republican principles and institutions they were sworn to defend.

By the time the first cadets arrived at West Point in the early fall of 1801, the academy was ready for operation. The post, which had until recently quartered three of the four active artillery battalions, was more than adequate to accommodate the new academy. Facilities were actually little changed from Revolutionary War days when the post was first created to secure the upper reaches of the Hudson and prevent the young nation from being split. The two-story academy, with its green benches and blackboard, had been built sometime before 1780, but was little larger than a country schoolhouse.[44] It was situated on a large plain which overlooked the river and which was bounded by hills that reached up 400 feet to the still unfinished Fort Putnam. In the early years, officers and cadets alike were housed in small quarters, scattered about the base of the hills at the edge of the plain. There they organized themselves into messes. By 1807, after

Long Barracks at West Point by an unknown artist.
WEST POINT MUSEUM COLLECTIONS, UNITED STATES MILITARY ACADEMY.

This view of West Point shows an old Revolutionary War barracks and other buildings much as they stood in 1801. The two-story "academy" stands just above the line of troops. The long barracks was renovated for the use of the cadets—the first facility large enough to accommodate the entire corps—and stood as a landmark long after more modern buildings were constructed.

some extensive renovation, the cadets were moved into an old Revolutionary War barracks—a "commodious tenement" large enough to accommodate all who were attached to the academy.[45]

Baron began instruction to the first cadets in September 1801. Morning lessons, beginning at eight, consisted of four hours of instruction out of Hutton's *Mathematics*, "accompanied with a lecture from Mr. Baron upon its application." The afternoons were sometimes occupied with "brief military exercises," but were more often devoted to spirited field sports.[46]

Classes were suspended just two months later, however, when Baron was placed under arrest on charges stemming from an altercation he had with a cadet. The cadet, Joseph Swift, upon arriving at West Point, had moved into the "artillery mess" of Lieutenants William Wilson and Lewis Howard. Baron did not approve of this arrangement and ordered Swift to join the cadet mess. Swift objected that the cadet mess was both uncomfortable and irregularly organized.

Soon after my stating this objection to Mr. Baron, he sent his servant with a verbal order to me on this subject of mess. I declined receiving any order from the mouth of a servant. In an hour after [,] Mr. Baron appeared at the fence of the yard called the old artillery quarters, in which I was conversing with Lieutenant Wilson. He said to me, "Do you refuse to obey my orders?" My reply was, "No, sir, but I refuse to receive a verbal order by any servant." Mr. Baron replied, "You are a mutinous young rascal." I sprang over the fence to assault Baron. He fled to the academy, and thither I followed him. He bolted the door in my face, and from the window of the upper story . . . applied course epithets, and to which I retorted.[47]

Baron took the issue to Dearborn who at first instructed Swift to apologize or face dismissal, but later reconsidered. The officers on post had advised the young cadet to stand his ground, and themselves preferred charges against the professor. The spotlight had now been turned on Baron. This was how matters stood when Major Jonathan Williams, the new superintendent, arrived in mid-December. Williams, it will be recalled, was recruited by Dexter in the latter days of the Adams administration with this post in mind. Jefferson and Dearborn had soon concurred in that judgment.

It was decided that Baron should have a formal hearing on the charges, which specified that he had—among other things—habitually collected at his house "many citizens of the lowest rank and the most depraved character" and disturbed the general peace. His practice of degrading the military officers of the post and his ill treatment of his own wife and children were also issues brought before the inquiry. Baron finally offered to resign and left the post in early February.[48]

As distasteful as the affair was, it did allow the new Superintendent to establish firmly his own philosophy concerning internal relationships in the academy. "While it is my opinion," he wrote,

that every officer and cadet should be treated with the politeness and attention becoming military men, it is my determination to exact the most pointed attention to all academic Duties and Rules, whether relating to study, dress, deportment or anything else. The interior of our Academy (in the hours allotted to Instruction) must be considered like a parade among military men when on Duty, and only the objects of the Instruction must be permitted.[49]

Williams took over the teaching responsibilities upon Baron's departure and added geometry to the arithmetic and algebra already being taught. This new start, however, was short-lived. Williams became ill in March and took leave in order to recover. Classes were once again suspended. Progress toward the firm establishment of the school was, nevertheless, being made. The new Military Peace Establishment Act, which formalized Jefferson's creation of the new school, passed the Congress and became law in March. The new Corps of Engineers, it provided, shall "be stationed at West Point . . . and shall constitute a military academy."[50]

III

The act which created the academy, and which was proposed and supported by the administration, was carefully drawn to provide the President with exceptional powers over the new Corps of Engineers and the academy. The officers of that new branch were peculiarly beholden to him. The act called for a tiny engineer corps of seven officers (and ten cadets)—one major, two captains, two first lieutenants, and two second lieutenants—but added that,

the President is . . . authorized, when he shall deem it proper, to make such promotions in the said Corps, with a view to particular merit, and without regard to rank, so as not to exceed one colonel, one lieutenant colonel, two majors, four captains, four first lieutenants, four second lieutenants, [a total of sixteen officers] and so as that the number of the whole corps shall, at no time exceed twenty officers and cadets.[51]

In this corps Jefferson was not bound by the traditional promotion by relative rank and seniority that was the rule in the balance of the army. This corps, more than any other, belonged to him. A clue to the necessity for this very liberal arrangement lay in Jefferson's desire for particular control over those to whom he planned to entrust this new institution and the Republican sons who were to be educated there.

The search for a faculty had been begun early. Major Jonathan Williams and the unfortunate Baron were selected only days after the administration took office. In Baron's case the process may have been speeded by the fact that his politics were correct—he was a Republican—and he was known to close administration supporters. Not all choices were that easy.[52] In their consideration, Dearborn and Jefferson took care to avoid the selection of men whose strongly Federalist sympathies might hazard the project. Nonetheless, the same shortage of qualified Republicans that prompted the school in the first place made it necessary to cast an especially broad net in the search for instructors. Though Jefferson could hardly avoid choosing some whom he might label "Republican Federalists," he did reject all who were tainted by loyalties to the Hamiltonian faction. It surely would not do to have strongly antiadministration role models for young men who were to mature as administration supporters.

Williams, who was selected to superintend the new school, was the first military member of the faculty to the chosen.[53] A nephew of Benjamin Franklin, and for a time secretary to the old sage in Paris, he was a lay scientist and an officer of the American Philosophical Society. Jefferson had been acquainted with him in both capacities for a number of years. They had corresponded both in reference to society business and scientific endeavors. Williams was a moderate Federalist, but if Jefferson had any concerns about his loyalty, Williams made every effort to dispel them. In a solicitous letter to the new President just days after the inauguration, Williams took pains to assure Jefferson that his recent appointment to the army by Adams had had no political basis. He included with his letter his recent translation of H. O. de Scheel's *Treatise of Artillery* in the apparent hope that this might focus favorable attention on him. It may also have been that his correspondence with the former Secretary of War—his last letter to Dexter, written just a week before Jefferson took office, had indicated that he was preparing a plan of instruction appropriate to such an institution—was left for the attention of the new administration. Whatever the case, Dearborn offered him the new post after little more than a perfunctory interview.[54]

Jared Mansfield, another instructor of mathematics, came to the attention of the administration through the efforts of Abraham Baldwin,

Jonathan Williams (detail) by Thomas Sully.
WEST POINT MUSEUM COLLECTIONS, UNITED STATES MILITARY ACADEMY.

Jonathan Williams was appointed by Jefferson the first Superintendent of the Military Academy at West Point in 1801. A nephew and sometimes secretary of Benjamin Franklin, Williams was a long time member of the American Philosophical Society—a *lay* scientist with particular interest in the military art.

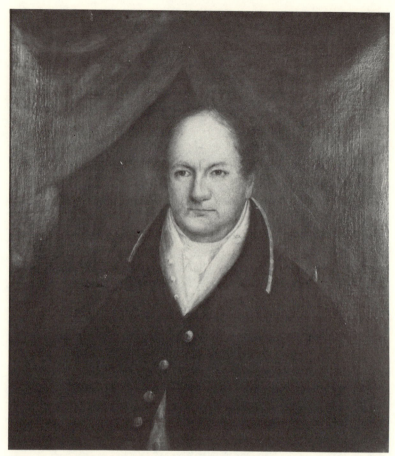

William A. Barron by an unknown artist.
WEST POINT MUSEUM COLLECTIONS, UNITED STATES MILITARY ACADEMY.

Captain William Barron was an early appointee to the faculty at West Point. During Jonathan William's frequent and sometimes extended absences, Barron was left in charge of the academy. Under his tutelage, however, it languished. He was dismissed in 1807 after he repeatedly ignored warnings concerning his personal conduct at West Point. That conduct prompted one legislator to seek a formal prohibition of *concubinage* in the regulations governing the army.

a Republican Senator from Georgia. Baldwin, formerly from Connecticut, had once been a student of Mansfield's and had been associated with him in local Republican politics. Mansfield was the most
politically active of the instructors at the military academy and among
the few longtime Republicans.[55] But, Mansfield had more to recommend him than mere politics. He had taught mathematics at Yale and
in 1801 had published a book, *Essays Mathematical and Physical,* which
included a chapter on the "Theory of Gunnery." Baldwin brought the
book to Jefferson's notice and the President ordered a number of
copies.[56] Mansfield's work had a practical bend—here, Jefferson concluded, was a man who would be comfortable with the Hutton text
which had been chosen for use at West Point. Baldwin was asked to
sound out Mansfield on the prospect of his teaching at the new school.
He did so in April 1802, and soon received a reply expressing interest
in the position. Dearborn offered Mansfield a commission the next
month and ordered that upon acceptance he should "repair with convenient dispatch to the post of West Point."[57]

Rounding out the new faculty was Captain William Amhurst Barron, the man who had been John Adam's first choice to head the
mathematics instructors. Thomas Cushing, the adjutant general, had
likely been aware of the earlier consideration of Barron and may have
brought him to Dearborn's attention. In any case the Secretary suggested the officer's name to Williams who replied that, though he did
not know him, "a teacher belonging to the corps would tend to har-
monize with the students and the officers of the Garrison."[58] Barron
had been serving with the Artillerists and Engineers since appointed
by Adams in 1800. He was a Harvard graduate and had tutored there
in mathematics. He was a moderate Adams Federalist of the ilk Jefferson believed compatible with republican institutions and a Republican administration. Barron, like Mansfield, was appointed an assistant professor of mathematics.[59]

Lieutenant Joseph G. Swift, who despite his early difficulties became the first graduate of the military academy in 1802, is often counted
among the early faculty members. Though not formally assigned to
the academy, he was commissioned in the Corps of Engineers and
stationed at West Point. When available he assisted with the instruction in mathematics. (He was at West Point for much of the academic

years 1803 and 1807, and during parts of others.) Swift was a moderate Federalist. He noted, however, that "politics were not generally discoursed upon at the Point, although the political opinions of every person there was well known, and newspapers of both parties were taken." Swift was interrogated personally by Jefferson concerning his politics and received the presidential admonition that the Republican party was the "rising power."[60]

In the spring of 1802, as his health mended, Williams began once again to organize the affairs of the fledgling academy. As he soon discovered, however, everything came under the watchful eye of the administration. Every change or addition encountered scrutiny and delay. When he had earlier attempted to introduce practical geometry into the curriculum, the absence of mathematical drawing instruments had thwarted his efforts. Williams immediately ordered twelve sets of the instruments and then put Dearborn on notice that it would "soon be necessary to have a good drawing Master."[61] Likewise, it had been necessary to order the surveying and mapping instruments required in both field work and practical exercises. In the spring he found it necessary to renew these requisitions, and added to them a request for one hundred copies of his own book (the translation of Scheel's work on Artillery) for use at the academy.

"I will consult the President, and will write you an answer," responded the Secretary of War to this renewed request for the instruments and books.[62] A few weeks later the promised answer arrived. "You will observe the notes made by the President on the margin of your list," wrote Dearborn, who then instructed Williams to procure those items that had been approved.[63]

Mansfield and Barron arrived at West Point in late spring—while Williams still convalesced at his New Jersey home. Based on his instructions, however, they once again opened classes. Just as he himself had attempted earlier in the winter, he directed the instructors to "proceed to theoretical and then to practical geometry, before the students acquired the higher parts of algebra; it would . . . be a loss of time to wait until a student becomes a perfect algebraist, before he is even a theoretical geometrician."[64] The system worked quite well and by late August, with the required equipment now in hand, the cadets were ready to proceed to field work where they could practice the problems of practical geometry. There they learned to measure "heights and relative distances" and the other skills, including drawing, necessary to make "a military map."[65]

With the addition of this field training the work day grew longer for the handful of cadets at West Point. Classroom work now began at 9 a.m. and continued until 2 p.m. every day except Sunday. Four afternoons each week from 4 o'clock until sunset, they met for field exercises.[66] Williams watched their progress with obvious pleasure. "My only regret in pursuing this plan," he wrote Dearborn, "is to see so few students; it would give me great pleasure to have my full number of cadets."[67]

The administration, however, moved very deliberately in its selection of cadets—a process that demonstrates the key role West Point was designed to play in Jefferson's reformation of the army. Dearborn and the President were diligent in their efforts to select cadets from within the country's Republican ranks. Applicants whose recommendations came from Federalist sponsors stood little chance; nomination by some High Federalist meant almost certain rejection.[68]

The political affiliation of academy applicants (or of their family) was a common and important subject of mention in letters of recommendation. The files of the very early years are fragmentary, but those that exist are indicative. "His father . . . is a Republican and I am informed the young man is also," reported one correspondent.[69] "He is . . . of reputable parentage, the family have all be[en] considered as thoroughly attached to republican principles," wrote another.[70] You will not take exception to "his moral character, his education [or] his political creed," reported still another.[71] These young men were all offered cadet warrants, though not all accepted them.

The failure to obtain an appointment was equally subjected to political interpretation. One such application noted that he published a Republican newspaper in New York state and that he had always been "attached to the principles of republicanism and your administration." When his letter met with silence he complained that "perhaps I may be suspected in my politics." The circumstances supported his conclusion. His paper had backed candidates who—in the

Thomas Jefferson by Thomas Sully.
WEST POINT MUSEUM COLLECTIONS, UNITED STATES MILITARY ACADEMY.

Jefferson created the military academy to help break the Federalist monopoly of office and opportunity. By providing training to otherwise, often ill-prepared Republican youth he opened the commissioned by the officers of West Point in 1822, honoring the founder of the military academy.

shifting factions of New York Republican politics—had allied themselves against Jeffersonian interests. The young editor was convinced that this had disqualified him in the President's eyes. "I was always a friend of his administration," he again pleaded, but the appeal fell on deaf ears. The young man's brother, who apparently was not tainted by the family association, received an appointment straight away.[72]

Jefferson knew from the beginning that it would be easier to create vacancies in the army than to fill them with qualified men of Republican persuasion. Federalists, on the average richer and more likely to have obtained an education, held the upper hand. Moreover, the colleges of the day tended to be Federalist and were often active in the political culture.[73] "The children of illustrious families," wrote John Adams, "have generally greater advantages of education . . . than those of meaner ones, or even those in middle life."[74] How was Jefferson to create a Republican army if Republican sons were unprepared for officership?

To break the upper-class monopoly of office and opportunity something had to be done to break the upper-class monopoly of education.[75] If the commissioned ranks were to be accessible to all classes of citizens; if the aristocracy of wealth and birth in the army was to be replaced with the aristocracy of virtue and talent; if men were to be used who lacked the advantages that wealth and position offered: education and training would have to be provided that would equip them to lead. It was no coincidence that the act which was the basis for the reform of the army also formalized the establishment of a military school on the Hudson. The new establishment of Republicanism in the army necessitated the academy that Jefferson created at West Point. His new military school would train men from the Republican stock of the country for positions of leadership in the new army.[76] For many it would provide the education they could not otherwise acquire. It was a key component of his new military establishment. Its creation was a conscious, purposeful act of an eminently and consistently political man. Far from being a school of science or engineering, the academy was created to provide Republican sons with the fundamental skills they would need to officer Mr. Jefferson's army.

CHAPTER 4

A More Republican Establishment

Henry Dearborn, as Secretary of War, inserted himself immediately into every aspect of his department—from strategy formulation to the everyday life of the soldier. Dearborn was not without experience: for a time he had served as deputy quartermaster general in the Revolutionary War under Washington; and in Congress he had been a close follower of military affairs—and a strong voice for economy in such affairs.

In the administration of his department he was ubiquitous—negotiating contracts, making assignments, settling arguments, inspecting, recruiting, and encouraging the design and construction of new equipment. "I like your Secretary," reported the Marine Commandant, "for he seeks to know what officers are doing."[1] He was interested in everything, looked everywhere, and asked question upon question. His interest, however, was pointed; the Republican imprint was unmistakable on all Dearborn touched. Daily the army became a more Republican establishment.

I

The most dramatic alteration to the staff in the new Republican establishment was the elimination of the quartermaster general. Dearborn

General [Henry] Dearborn by Charles B.J.F. de Saint-Memin.
NATIONAL PORTRAIT GALLERY, SMITHSONIAN INSTITUTION, WASHINGTON, D.C.

Dearborn's interests in his military establishment were all encompassing. He looked everywhere, examined every operation, and reformed the whole. A Republican imprint was unmistakable on all he touched.

made his own office the focal point of requisitions, though supplies were dispersed through three new civilian military agents and assistants appointed from among the officers in the field.

For administrative ease the country was then divided into three departments, each headed by one of the new military agents. Peter Gansevoort was appointed to the Northern Department in Albany, and served the posts in northern New York, those on the Great Lakes, and Fort Wayne. Abraham D. Abrahams was military agent for the Southern Department, first at Savanna, Georgia, and then at New Orleans after the acquisition of Louisiana. His department included all the posts from Georgia to the Territory of Orleans. The Middle Department was headed by William Linnard, whose responsibilities included the posts along the seaboard from Norfolk to Portsmouth, and in the west along the Ohio and Mississippi rivers, including Vincennes, Chickasaw Bluffs, Fort Adams, and Mobile. Upper Louisiana was later added to the Middle Department.

Linnard had the largest territory and the greatest responsibility. He not only shipped the military supplies within his own district but transported goods from Philadelphia and the other cities in his territory to the other districts. Gansevoort and Abrahams were allowed to purchase supplies locally, if available at a savings, but for the most part that was not the case. Linnard was a particularly good choice for this key position. "His integrity," Winfield Scott recalled, was "proverbial." For years,

he made . . . all disbursements on account of the army [except pay], amounting to fifty-odd millions, without the loss of a cent, and at the smallest cost in storage, clerk hire, and other incidental expenses ever known.[2]

Dearborn, however, supervised the process closely, requiring the agents to seek his authorization before making any expenditures that exceeded fifty dollars. This did keep spending down, but it also kept him immersed in petty details and often meant delays.

The administration made every effort to reduce dependency on foreign sources for materials essential to the nation's defense. Weapons and uniforms were among the first necessities, and domestic manufactur was encouraged. Muskets, for example, were ordered from several dozen private American contractors in addition to the national armories at Springfield, Massachusetts and Harpers Ferry. The administration's encouragement of Eli Whitney and his methods—and their patience with him—are particular evidence of this spirit.[3] Likewise, in the procurement of cloth and other manufactured products they sought domestic sources—choosing in favor of the American producers whenever possible.[4]

The purchase of clothing and most other manufactured items was the responsibility of the Purveyor of the United States, a position filled by Tench Coxe throughout most of Jefferson's two terms and beyond. On the orders of the Secretary of War he purchased—on the best terms available—the necessary supplies: uniforms, blankets, arms, hospital stores, and camp equipage. Though the newly created military agents were also empowered to purchase items under specific circumstances, the Purveyor remained the principal purchasing agent. He provided these goods to the Superintendent of Military Stores who either stored them or sent them, via the military agents, to the field.

By law, soldiers were to be provided a new uniform issue each year. If they needed more, they could draw them from surplus stocks and pay the contract price out of their monthly pay. As a rule the assistant paymasters were charged with the local issue and accounting for uniform items.

Troop complaints, in 1803, about the quality of clothing being supplied, set off a feud between Coxe, the purveyor, and William Irvine, the superintendent of military stores. Both faulted the procedures the other used in inspecting the goods. The conflict between the two men, however, went beyond that simple issue. It had roots in the continuing struggles within the Republican party in Pennsylvania, and the feuding and bitterness was not diminished when Callander Irvine succeeded to his father's position upon the latter's death in 1804. Coxe, who had been instrumental in Thomas McKean's successful gubernatorial campaign in 1800, could count on a network of close Republican friends throughout the country. The younger Irvine's support was, however, no less impressive; "a good push now," wrote one backer, General James Wilkinson, "and Tench will go—Mr. Gallatin is dead for it—the fellow [Coxe] is utterly incompetent."[5]

Dearborn tolerated both men and their antics well beyond the point where the interests of the nation were best served. Shortages in the field became a way of life. In the spring of 1808, when the army was rapidly expanded, the need of uniforms for the new troops became critical. Still, Coxe and Irvine feuded. Try as he might the purveyor could not get cloth that Irvine would accept. The impasse continued into the fall, long past the time when supplies could be safely shipped to the isolated frontier posts. The two men bickered and the army in the field suffered.

Critics have argued that Dearborn's organization of the department promoted inefficiencies.[6] Still, administrative organization was less of a factor than personal animosities and the peculiarities of the procurement system. There seemed no means to convince the principals to cooperate, or to force low bidders to perform according to the dictates of their contracts. Neither problem was unique to Jefferson's administration, and neither admitted any easy remedy. Still, under the watchful eye of Dearborn, the system worked reasonably well—in peacetime. It did not, however, prepare the army for war. Still, it is unlikely that any system would have. Dispersed as the army was in small, isolated posts—with garrisons seldom larger than a single company—there was little opportunity to learn the lessons of supply on the larger scale that would be required in wartime.[7] In any case, the lessons taught by the one significant campaign of the period—that on the Sabine in 1806—were forgotten in the turmoil of events that followed in its trail.

Dearborn was never hesitant to try new ideas. Convinced, as early as 1803, of the desirability of rifles, he directed Joseph Perkin, superintendent of the armory at Harpers Ferry, to start their manufacture—despite the fact that the army, as then constituted, had no riflemen. By 1807, over 4,000 had been produced. The next year, when the nation created a rifle regiment as part of a broad expansion of the establishment, the arms were ready.[8]

The Secretary's interests were legion. He was concerned about the quality of American gunpowder and, in 1803, initiated tests of various brands, including the eagle bearing packages from E. J. Du Pont de Nemours. Du Pont's powder was widely celebrated—even in verse—for its supposed excellence:

> foaming Brandywine's rough shore it came,
> To sportsmen dear it merits and its name;
> Du Pont's best Eagle, matchless for its power,
> Strong, swift and fatal as the bird it bore.[9]

But Dearborn was not purchasing powder for sport, and he remained convinced that the products of the young American gunpowder industry were inferior to those of the British and French. He continued the testing and the efforts to improve the American product until war threatened in 1808.[10]

Similarly, he pursued improvements in gun carriages for both light artillery and heavy guns.[11] In this effort he worked through Colonel Henry Burbeck, the commander of the artillery regiment. Burbeck, whose units were scattered throughout the country, was posted in Washington where, in effect, he served as Dearborn's principal assistant on technical artillery matters.[12]

In keeping with the general thrust in procurement, Dearborn and Burbeck energetically pursued the production of American-made cast-iron guns. Not only were the iron cannon cheaper—only one-fifth to one-sixth the cost of those made of brass—but the country had vast reserves of iron ore, and little or no copper and tin for brass. Dearborn was so confident in these experiments that he ordered the purchase and casting of brass cannon stopped until iron guns could be proven. He followed the progress of the experiments closely and sought out advice on all the details of design and construction. By measured steps the weight was reduced to that of similar brass pieces; in the end the work proved eminently satisfactory.[13]

Light, or flying artillery had come of age on European battlefields, and it was an innovation that Dearborn hoped to introduce into America. When light artillery was finally authorized in 1808, the Secretary lost no time in organizing the first company. It was an experiment in field artillery proper. George Peter, formerly an aide to Wilkinson, was promoted to Captain and given command of this unique unit. Established in Baltimore, the original test of such an organization's capabilities centered around two brass six-pounders which had been recently acquired from the French—part of a large artillery park they had left at New Orleans. Artificers at Fort McHenry were ordered to build gun carriages and limbers. They were to be patterned after those introduced into the French army in the 1760s by Jean-Baptiste de Gribeauval—an innovation which had made the French artillery mobile, accurate, and (until copied) superior to any other. They also built caissons for hauling ammunition. Dearborn's instructions were specific; the caissons should hold fifty cartridges, "ten of which ought to have round shot, and ten of grape or canister." As soon as one of the guns and its accessories was readied, Captain Peter was ordered "to proceed, at the rate of five or six miles an hour, from Baltimore to [Washington], and to make some experiments [there] by maneuvering the cannon at different directions."[14] These experiments proved so successful that the administration ordered the company, or as much of it as was ready, to march in the 4th of July parade just a few weeks later.

When completely outfitted, Peter and his command were ordered to New Orleans. As a test of their capabilities in the interior, they were sent overland to Pittsburgh and then by barge to their destination. They departed the day before Christmas, 1808, and despite the winter weather, made the trip with relative ease. "The performance of the new light artillery in the late march has exceeded my most sanguine expectations," Peter reported to Dearborn. "The gun carriages, ammunition wagons, fixed ammunition, etc, have arrived without the smallest injury." The trip, he surmised, could have been made in ten days if the luggage wagons had been able to keep pace with the guns.[15]

Light artillery had demonstrated its utility in America, but the experiment came late in Jefferson's second term and Dearborn had no opportunity to extend it. The next administration had no interest in such contrivances, and abandoned the project and sold the horses.

The reorganization of the staff, though motivated by political concerns, was achieved at little loss of efficiency. That is not to say that the new system was particularly good, only that it was no worse than the old one. Neither was geared to respond to the needs of a rapidly expanding army such as might have to be created in times of crisis or war.

The adjutant general's affairs were little altered. In fact, order brought by the new administration had been a welcome relief from the turmoil that had surrounded the latter period of the Adams presidency. Under the former President, cabinet changes, the move to Washington, and then the War Department fire had made a shambles of any administrative efficiency that had existed. As the change of administrations had approached matters had grown even worse. Cushing complained to Wilkinson that there was,

great difficulty . . . in getting business properly done in the present per-
plexed state of things. . . . In short everybody and everything here are so
much out of tune that I wish with all my heart that the period was arrived
for transferring the public functions.[16]

Promotions made throughout 1799 and in the first half of 1800 were
neither properly announced nor recorded; as a consequence both personal accounts and public records were in disarray.[17]

With the new administration things proceeded more smoothly.
Cushing was still harassed by the work load but now at least he received additional compensation for his efforts. He once asked Dearborn for an additional clerk but got nowhere. With only one clerk to
assist him he sought a means of cutting down on his correspondence.
"Were I to answer every letter I receive from more than fifty corre-
spondents," he wrote one officer, "my whole time . . . would not be
sufficient for the purpose." Under the pressure of "great labour and
fatigue," he adopted a strict rule:

Never write a letter merely to acknowledge receipt of one, or to converse on
subjects with which I have no connection and over which I have no control;
but when it is necessary for me to write[,] to examine and acknowledge the
receipt of all letters from that correspondent.[18]

Faithful to this rule, he acknowledged in this note the receipt of six
letters that had accumulated from the addressee during the preceding
seven months.

Cushing's role as inspector suffered both from the demands of his
other position and from the elimination of his deputies. He made a
few brief inspection trips, but by and large this duty was neglected.
Training and tactical doctrine or "discipline"—two areas under the
preview of the Inspector—had been neglected for years and received
no immediate attention under the new administration. With renewed
hostilities in Europe in 1805, however, this deficit in American military thought became more clear. In the American army both training
and discipline were still prescribed by Baron Frederick von Steuben's
Blue Book, the thin Revolutionary War classic. Though an American
work or two had been produced on artillery, virtually nothing had
been written in this country to modernize the employment of infantry, cavalry, or riflemen. Elsewhere, however, under the combined

influence of the French Revolution and Napoleon Bonaparte, old systems had given way to the newer methods. America's drill and discipline had become outmoded.

In the years of peace between 1801 and 1805, Napoleon reorganized his armies along lines that made possible almost unlimited decentralization under a single supreme command—a scheme that would ultimately be adopted by all European forces. The flexibility gained through this organization, combined with his genius for their employment, made the French army a devastatingly effective instrument. Though not all the advances in European military thought had applicability to the minuscule army of the United States or its mission on the frontier, some developments did seem ideally suited to both the physical and political climate of the young nation.

It was William Duane, publisher of the Republican *Aurora,* and a militia officer in Philadelphia, who first attempted to adapt what had been learned in Europe to the American experience.[19] Closely associated with the administration, his efforts in this behalf were carefully encouraged by Dearborn. When Duane seemed to falter in 1808, as his economic fortunes declined, the administration offered him a lieutenant colonelcy. Duane accepted and completed the work the next year while an officer of the regular establishment.

To Duane, elements of French experience in the first years of the Revolution seemed applicable to the American situation. When the drilled and disciplined units of the old Royal Army dissolved, the gaps had to be filled by men who had patriotic fervor but no inclination to accept the discipline essential to traditional infantry. "On the first moments of the French Revolution," Duane wrote in 1807, "endangered by the defection of so many military men . . ., they saw the necessity of a new organization for raw troops." That new organization was the rifle corps or light infantry. Duane saw applicability to the American experience. "It is upon *rifle corps* and horse or *flying artillery* . . . that we shall have to rely principally . . ., because," he wrote, "they are the means best suited to the nature of our country."[20] As a modern scholar put it,

the revolution armies made a virtue of necessity, elevating the Rousseau-ite concept of 'the natural man' to a guiding principle. . . . They were fighting as free men to defend freedom, and for free men a combination of individual skirmishing and mass columns of attack to cries of *a la baionnette!* was the natural mode of fighting. Indeed it was the only possible mode of fighting for troops who had only handled a musket for the first time a day or two before the battle.[21]

Americans too would attempt to make a virtue of the same necessity. The light troops on the French model, with riflemen and skirmishers, were a "republican" solution—a social reformation. It was natural then that the greatest proponent of this new discipline in America was one of the foremost Republican pundits of the day.

The general catalyst for Duane's thinking was a new threat of hostilities with England; the proximate stimulus, a military work by Maximillian Godefroy which had appeared in August 1807, just after the menacing *Chesapeake-Leopard* encounter.[22] Godefroy examined America's defense, and found it wanting. He rejected two of its staples—the militia and Steuben's old system of discipline. Only regular forces trained in the modern French modes, he argued, could meet the new European armies on equal terms.

Duane debated Godefroy in two extended essays in his *Aurora*, and conceded much of the latter's argument.[23] Recent changes in warfare, Duane agreed, had made Steuben's military tactics largely inapplicable; Americans should adopt the new French doctrine.[24] The militia was ineffective—"courage and good intentions," he granted, "do not alone make soldiers." Still, he would not concede that the militia should be replaced.

Duane's solution was a new militia organization of cavalry, artillery, and infantry, with emphasis on the light elements of these, particularly the flying artillery, light infantry, and riflemen. This new militia, Duane argued, could be prepared to meet and defeat the enemy. No great "scientific acquirements" were necessary. "Modern tactics," he asserted, "is the result of that experience, which men of intelligence, have derived from the study of history, and the study of mankind."[25] By the time Duane penned these lines he had already settled on a plan to assemble as much of this history and thought on the art of war as possible, and to make it readily available. Thus the genesis and schema of his *American Military Library*.

Duane collected, in his personal library, more than 350 volumes of military works, and read widely in it. He was particularly impressed by the works of Guibert, Bulow, and the contemporary writing of a young Swiss officer on the staff of Napoleon's army, Antoine Henri Jomini. When Jomini's thin volumes on the campaigns of Frederick the Great *(Traité des grandes opérations militaires)* began to appear in 1805, Duane seized on the work.[26] He sought out each new volume as it appeared, and had it quickly translated as he prepared his own manuscript.

His early attention to Jomini is both remarkable and revealing, for this young interpreter of Frederick (and later Napoleon) was to become one of the most influential figures in modern military thought and was to have a profound impact on American military thinking (though it was to be another three decades before this influence was truly felt.) Duane sensed the significance of this young writer's insights long before most others.[27] Jomini's particular fame lay in his systematic attempt to identify basic principles in warfare. The brief concluding volume of the *Traité* contained his first effort to identify the fundamental precepts inherent in all military questions. "There have existed for all times," Jomini wrote, fundamental principles, on which good results in war depend . . . [and which] are unchanging, independent of the kind of weapons, of historical time and of place."[28] Jomini later concluded that there was a single organizing theme underlying all the operations of war—*mass*, or throwing the preponderance of one's forces upon the decisive point—but the detailed explication of this did not appear until 1836. Hints of it, however, or more precisely Jomini's own working out of this proposition, can be found throughout the *Traité* and it was from that process that Duane drew his understanding.[29] Achieving mass, of course, required precise maneuvers and marches—an essential ingredient if forces were to be put into action speedily and in unison. Duane came amazingly close to Jomini's larger meaning when he argued that,

The first axiom of military institution is, that the unity of force constitutes the military power, to produce this unity or consentaneous action of numbers, is the object of discipline.[30]

Duane, however, was less interested in principles than in practices—the stuff of discipline and training. The unstated principle may have been *mass*, but the practice that allowed one to concentrate forces was the ability to determine how long it would take to march each of several dispersed units to a given point. Accurate calculations of the march required established norms of both pace (the length of step) and cadence (the number of steps per minute). Duane grasped this point immediately. "The great importance of the length of *pace* and *cadence* . . . is not sufficiently understood or appreciated," he pointed out. "It can never be repeated too often . . . [that] uniformity in marching, the length of pace, and the unity or cadence of the step . . . is the most important part of military discipline."[31]

When completed, however, the *American Military Library* proved both too extensive and too unfocused to be useful as a drill manual. Whatever Dearborn's hopes for Duane's work, the administration left office before it was published and it was never adopted by the army. William Eustis, the next Secretary of War, had little interest in such subjects. The American army struggled along without effective doctrinal reform until after the War of 1812.[32]

In the process of reform, the administration decided to update the old Articles of War—created in the midst of the Revolution—that were still the legal framework of the military establishment.[33] This code was long out of date; it did not even reflect the changes in governmental form effected by the new Constitution. Since its drafting only the articles relating to the administration of justice had been revised in any important way.[34]

Though the revised Articles prepared in early 1804 followed closely the original, the new code did reflect the larger role of the Executive that was defined in the new Constitution, and did consolidate some new power into the hands of the president. For example, they gave him the sole authority to institute military courts of inquiry, curbing the power of the army's senior officers who had sometimes used courts as a means of asserting their own influence and power. Most changes were modest: the functions and status of the new Corps of Engineers were spelled out; new limits were placed on corporal punishment (only fifty instead of a hundred lashes were now permitted); courts-martial were prohibited from trying an offender more than once for the same crime; and the President alone was to be authorized to pardon a death sentence.[35]

Only one administration proposal proved contentious—a charge that, on the surface, was no more than an editorial rewording to reflect constitutional alterations. In place of the earlier prohibion against "traitorous and disrespectful words against the *authority* of the United States in Congress assembled," the new article prohibited the use of "traitorous or disrespectful words against the President" or other members of any of the branches of the federal or state governments.[36] The new wording, however, protected both the *authority* and the *person* of the President and government officials, and the more radical republicans objected. Joseph Nicholson said, "it was not his wish to fence round the President, Vice-President, and Congress, with a second sedition law." If officers conducted themselves improperly, he argued, there were other means available to discipline them.[37]

While Nicholson and others might have objected, the administration felt the necessity of such a provision. Some elements of the army remained politically alienated; among the infantry in the West, all the officers of some commands were reported to be "non-Jeffersonian."[38] The administration counted this provision essential, and rather than lose it, the entire bill was allowed to die.

The bill was reintroduced in 1805. Again, it was amended in only minor ways: officers from the marines and army were allowed to serve on each others' courts-martial; it provided defendants the right to challenge (for cause) officers sitting on their court; and it created a statute of limitations of two years for offenses under the new Articles.[39] Other reforms failed. The committee reported out provisions that would have specifically forbidden "concubinage," the "playing at cards or Dice," and "frequent intoxication," but these were rejected. Robert Wright, of Maryland, who suggested restoring the privilege of dueling, could not secure even a second for this motion.[40] The new bill appeared headed for passage.

Suddenly, however, this issue became intertwined in a controversy between General Wilkinson and Colonel Thomas Butler. The issue was Wilkinson's order for the army to cut or crop their hair and Butler's continued refusal to do so. A memorial from the Tennessee militia officers requesting relief for Butler portrayed this as an abuse of power which they suggested should be corrected in the new Articles.[41] When the Senate received the petition, a coalition of antiadministration and anti-Wilkinson men sent the matter to the committee which was then considering the proposed new code. Though the Senate refused to act on the petition the introduction of this issue added a level of emotion to the debate that proved an obstacle to effective deliberation. William Branch Giles became so vexed that he declared, "Soldiers & subordinate officers ought never to *think*—that they were bound to yield passive obedience & nonresistance in all cases whatever to the commands of their superiors."[42]

With this the administration abandoned efforts to secure passage of the bill in that session, but did reintroduce it in the first session of the next (9th) Congress. There one further article was added, giving the President power to prescribe the uniform.[43] Approval now came after only brief consideration. The new Articles of War were set in place in 1806. It had taken two years to get the measure passed. In the end, however, the only concession made on the point of early contention— conduct toward the executive—was to change the word "traitorous" to "contemptuous," a move that seems to have strengthened, not weakened, the provision.

The difficulty that the administration experienced in pushing through this rather straightforward revision of the out-of-date, Revolutionary War era Articles, was partially a result of the fragmenting of the Republican party that had begun to occur by the end of Jefferson's first term. A faction of Old Republicans associated with John Randolph saw the Jeffersonians as too moderate—as having abandoned basic republican principles. Until they themselves split on the army issue in 1808, they opposed any strengthening of the regular establishment or any efforts to enhance federal authority over the existing force—proposals which, for reasons seldom exposed to public scrutiny, the administration almost universally sponsored and supported.

II

Dearborn took a personal interest in the welfare of the soldiers. He watched the monthly troop returns closely; if he sensed that men were becoming ill because of an unhealthy site, he ordered corrective measures taken or detachments moved. To leave troops in an unhealthy place (unless necessitated by some urgent military requirement) would,

he instructed Wilkinson, "be considered as sporting with men's lives."[44]
Dearborn also followed the individual situations and performance of
his officers. He moved the aging and infirm Zebulon Pike to a less
demanding and more remunerative job, and when the old soldier was
no longer able to perform even those duties, allowed him "to retire to
such place as is most agreeable and to continue in furlough [with pay]
until further orders."[45]

The Secretary, however, insisted that as a norm duty must take
precedence over mere personal convenience. He was particularly irri-
tated when officers resisted the transfers he ordered. "It would appear
that you as well as many other officers of the army," he wrote one
lieutenant, "consider a military commission" a mere convenience and
whenever "military duty in any degree interferes with private concerns, the service is no longer an object worthy of attention."[46] "It
has become too common," he wrote another, "for Officers when ordered on duty" to complain that it was "very inconvenient for them
to comply" rather than giving "that prompt obedience, which is so
essential to a military system."[47]

This went hand-in-hand with a natural, Republican interest in
economy—which the secretary counted both in virtue and a necessity.
"I have too much reason for believing that you are not as attentive to
the rules and regulations relating to expenses," he wrote Lieutenant
Colonel Thomas Hunt who was soon to take command of an infantry
regiment. He expected more, he said, "from an officer of your rank
and experience." It was becoming "fashionable," he lamented, for officers to pay less attention "to minute parts of their duty than to other
considerations" that related more "to private convenience than the good
of the service."[48]

It was considerations of economy which provoked Dearborn to remind his commanders that in the interior it was not necessary to build
elaborate earth and masonry fortifications. There they would need
only stockades with blockhouses that would provide "flank fire from
every part of the post." He repeatedly specified how these were to be
organized and built, and often provided sketches and designs. A
stockade for a company of troops was to be "constructed of timber
slightly hewed . . .; the magazine for powder to be of brick of a conic
figure" capable of holding fifty to one hundred barrels. "The block-

Fort Washington, on the Site of Cincinnati.
NATIONAL ARCHIVES.

Fort Washington was similar to the timber forts Dearborn prescribed for many locations in the interior. Blkock houses at each corner provided covering fire along each parapet or wall. Heavy earth and masonry walls were unnecessary where the enemy seldom had cannon—and never had them in significant numbers.

houses are intended to be so placed as to secure from the upper & lower stories the whole of the lines." Leaving nothing to chance, Dearborn specified the size of rooms and even the number and size of panes of glass for windows.[49]

The soldiers' day-to-day routines—whether in a coastal garrison or a frontier fort—were quite similar. Fatigue or work details alternated with drill, parade, and roll call. The daily life of a soldier was a series of responses to the beat of a drum. It called him to work, to church, to witness punishments, to eat, and even to receive his daily ration of whiskey.

The daily subsistence ration, inexplicably reduced in 1799 was re-established in 1802 at a rather liberal level.

1 ¼ pounds of beef (or ¾ pounds of pork),
18 ounces of bread or flour, and
1 gill of rum, whiskey or brandy.

In addition, the contractor was required to supply—with each hundred rations:

2 quarts of salt,
4 quarts of vinegar,
4 pounds of soap, and
1 ½ pounds of candles.[50]

Rations were provided in the same manner as they had been since the Revolution—through contracts to the lowest bidder. But, subsistence contractors sometimes found it impossible to supply rations to the far-flung frontier posts at the prices agreed—and still profit in the trans-action. Too often they simply refused to perform as agreed. At best, this arrangement created a situation that guaranteed rations of mar-ginal quality. Jacob Kingsbury reported, in October 1805, that he was about to order his men to begin hunting to supplement the supply of rations he had been receiving.[51] Even less isolated posts had their dif-ficulties. "There exists, at [West Point], a serious evil respecting ra-tions," complained the instructors at the academy, who went on to explain that there had been no fresh meat delivered in over two-and-a-half months.[52]

Troops were encouraged to grow fruits and vegetables to supple-ment this diet and enhance the nutritional balance. Garden plots were a regular feature in the layout of posts or garrisons. In addition, su-tlers, who operated stores at the garrisons, were authorized to sell the troops a wide variety of items that were not issued, and to augment certain portions of the official issue—such as the liquor ration.

The liquor ration was a rather generous one in any case. The ad-ministration had set the daily portion at one gill (¼ pint) of either rum, brandy, or whiskey. (The ration had varied over time from a high of one gill to a low, in 1799, of ¼ gill.) In 1803, Dearborn pressed his commanders to substitute beer for the hard liquor and actively promoted the effort. "Although there appears to be large proportion of your men who prefer Whiskey to Beer, it may be proper to make an experiment for two or [three] months and if after such an experiment they continue to prefer Spirit they may have it."[53] Despite this promise, Dearborn ignored the soldiers' preference and continued to promote beer. "Good malt Liquor with a due proportion of Hops therein, is much more healthy than the use of ardent spirits," he argued, and insisted that his officers should "endeavor to convince the troops of the usefulness of the change."[54] When they objected that beer was not available to them, Dearborn arranged for it to be shipped from Philadelphia.[55] The next year he secured legislation permitting the substitution of "malt liquor, or low wines" for the usual spirits, and ordered contractors to furnish it, where available, from July 1 though mid-October.[56] This effort, however, proved both unsatisfactory and unpopular. Local beers often proved inferior and wine was not readily available except when imported—a limitation that made it undesirable due to cost even before the embargo precluded it. This experiment was ultimately chalked up as a failure and abandoned.[57]

The sutlers were closely supervised by the post commanders who when necessary, could set their prices and even close them down. Liquor was often the source of problems. Captain John Whipple, on the frontier at Fort Wayne, had so much trouble with intoxication among the troops who frequented the sutler's establishment that in December 1804, after repeated threats, he shut down that dram seller. He relented, however, on Christmas Eve and, in the spirit of the season, reopened the bar.[58]

The true norm of a soldier's life was manual labor or fatigue duty. The special fatigue uniform issued each man testified to the universal nature of this employment. Work on stockades or fortifications, buildings, roads, gardens, and all the facilities necessary to frontier (or coastal) army life, occupied the bulk of the day.

Still, parade and ceremony remained an important feature. Dress reviews, roll call, guard mount, and simple marching were part of every soldier's daily routine. Drill and discipline were the art form of the professional military. The prescribed manner of combat—to the degree that it was prescribed for the American army—was to form ranks and move shoulder to shoulder and fire volley after volley into a similar line of enemy. Only constant drill could instill the discipline necessary to act in such unison in the face of enemy fire. But, most American officers had long since concluded that combat in the wilderness did not—and would not—bear resemblance to that formal practice. As a consequence little time was spent in such drill. At the same time there was little incentive to seek an alternative more suited to the American situation. The army was effectively without such a discipline, but when Lieutenant Colonel Constance Freeman suggested modifying Steuben's drill, he was instructed by the War Department not to innovate.[59] Duane's later work, prompted by the threat of war in 1807, was a recognition of this deficiency—though, as a beginning, it proved unrewarding.

Reflecting the ongoing political and social reform, the army took on a more republican appearance. Despite some opposition, the new establishment moved inexorably toward a new look. Thus, military dress edged toward plainer fare. Trousers—with short socks and half-gaiters—became uniform items; knee breeches, stylish shoebuckles, and long socks were dispensed with. Lace and other trims also began to disappear.[60]

Shortly after Jefferson took the oath of office, General Wilkinson ordered officers and men alike to cut their hair short, and to dispense with the practice of powdering it and putting it up in queues. This innovation owed much to trends in Republican France and their popularity with many in the new administration—though the general insisted that cropped hair was simply more healthy. Still, he broadcast the fact when Jefferson cut his hair. "You will be pleased to signify to the Gentlemen of the corps, that the President of the United States . . . has thought proper to adopt our fashion of the hair, by Cropping," Wilkinson wrote to urge compliance.[61] Regardless, some officers strongly opposed the change. Several threatened to resign over the issue of giving up their queues, and at least one did. Another, Colonel Thomas Butler, went before a court-martial twice for his failure to comply with the order.[62]

Attracting young men into the army was not always easy. In a land of so much opportunity there was no rush into the ranks. Proximity to the frontier and the promise of opportunity in general hampered recruiting. Republicans had traditionally applauded this situation. Jefferson had pinned his hopes of forestalling Hamilton's misuse of the New Army precisely on the inability to recruit any but officers. The new administration now found that the same conditions worked against their efforts. "The Universal prevailing principles of Republicanism, [by which] I mean Equality, Render the Recruiting business almost entirely insuccessful [sic]," complained one recruiter.[63]

The Military Peace Establishment Act of 1802 spelled out the ground rules for recruiting. For every "effective, able-bodied citizen of the United States . . . at least five feet six inches high, and between the ages of eighteen and thirty-five years" who was enlisted for a term of five years, the recruiting officer was paid two dollars. Recruits under the age of twenty-one were required to obtain the consent of their parents or guardians. Fraudulent enlistments by underaged youths was the most common problem. Officers who were under pressure to procure recruits were sometimes less than diligent in checking the age of young men who, despite their fuzzy-cheeked appearance, claimed to be twenty-one. The Secretary of War investigated numerous complaints and usually agreed to discharge the underage soldier though he sometimes insisted that a substitute be found, or that bounties or uniforms be returned.

Recruiters approached the difficulties of their task in different ways. Lieutenant Alexander Macomb "hired music to facilitate the Recruiting Service"; others resorted to more underhanded methods.[64] "I hope the difficulty in procuring recruits," wrote Dearborn to one, "has not induced you either [to] enlist improper characters or to take advantage of anyone while in a State of intoxication." Both, he pointed out, "are strictly forbidden by law as well as by every principle of propriety."[65] When he received complaints alleging that a man "in a state of brutal intoxication," had been induced to enlist, he immediately ordered the man discharged. "Consider yourself fortunate," he wrote the officer who had enlisted him, "in escaping with no other inconvenience than of paying all expenses incurred by [the] enlistment."[66]

The center of recruiting activity for each area—the rendezvous— was manned by a captain or senior lieutenant, and a sergeant. Dearborn specified that officers should be drawn from those with more experience. "Young officers," he said, "are not usually suitable for such service."[67] These sites were generally opened in the late winter or early spring and remained in operation until they had filled the companies they served. It was here that recruits were assembled and given some rudimentary training in drill and discipline—"the men at drill are to be taught how to stand, to fact, to march & to wheel before arms are put into their hands," directed Wilkinson.[68] Here, they were provided with a uniform and given half of the twelve dollar enlistment bonus that had been promised. Upon joining their companies they received the balance of their bonus and the remainder of their uniform issue. The recruiting officers were provided funds to pay the bonuses and to procure temporary billets. Uniforms and muskets for training were issued based upon the numbers recruiters were expected to enlist. When a sufficient number of trained men had been assembled they were marched off to join their companies. As a rule, to save marching, the rendezvous served those companies to which they were closest or most convenient. Through monthly reports to the Adjutant General, Dearborn kept track of the pace of recruiting and occasionally interceded to direct recruits to units being readied for particular operations.

With the reorganization in view, little or no recruiting had been undertaken in the winter and spring of 1801–2. As a consequence the strength of the army declined throughout the next year. By December 1802, Dearborn concluded that a new program of recruiting was essential. He directed that each regiment should fill its own ranks and specified the sites at which recruiting rendezvous should be located. "I have avoided the large Seaport towns from a conviction that Soldiers recruited in those places are far inferior to those recruited in Country places, and much more frequently desert."[69] It could not have escaped Dearborn's notice that such a plan—recruiting in the more staunchly Republican countryside, recruiting yeoman farmers rather than urban mechanics—would promote a more Republican army.

Except in 1803, when an unusually large number of men finished the five-year tours they had begun in 1798, this recruiting tactic kept the army's regiments reasonably well filled. Aside from Philadelphia, the larger cities were not tapped until the dramatic expansion of the army is 1808.

Recruiters followed the population westward. By 1805, officers were canvassing settlements in Kentucky, Tennessee, and along the Ohio and Mississippi rivers. There is some indication that either recruiting became easier as time went on or that recruiters became more efficient. Whichever the case, the number of rendezvous declined from twenty in 1803 to seven in 1805 despite some increase in the number of recruits required. Dearborn sought about 400 recruits in 1803, 1,000 in 1804, and from 600 to 700 each year thereafter until 1808.[70]

Duty on the frontier and in isolated garrisons sometimes brought danger, but the more constant threat was loneliness. Fort Pickering, at Chickasaw Bluffs on the Mississippi, was "shut out from all communication with the world," complained Lieutenant James Swearingen, the post commander. It is "situate[d] in a savage country . . . [with] not a companion, [and] no society except two families of Indians." "I can justly use the term of the Poor Irishman," he said, " 'two thousand miles from home and forty miles from any place.' "[71] There was danger, but it lay more often at the hands of friends, or in accidents and illness, than in actual hostilities. The records of the eight years of Jefferson's two terms have revealed only one soldier killed in action—a member of Lieutenant James B. Wilkinson's party who was killed by Indians while exploring the Missouri River in 1805.[72] Many more died in fights or duels, and even more from the effects of weather and disease. Yellow fever was prevalent in the south and periodically took its toll at army posts. As the time to occupy New Orleans neared, in 1803, General Wilkinson called for "rotation of duty during the summer season." Otherwise, he said, they should "calculate on the death of one forth our troops the first season." Though his concern might have seemed misplaced in the light of the immediate experience, events only a few years later would justify it.[73]

For all of its drawbacks, life on the frontier—far from the diversions of civilization—did hold some advantages for the soldier. In the midst of the citizenry, soldiers seemed naturally drawn to trouble—the catalysts were most often drink or women, or both. But, even in official dealings the soldier was often at a disadvantage. "A soldier has a bad time of it in a dispute with a Citizen," wrote William Burrows, the marine commandant. "If he neglects his Duty, he will get 100 lashes;

if he does it, he will probably get hung."[74] Life in the wilderness precluded much of this danger.

Burrows lament—and Albert Gallatin's oft cited quip that the army should be consigned only "to distant garrisons"—was prompted by an incident at a Fourth of July gathering for the luminaries of Washington society, where marine sentinels were provided to insure that guests were not disturbed. When one citizen became abusive upon being ordered away, an overzealous marine enforced compliance with his bayonet. "The very sight of a bayonet to preserve order amongst citizens rouses my indignation." wrote Gallatin to his wife concerning the incident. "I never want to see the face of [a soldier] in our cities and intermixed with the people."[75]

Yet, Gallatin's piqued remark illustrates neither his own nor general Republican attitudes toward the military—those of John Randolph and a few other Old Republicans excepted. Despite his outburst, Gallatin made no effort to effect the removal of the army to the frontier or to keep "that perhaps necessary evil" out of the populous regions. Nor was there ever any such intent on the part of the administration. Though much of the army was assigned on the frontier, fully one-third of it was stationed in and around many of the nation's most important eastern cities. In the summer and fall of 1802, fourteen of the army's twenty artillery companies garrisoned forts along the Atlantic seaboard. There were troop contingents—often two companies strong—in Portland, Portsmouth, Boston, Newport, New London, New York, Philadelphia, Baltimore, Norfolk, Charlestown, and Savannah. More were added in 1807. Washington, in turn, was garrisoned by Burrows's marines.[76]

Gallatin was rightly appalled by the marine's bayoneting of a citizen, but his angry words were just that. Though he had no affection for the military, neither did he abhor them. He had been an early advocate of Republican cuts in the military establishment, but economy had been his goal. As we have seen, the "reduction" that was ultimately effected sought a different objective. And, just a few years later, it was Gallatin who urged the use of the army in port cities and border towns to enforce his faltering Embargo.

Jefferson's *chaste reformation* moved doggedly to adjust the make-up of the army, its routine operations, and the day-to-day life of the soldier.

Over time, each began to display unmistakable marks of republican character. Dearborn insisted on economy in all affairs and usually achieved savings without significant loss of effectiveness. New debates arose over military doctrine—over how to fight—and again these bore a marked republican imprint. Even the soldiers took on a more republican look: cropped hair in place of queues and powder; and trousers instead of knee breeches, long socks, and buckled shoes.

The Secretaries of War had always been involved in the routine administration of their department, but with the Republican reforms, Dearborn became even more closely associated with day-to-day matters throughout the army. That, of course, was by design—a part of the social and political reformation he had helped to craft.

CHAPTER 5

The Army in the Field

Jefferson and Dearborn did not forget, as they pursued their ongoing reformation, that since the initial reorganization in 1802 the army in the field and its general had largely escaped the reach of their efforts. The implications were troubling. There had been frequent talk of breaking up the Union—first from those in the West and, as time went on, from those in the Northeast. The nation had existed a bare two decades, and for less than that under the new Constitution. National identity and allegiance were not yet firmly fixed.[1] In this regard, the loyalty of the army was a special concern.

Dearborn kept a watchful eye on the army and on Wilkinson. As a safeguard, however, the administration cautiously cultivated divisions within the ranks that would lessen the general's influence.

I

The army existed to be an instrument of national power and policy, and that fact was not lost on the President or his Secretary. An examination of the record shows not only a consistently high level of involvement on the part of the administration in army affairs, but an elevated understanding of the value of that force as an element of power. As Mary P. Adams has very adequately demonstrated: while attempting to resolve problems through diplomatic means, they "at

the same time made adequate military preparations in the event that
war should occur."[2] Adams focused on Jefferson's second term, but
is now clear that from the beginning orders to the field were purposeful and part of a coherent strategic design. Troop deployments, the
establishment of fortified posts, and even mundane road building were
all elements of a larger scheme.[3]

The disposition of troops reflected the relative concerns of the ad-

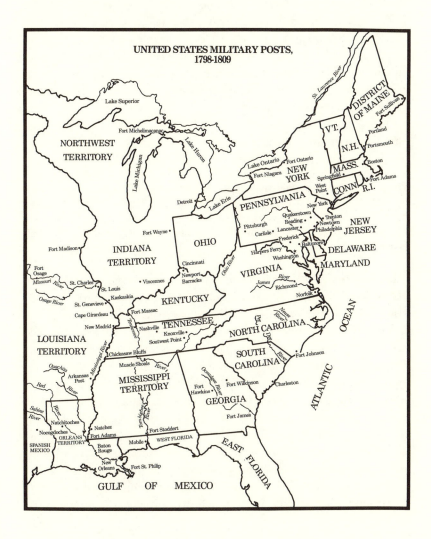

UNITED STATES MILITARY POSTS,
1798-1809

ministration, The English, French, and Spanish were all potential adversaries; therefore every border had to be defended. Along the maritime frontier it was artillery companies that garrisoned the forts. Elsewhere the infantry prevailed, though some artillery companies were also posted in the West. In the beginning, ten companies stretched across the northern frontier from Fort Ontario at the eastern end of that lake, through Niagara to Detroit, Michelimacanac (later called Mackinac), and Fort Wayne. On the southern and western borders, nine companies manned posts form Kaskaskia through Fort Massac, Chickasaw Bluffs, and Fort Adams (on the Ohio and Mississippi), to Fort Stoddert on the Mobile. Seven more occupied Vincennes in the Indiana Territory, Fort Wilkinson in Georgia, and Southwest Point in Tennessee, where they attempted to protect white settlers from the Indians and vice versa.

During his first year in office, President Jefferson listened with concern to rumors of Louisiana's retrocession from Spain to France. In April 1802 he wrote his minister to France, Robert Livingston, that:

There is on the globe one single spot, the possessor of which is our natural and habitual enemy. It is New Orleans, through which the produce of three-eights of our territory must pass to market, and from its fertility it will ere long yield more than half of our whole produce, and contain more than half of our inhabitants.[4]

In the days just before this letter was written, the administration had reviewed its military stance along the Mississippi—opposite Louisiana. The reorganization under the Military Peace Establishment Act had left two companies of artillery and four of infantry at the two posts on the river—Fort Adams (30 miles south of Natchez) and Fort Pickering at Chickasaw Bluffs (present-day Memphis). Both were resupplied via the river. If hostilities broke out, that avenue would be problematical; the enemy occupied the opposite bank and might choose to close the river. Under those circumstances an overland route was essential, and Dearborn ordered the construction of a road from Muscle Shoals, on the Tennessee, to Natchez. Supplies could then be moved down the Ohio, up the Tennessee, and thence overland if the situation required. That road and others being built would also link the region with Nashville and through that settlement to other points.

"The opening of the road from [the] Tennessee to Natchez," Dearborn stressed, was "highly interesting to the public." To spur progress he suggested rotating the military work parties every sixty days. The Secretary had earlier provided for additional pay for the troops employed in such enterprises and now promised added compensation to the officers. He urged that the reorganization which had just been ordered under the new Military Peace Establishment Act not delay the project.[5]

It was uneconomical, Dearborn said, to open a wide road in regions where traffic was to be light. "Such part as is not actually used in traveling," he noted, "will soon be overgrown in bushes and be more difficult to pass than if the original growth was standing." Instead he directed that the right-of-way be cleared to a width of only twenty (and later sixteen) feet, and that the road itself be only half that width. The roadway, he directed, should be "cut close to the ground, and smoothed for passengers. . . . Swamps and streams should be causewayed & bridged." "The great object," he observed, "is to have a comfortable road for horses and foot passengers."[6]

When the road was completed in 1803, Dearborn stationed small detachments of troops along it to protect travelers and shipments. The President had suggested sending "a small body of cavalry, or mounted infantry, to be perpetually scouring the road [to Natchez]," presumably forgetting that the cavalry had recently been eliminated and that he had no mounted infantry (or dragoons) in the regular establishment.[7] When and where national interests directed, Jefferson immediately moved to secure overland communications, but, in regions where roads were of less strategic importance the federal government did little to aid the local officials.[8]

In August 1802, when the Spanish commandant closed the Mississippi to navigation and denied Americans the right to ship their goods through New Orleans, the administration undertook a cautious program of augmenting the American forces along the river. The ultimate solution, however, lay in acquiring New Orleans. In January 1803, Jefferson dispatched James Monroe to assist Livingston with the negotiations to purchase the city. What would happen if the mission failed was a matter of wide speculation; many in the army anticipated war. "If Mr. Monroe succeeds all will be well, but if he should fail, we shall have noise, bustle & Bloodshed," wrote James Wilkinson. "Keep your sword with a good Edge, & be quiet," he advised.[9]

Dearborn informed Wilkinson that though the country had "assurances of the friendly disposition of the French and Spanish courts," it would be "advisable to make some preparation for a different state of things."[10] With that in mind the Secretary ordered the further reinforcing of Fort Adams, at the edge of the Spanish-occupied territory. Companies from Chickasaw Bluffs and Pittsburgh were ordered to the fort. He sent additional cannon and an engineer who could supervise the construction of new fortifications. Two further companies at Southwest Point were alerted to be ready to move on order. Congress took the same cue and authorized a new arsenal and magazine for the western reaches which would hold 8–10,000 stand of arms. Dearborn chose to put it in Kentucky within easy reach of the Ohio river, and via that to the Tennessee or Mississippi Rivers.[11]

Wilkinson reported, in July, that the troops at hand—with those from Southwest Point—would suffice to accomplish a *"coup de main"* if the Spanish were not alerted in time to reinforce from Havana. At the same time he grumbled bitterly about the failure of the administration to consult with him or even to keep him informed of its intentions. "If anything professional is to be done which may imply trust & hazard—I hope you may confide the execution to me, or give an order to someone to knock me in the Head."[12]

Any plans for a strike to seize the Spanish port, however, were soon overtaken by word of the purchase of Louisiana. Eyes now focused on the upcoming, rightful occupation of New Orleans. Decidus Wadsworth, the engineer who had been sent to Fort Adams, was told to stop work there and try to learn what "repairs may be necessary on the Fortifications & Barracks at New Orleans."[13]

The army now began to prepare for a new mission. To the North, along the Mississippi, Amos Stoddard was ordered to cease work on a new post on the east bank just below St. Louis. Instead, he was directed to prepare to take charge of the newly purchased territory to the west.[14] The army was charged with the governance of the new territory until a permanent civil government could be appointed and organized. But, officers were carefully instructed "to conciliate the feelings of the people" and to assure them "that they will be secured in all their rights civil & religious."[15] While the army prepared for this new role, Jefferson, at Monticello, toyed with plans for exploring the new domain.

Suddenly, in September, the Spanish ambassador announced that, "France has no authority to [sell Louisiana] without the approval of Spain," and that no such approval had been given.[16] A short time later he amplified that message. The sale of Louisiana to the United States was founded on the violation of the treaty by which France had gained the territory and therefore "the treaty of sale made between France and the United States does not give the latter any right to acquire and claim Louisiana."[17] In the meantime, word had arrived that France itself was having second thoughts about the sale. As a precaution Jefferson urged that Congress act "with as little debate as possible" to consider the treaty consummating the sale. Approval quickly followed. Jefferson immediately called a cabinet meeting "to decide . . . definitely on our measures to be dispatched Westwardly."[18]

Jefferson had no intention of losing this prize; military force would be used, if necessary, to secure it. In a personal note to Dearborn, the President advised him to see Senator John Smith of Ohio, who during the summer recess had visited New Orleans and who had "very important information as to the force, [and] the dispositions [of the Spanish], and the topography of the country."[19] The chief executive considered dispatching orders immediately to General Wilkinson to effect the occupation, but delayed until Congress passed an enabling act. That done, he issued orders to take possession of New Orleans. Wilkinson was advised that if the Spanish resisted, and if he considered his force adequate, that he should take whatever measures were necessary to seize the city and to capture Baton Rouge en route. At the same time Dearborn ordered the militias of Kentucky and Tennessee—and boats to move 4,000 of them—to be prepared to help, should force prove necessary. Governor W. C. C. Claiborne of the Mississippi Territory, who with Wilkinson would receive Louisiana, was ordered to march immediately with whatever militia was available to join the regulars and take the city. Delay might allow the Spanish garrison to be reinforced. The government moved forcefully to secure its purchase of New Orleans and Louisiana.[20]

After the orders were issued, there was little more the administration could do. Transit time for dispatches, each way, was roughly a month—no word in return could be expected before the end of the year. In the meantime, Jefferson began the task of organizing the government of the new territory, and Dearborn turned his attention to the events at Fredericktown, Maryland where Colonel Thomas Butler (and his quene) stood before a court-martial. Still, these diversions were not enough to keep those in Washington from fretting over what might be happening along the southern reaches of the Mississippi.

Finally, on January 6, 1804, unofficial letters arrived indicating a "tranquil state of things at New Orleans." Three days later more such reports were received, but there was still no official news from either Wilkinson or Claiborne. Dearborn, in frustration, wrote a bitter reprimand to the general. This was "the only period for several years past, when information had been highly important relative to any Military operations" and he had expected prompt reports. "Some explanation will be necessary." "You have taken no notice of any of my previous letters," the Secretary charged, and he ordered Wilkinson back to Washington as soon as essential security arrangements were made at New Orleans.[21]

Communications from Wilkinson concerning the situation were, of course, on their way. The orders to occupy New Orleans had arrived in the first days of December. On December 4 Wilkinson had ordered his troops to be prepared to leave at a moment's notice, but preparations were slow and the force did not actually embark for almost a week.[22] They proceeded slowly but without incident and reached a point two miles above the city on December 15. There they camped while arrangements for the transfer were worked out. Wilkinson, mindful of his instructions, cautioned his men that the upcoming days would require "much self denial & restraint." These were "a polished people" he warned, but "strangers to our manners, our law & our language" and we must "receive them into the great family of our country with cordial embraces."[23] It was from this camp that he dispatched his first report to Washington. That letter and two later reports which recounted the peaceful transfer of the territory arrived in the Capitol on January 16.[24]

On the day appointed for the ceremony, December 20, the troops

Raising the Flag by T. de Thulstrup.
FROM THE COLLECTIONS OF THE LOUISIANA STATE MUSEUM, NEW ORLEANS.

Despite the formal transfer of Louisiana, many citizens of the region had little to bind them to the United States. That lack of allegiance was problematic in light of the region's strategic vulnerability, and the proximity of the Spanish. The Burr conspiracy highlighted that vulnerability.

entered the city and took up their positions in the Place d'Armes. The occasions went smoothly. Pierre Clement Laussat, the French commissioner, exchanged credentials with Claiborne and Wilkinson, then formally transferred title to the delegates of the United States, absolved the people of their former allegiance, and presented the keys of the city to Claiborne. Claiborne, in turn, spoke to the crowd and assured them of the protection, under the new government, for the full enjoyment of their liberty, property and religion.[25] While many of the inhabitants had reservations, they refrained from any overt demonstration, and the transition began in a quiet, orderly fashion.

Wilkinson immediately took measures to gain control over the territory. He sent a detachment down the Mississippi and occupied Fort St. Philip. At the same time, he sent other troops upstream to occupy a post at the mouth of the Arkansas River, and inland to the key post at Natchitoches. Later, as they were freed from other duties, American troops also took possession of the posts at Ouachita, Opelousas, and Attakapas.

Wilkinson's greatest concern was about facilities in New Orleans which the Spanish still occupied and which they insisted need not be turned over immediately. About 300 Spanish troops remained. He felt it essential to retain a sizable contingent of this own in the city until these Spanish forces departed.[26] The bulk of these were removed from New Orleans in the spring, but their presence, until then, had tied down the available American troops and delayed the occupation of some inland posts. United States forces now faced the Spanish in Texas across a long and often ill-defined boundary—a situation that promised difficulties.

In Washington, meanwhile, the administration began to consider how it would defend the new possessions. The forces that had earlier been collected at Fort Adams were already in New Orleans—three artillery companies and four companies of the 2d Infantry Regiment. This was the greatest concentration of forces in the nation. Nonetheless, at the end of January, Dearborn ordered three more artillery companies from the East Coast to move there and redistributed the remaining forces in order to garrison all the key eastern fortifications.[27] He wrote Wilkinson that the three artillery companies would be on their way as soon as possible, but that no decision had yet been made as to how many more troops could be dispatched. He did advise, however, that gunboats would likely be built to help protect the mouth of the river and Lake Pouchartrain. He reassured the general that all measures necessary were being taken to "render the Government of Louisiana sufficiently secure."[28]

Rumors of troop movements were rife in Washington.[29] Dearborn had scoured the coast for troops and had sent all he could get his hands on to New Orleans.[30] Meanwhile, he pressed the recruiting effort and made plans to bring the army to full strength.[31]

The strategic importance and the peculiar vulnerability of New Orleans were quite clear to the administration, and they moved with decisiveness to consolidate the new position. Isolated as it was—distant from the mass of the nation's population—the traditional reliance on a militia force to provide a defense was not practicable. Moreover, there was no certainty that what local population there was would prove loyal to the American government so recently imposed on them. Regulars were essential to any defensive arrangement at New Orleans and the administration moved unhesitatingly to shift forces to accommodate the situation. Dearborn ordered Lieutenant Colonel Constance Freeman to proceed to New Orleans to take command of the posts in that region.[32] The importance of the post, and the number of troops, required a senior officer. Freeman, who was second in command of the Corps of Artillery—many of whose scattered companies were now in, or en route to, that city—was a logical choice. Wilkinson was told to depart as soon as Freeman arrived.[33]

With the situation temporarily in hand, plans went forward to gather, in Washington, a group that could formulate a permanent solution for the defense of New Orleans. Wilkinson would soon be on his way and the engineer, Wadsworth, who had been studying defensive needs of the city, was also ordered to the capital to confer.[34]

In the meantime, the administration made a series of decisions that were designed to strengthen the allegiance of the populace in the newly acquired regions. The existing militia establishments were cautiously accepted, including a "Corps of Freemen of Color." But Claiborne was instructed to proceed with caution—particularly where the selection of officers was concerned.[35]

On a strategic level the need for better communication with the new territory was clear. "[It] is becoming indispensable" wrote the President, "for us to have a direct communication from the seat of our government with that place, by a road." The route he suggested was one that would "keep below the mountains, the whole way" and would run through Creek country in Georgia (and what would become Alabama). In exchange for the right to build such a road he suggested that the Creeks "will have the advantages of keeping taverns for furnishing necessities to travellers, of selling them provisions & receiving a great deal of money in that way." Only months before, Georgia officials had been told that such projects would be left to the states. Strategic necessity now dictated otherwise.[36]

In St. Louis, on March 9, 1804, Captain Amos Stoddard formally took possession of Upper Louisiana from the Spanish—first in the name of France, for whom he also acted, and in turn for the United States. He had waited on the east bank of the Mississippi almost nine months for this day. His instructions from Dearborn had been simple and to the point: take possession of the territory and secure the allegiance of the inhabitants. "Conciliate the feelings of the people," Wilkinson had written in July of the year before, with the first word that the transfer was forthcoming. In November he wrote again in the same vein, "You will treat the Officers and inhabitants in a most polite and friendly manner and take every measure in your power to protect the inhabitants in their rights and privileges."[37]

For a time Jefferson considered the possibility of reserving much of the west bank of the river as a vast Indian territory. "The inhabited part of Louisiana [Orleans]," he wrote John Breckinridge, would immediately become a territory and soon a state. But above that, the best use he could see for the country "for some time" would be to exchange it with Indians now to the east of the river for their present lands.[38] He hoped, he said, "to transplant our Indians" across the river "constituting them a Marechaussee to prevent emigrants crossing the river, until we shall have filled up our vacant country on this side."[39]

To complete the circle, the administration toyed with the prospect of removing the whites who had already settled on these prospective Indian lands. In December, 1803, after brief visits to a few of the settlements in the new territory, Meriwether Lewis, recently the

President's Private Secretary and therefore privy to much of his thinking, wrote Jefferson that he believed the "wish to withdraw the inhabitants of Louisiana" could be accomplished "in the course of a few years" if the country was "justly liberal in its donations" of land in the regions to the east. "The American emigrants," he went on, "will be more readily prevailed on to come into the measure than the French."[40]

In the end, the impracticability of such a course prevailed and the administration scaled back its plans and turned again to the task of winning over the inhabitants of Upper Louisiana. Lewis accompanied Stoddard to St. Louis to accept the territory, and assisted and advised him while final preparations were made for his own departure with Clark to the westward reaches the next spring. Stoddard had been directed to act as Commandant of Upper Louisiana until a civil government was appointed. Subordinate to him, the federal government commissioned four district commandants—Samuel Hammond, Return Meigs, Richard Kennon, and Seth Hunt. Their first task was a "complete organization of the militia" in the key districts of St. Louis, St. Charles, Cape Girardeau, and St. Genevieve. Dearborn warned that the creation of a loyal force would hinge on "a judicious selection of officers."[41] Bringing the region under effective control was an urgent concern. Winning over the principal provincial leaders was the key.

It was probably Meriwether Lewis who suggested that the new military academy at West Point could be used to aid in that process. Lewis had surely been aware of the motives that led to the creation of the school and was therefore keenly aware of the political utility of the institution. The plan was simple. The sons of the area's leading citizens should be made cadets and sent to West Point. What better way to bind these families to the new nation—and to the administration? It was agreed without hesitation.

Within less than a month after accepting the territory for the nation, Lewis and Stoddard had recommended three young men—Charles Gratiot, Auguste P. Chouteau, and Augustus Loramier—as cadets. The Gratiots and Chouteaus were two of the most prominent families of St. Louis; Loramier was the son of the former commandant of Cape Girardeau, a district second only to St. Louis in importance. Before the end of the year three more were added to the list: Louis Valle, whose father had been Commandant of St. Genevieve; Pascal Vincent Bouis of St. Louis; and a second Loramier son, Louis.[42]

Stoddard, who was less attuned to the political advantages to be achieved, objected to the appointment of Louis Loramier because "he exhibited too much of the Indian in his color." "This circumstance," he continued, "may make his situation among the cadets at the school rather disagreeable."[43] Dearborn and Jefferson ignored the advice and the young man was enrolled. Despite Stoddard's fears (or prejudice) the younger Loramier spent two years at West Point without recorded incident, graduated, and was appointed an ensign of infantry in November, 1806.[44]

II

Though exploration occupied but a small part of the army, it was an important function—often directly linked to contingency planning and the gathering of intelligence. It is unnecessary here to repeat in detail the well-known stories of these expeditions, though it is important to recall that they were essentially military expeditions and one more role in which Jefferson had cast his small army. The Lewis and Clark adventure, in particular, caught the nation's fancy. Their return in September 1806 was an occasion of national celebration.[45]

In May 1804, after several months in St. Louis, Meriwether Lewis and coleader, William Clark, were prepared to head up the Missouri. The expedition was conceived in late 1801 and, as Donald Jackson has so aptly demonstrated, was prompted by—or was Jefferson's response to—descriptions of an earlier overland passage through Canada to the Pacific.[46] Planning, coordinating, and training had occupied the better part of two years. The party had chosen to spend the winter of 1803–4 on the eastern shore of the Mississippi, roughly opposite St. Louis, correctly judging that the formal transfer of Upper Louisiana to the United States would eliminate many problems of coordination.

President Jefferson had been succinct in pointing out that the object of their mission was to explore the Missouri river" and to attempt to find "communication with the waters of the Pacific." He had been more minute in detailing how they should proceed. He wanted a full account of the peoples they encountered, and specified a long list of "objects worth of notice"—animal, vegetable, and mineral. Moreover the group should be "friendly & conciliatory" with the natives and assure them "of our wish to be neighborly, friendly & useful to them."[47]

In the spring of 1805 Wilkinson was appointed Governor of the newly organized Louisiana Territory (formerly Upper Louisiana).[48] Jefferson meant this to be a temporary expedient, a transition from the formal military rule under Captain Stoddard to a full civilian government. But there were advantages in this transitory arrangement; the army was particularly suited for the special missions of exploration that Jefferson and Dearborn—for essentially different reasons, the one scientific, the other strategic—desired to undertake.

Immediately upon his arrival at St. Louis in late July 1805, Wilkinson began making plans for "three or four small expeditions."[49] In August he ordered Lieutenant George Peter with Jean Pierre Chouteau, a prominent St. Louis fur trader, to ascend the Osage River and obtain permission of the Indians to establish military posts.

A few days after Peter and his party had departed, he sent Lieutenant Zebulon M. Pike north on the Mississippi to explore the sources of that river. In addition to their primary mission, Wilkinson assigned secondary tasks which reflected the President's interests. They were to map the rivers by "magnetic needle" and time measurements, "noting whatever may be remarkable on their banks." Their orders contained quite specific instructions:

Direct your attention particularly to ye productions of the Animal, vegetable, and Mineral Kingdoms. . . . [Send back] whatever curiosities you may have collected. A Skeleton of the nondescript animals whose bones are found in the Country is highly desirable and also Mineral Salt, ores, stones and even wood which may be new to us.[50]

An additional object of these explorations—one prescribed by Dearborn, though apparently without written instructions—is clear from the general's correspondence with the Secretary. The general had been instructed to conduct reconnaissance and prepare plans for contingency operations against Mexico. He was delighted at the prospect and hinted of this in a letter to Jonathan Williams a few days after Lieutenants Peter and Pike had departed. Commenting on the conjunction of an old ambition and his new station, he wrote: "For a Military Man of 30 who looked forward to the submission of The Mexican Kingdom, it [Louisiana] is a noble theater." Here he could scratch an old itch. "I shall ascertain every devious as well as direct route," he wrote, but added a note of melancholy, "I fear I shall not last long enough to avail me of my knowledge."[51]

In October he dispatched a third expedition under his son, Lieutenant James B. Wilkinson, ostensibly to move up the Missouri River to the mouth of the Platte River and establish a fort. Shortly after they left, however, word circulated that their true object was to create an advance base near Santa Fe. Whatever the truth of this, Lieutenant Wilkinson accomplished nothing. About 300 miles upriver—following the course Lewis and Clark had taken the year before—they ran into hostile Indians; a soldier was killed, and the party turned back. They were again in St. Louis by early December.[52]

Lieutenant Peter had better luck on the Osage. He completed his mission and returned to St. Louis in October. Pike also succeeded and returned the following spring, after wintering in the headwaters of the Mississippi. A trunk full of items gathered by these two officers and their parties was collected, tagged, and sent along to the President. Included in the potpourri were samples of river salts, iron, lead, spar, and pumice; a buffalo pelt and two horned toads; a "cluster of fruit from the cottonwood tree;" and a map that traced a route to Mexico City through San Antonio, Laredo, Monterey, Saltillo, and San Luis Potosi.[53]

Pike set out again in July 1806, this time with Lieutenant Wilkinson. Their orders set out several objectives, but the clear (though unstated) purpose was further reconnaissance of routes along the northern approaches to Mexico. First, some Osage prisoners were to be escorted to their village—retracing the route George Peter's party had taken the year before. Following that Pike was told to reach the Comanches and win their allegiance. He was also instructed to explore the headwaters of both the Arkansas and the Red Rivers. (The last order revealed a paucity of knowledge about these rivers, whose headwaters diverge rather than converge.) Pike and Wilkinson split up when they reached the Arkansas River. The latter turned downstream and returned to civilization, while Pike turned westward in search of the Rockies. He found them in November but they proved inhospitable. Without proper cold weather gear the small force suffered terribly through the winter. Late in February 1807, a Spanish patrol from Santa Fe found the group and escorted them to Santa Fe, then Chihuahua, and finally, in late June returned them to American soil.[54]

III

General Wilkinson had barely departed the Capitol for his new post in St. Louis in the late spring of 1805 when rumors began to circulate concerning connections between himself and Burr, and of clandestine meetings the two had held the winter before.[55] These rumors were further fueled by their meeting at Fort Massac in early June as both men traveled down the Ohio.[56] The former Vice-President was touring the West, making plans and securing allies for an adventure of the next year. He had detoured to Nashville to see Andrew Jackson, and had left believing that he had won over the general from Tennessee. Burr was now on his way to New Orleans.

The two men spent several days conversing and then parted ways. Burr began a leisurely trip south with several army officers who were en route to the city for the second court-martial of Colonel Thomas Butler—still the defiant possessor of his queue. Wilkinson continued on to St. Louis.

Precisely what the two discussed at Fort Massac is a matter of some conjecture. Had Burr's ultimate plan yet matured? Was Wilkinson a coadjutor? Burr seems to have believed that Wilkinson now supported him, but his judgment on such matters was often imperfect. As Mary-Jo Kline, editor of Burr's papers, has noted, Burr tailored his conversations "to the dreams and prejudices" of every audience. "He told each man what he wanted to hear."[57] Likewise, Burr heard only what he wanted to hear; many whom he counted among his supporters were either never a party to the completed design, or distanced themselves quickly from it when it was put into effect.[58] Andrew Jackson was certainly one of the latter.

Whatever Wilkinson's role, it would have been natural for them to have discussed military action against Mexico. After all, the general had just been instructed by the Secretary of War to give this subject serious attention, and discussions of how the army should move against the Spanish would have been a most natural topic for the two men. Wilkinson may, at the time, have been playing some role in Burr's intrigue—if, in fact, an intrigue had yet taken shape—but even lengthy discussions of a military assault on the Spanish is not, by itself, conclusive evidence of it.

There is no doubt that Wilkinson was party to some plan that involved Burr, but its scope is uncertain. As a minimum he hoped to help the former Vice-president find an elective office in the West. Beyond that, however, only conjecture reigns. Those who claim he was party to the ultimate plot—a second-in-command—have based their conclusion on the word of Burr or his admitted confederates, or on the flaws in Wilkinson's character that led him into the repeated employ of the Spanish. This evidence, however, is unconvincing when cast in the light of what we now know of subsequent events.

By late summer of 1805, rumors of Burr's intentions and of the general's involvement were everywhere. Daniel Clark wrote him from New Orleans that,

You are spoken of as [Burr's] righthand man. . . . The tale is a horrid one, if well told. Kentucky, Tennessee, the State of Ohio, with part of Georgia and part of Carolina, are to be bribed with the plunder of the Spanish Countries west of us to separate from the Union.[59]

The administration missed neither the rumors nor their implications, and Dearborn penned a strongly worded warning to Wilkinson.[60] However, neither that letter nor Clark's reached the general before he became even further associated with Burr, who was already en route to St. Louis.

Burr arrived on September 12 and stayed a week—lodging with his brother-in-law, Dr. Joseph Browne, the territorial secretary. It is almost certain that they again discussed an assault on Mexico—a subject that was still center stage in the mind of Wilkinson. He had written Dearborn, only a few days earlier, describing not only the route to Santa Fe, but laying out a campaign strategy to seize northern Mexico if war should start.[61] He almost certainly shared that information with Burr.

Burr left St. Louis convinced that Wilkinson supported him and his cause, but, if that was so, it was to change almost immediately. Clark's letter concerning rumors of his involvement with Burr is part of the explanation of this. It may have arrived before the former Vice-President departed, but if it did Wilkinson made no mention of its contents to him then.[62] "Amuse Mr. Burr" with the rumors in circulation, Clark had written, but Wilkinson found them quite unamusing. For the first time, he became suspicious of Burr's true intent.

More important than Clark's note in diverting the General from any further connection with Burr was the sharp warning from the Secretary of War. If the mails from Washington took their usual month in transit, this letter should have reached Wilkinson about a week after Burr departed. It was unusually direct. "There is a strong rumor that you, Burr, etc., are too intimate," Dearborn wrote. "You ought to keep every suspicious person at arms length, and be as wise as a serpent and as harmless as a dove."[63] Wilkinson now knew that his connection with Burr had been surmised, and of official disapproval. For all his faults and vices—and they were numerous enough—he was not foolhardy. It is inconceivable that he would have continued the relationship after this warning from Dearborn.

Wilkinson was chagrined, but there was nothing he could now do about the recent visit. He did not reply directly to Dearborn, but instead penned a letter to Robert Smith, the Secretary of the Navy. "Burr is about something," he wrote, "but whether internal or external, I cannot discover." He advised Smith to keep an eye on Burr.[64]

Wilkinson now tried to distance himself from the New Yorker and his schemes. In November he sent the former Vice-President a copy of Clark's letter—an indirect effort, it would seem, to caution Burr against any adventure, and thereby get himself off the hook. Burr, however, simply brushed aside the implied warning.[65] When his letters to the General went unanswered, however, he took note. "Nothing has been heard from the brigadier since October," he complained in April.[66] Historians have puzzled over Wilkinson's silence. Thomas P. Abernethy, in his careful analysis of the Burr conspiracy, wondered openly why Wilkinson had "failed to keep in touch with Burr." Milton Lomask, Burr's biographer, concluded that the general was "already thinking of exposing his collaborator."[67] But neither Abernethy, nor Lomask, nor other scholars appear to have discovered Dearborn's warning to Wilkinson. That document explains the silence. Following the advice from Washington, the General was attempting to disassociate himself from Burr's designs—but to do so without further implicating himself or without admitting even innocent involvement.

Burr, however, would not take the hint. In April 1806, after months without a word, he wrote Wilkinson that "our project is postponed till December." Still, he apparently now sensed some reluctance on the general's part, for he added, "The associates is enlarged and comprise all that Wilkinson could wish." Wilkinson responded to this letter but again used indirection without effect. He later claimed that, if this letter could be produced, it would exonerate him. Burr refused to reveal it.[68] Regardless, Wilkinson's hints that he would not take part were too circumspect for the single-minded Burr. The New Yorker saw only what he wanted to see in the general's last note.

IV

Shortly after Burr departed St. Louis, Wilkinson received word that a fellow officer, Colonel Thomas Butler, had died in New Orleans. As a rule such news would be cause for mourning, but Butler's death was an exception. For Wilkinson it was a victory of sorts; for the administration it was cause for new and continuing concern.

In early 1804, while in the midst of settling affairs after the transfer of New Orleans, Wilkinson had received the verdict of the first court-martial he had ordered for Butler. The offense had been the failure to comply with the order of April 30, 1801, specifying that "for the accommodation, comfort & health of the Troops the hair is to be crop[p]ed without exception the general to give the example." Butler had simply refused to have his hair shorn. Wilkinson had, at first, granted him an exemption from the order—"in consideration of infirm health"—but later withdrew it. When Butler still refused to comply, the general ordered a court-martial. When this board issued only a mild rebuke, the general was furious.[69]

Butler was second in seniority to Wilkinson and a veteran of the Revolution who, like the general, had taken the field again with Ar-

Colonel Thomas Butler, Jr. by Jose de Salazar.
COLLECTION OF THE MUSEUM OF EARLY SOUTHERN DECORATIVE ARTS, WINSTON-
SALEM, N.C.

Colonel Thomas Butler, second ranking officer in the army, was General
Wilkinson's nemesis. His sometimes overt challenges of the general's authority were tolerated—even quietly encouraged—by an administration that (at
least until late 1806) distrusted Wilkinson only slightly less than the army's
other senior officers. Butler's opposition to the general seems to have been
viewed as a means to reduce the latter's influence.

thur St. Clair. More important, however, he was Wilkinson's most ardent rival in the army. Their differences had begun years earlier, after St. Clair's ill-fated campaign of 1791. Butler had lost a brother in that expedition and had himself been twice wounded. He had not taken kindly to the criticism that Wilkinson leveled concerning the way in which the battle had been fought—particularly so since Wilkinson had not taken part.

Over the years the differences between the two men grew and, in time, those officers of the army who fell out with the General began to coalesce around Butler. By 1801 he was the focal point for the anti-Wilkinson sentiment. Normally such a division would have seemed undesirable. But, when Dearborn and Jefferson had the opportunity to drop the colonel in 1802, during the reorganization, they chose not to. In fact, they refused his specific request to be dismissed.[70] Clearly the administration saw value in the rift; it was one of the few checks on Wilkinson's power.[71]

The dispensation which Wilkinson had granted Butler concerning the haircut order served only to make him more independent. He had refused to publish the "cropping" order, and word reached Wilkinson that within the regiment, officers were saying that "The Col[onel] intended to wear his Hair & expects his officers would follow his example." To the general this "prove[d] a mutinous combination of a whole Corps," which could only be suppressed by humbling or destroying Butler. "If the Col[onel] will submit . . . I shall be content," he wrote Jonathan Williams. Otherwise the only solution was to "expose" and convict him.[72]

The sentence of the court—a reprimand—was from Wilkinson's perspective wholly unsatisfactory. It did more to enhance Butler's image than to destroy it, and Wilkinson knew it. Moreover, Butler knew it. In his effort to deflect Wilkinson he had engaged an important ally in Tennessee—Andrew Jackson. Jackson had attempted to get Jefferson to intervene and his efforts may have been partially responsible for the lenient sentence.[73] Wilkinson was not satisfied and ordered Butler to New Orleans for a new showdown. Dearborn interceded temporarily instructing Butler to remain in Tennessee until he received further orders.[74] Butler again appealed to Jackson, who replied: "I will have a remonstrance signed by all the respectable citizens of this District." The haircut order was, he said, "a wanton act of Despotism" and would certainly be set aside by the President or Congress.[75]

When Butler finally arrived in New Orleans in October 1804 to take command, Wilkinson discovered that the colonel had once again failed "to leave his tail behind." Emboldened by the results of the first court-martial and assurances from friends like Jackson, he was more contemptuous and disrespectful to the general than ever.[76] The memorial promised by Jackson was finally sent to the President in December and forwarded to the Senate the next month. The hostile reception it received from many in the upper house, including particularly such Wilkinson allies as Samuel Smith and William Branch Giles, should have been a warning to Butler, but it apparently was not. In July he was again brought before a court-martial. The charges were brief and to the point: "Willful, obstinate, and continued disobedience," and "Mutinous Conduct."[77] This time the outcome was more to Wilkinson's liking. "Guilty," ruled the new court, of disobedience to the original order and the order of the prior court, and "guilty" of mutinous conduct "by appearing publicly in command of troops . . . with his hair cued [sic] in direct and open violation of the General Orders." The board sentenced him to be suspended without pay and privileges for twelve months. Wilkinson approved the sentence, but it could not be carried out. Butler had died, of a fever, two weeks before.

"Butler has defected," wrote Wilkinson, and with these three words, marked the colonel's death. But even in death Butler mocked him, or so it was commonly said. As the story was told, a hole was cut in Butler's coffin allowing his queue to protrude—evidence he had retained in until death. This incident was immortalized by Washington Irving in his Knickerbocker's *History of New York*.[78]

"Thus ends the contest," wrote Henry Burbeck, who commanded the Corps of Artillery, "and I hope it will rest with him—and that the Army will never again be disturbed with a dispute so destructive to order and Military discipline."[79]

This "defection," however, eliminated the rallying point for anti-Wilkinson sentiment. Captain Edward Butler, the colonel's younger

Colonel Keldermaster in his Coffin by Felix Darley.
FROM WASHINGTON IRVING'S *Knickerbocker History of New York.* COURTESY,
AMERICAN ANTIQUARIAN SOCIETY.

Keldermaster "deserted from all earthly command," according to Irving, who
retold the Butler tale just a few years later (1809), "with his beloved locks
unviolated. His obstinacy remained unshaken to the very last moment, when
he directed that he should be carried to his grave with his . . . queue sticking
out of a hole in his coffin."

brother, resigned and left what resistance there might have been in
disarray. The vacancy at the top of the 2d Infantry Regiment would
normally have created a ripple of promotions from below. However,
shortly after the colonel's demise, Dearborn notified Wilkinson that
henceforth "no promotions are to be considered as having taken place
until the sanction of the President . . . shall have been made known."
Just in case that wasn't clear, Dearborn was specific: "No measures
should be taken in consequence of the death of Colonel Butler in regard to promotions until you receive further information from this
department."[80] The administration saw this occasion as an opportunity to infuse into the upper echelons of the infantry a man who was

both a fervent administration supporter and a Wilkinson opponent, and they meant to take advantage of it.

Command of the regiment had to be given to Lieutenant Colonel Thomas P. Cushing, who had long been the second in command. Though a staunch Wilkinson supporter—and therefore hardly the man the administration was looking for—he was too closely associated with the War Department (as adjutant general) and too widely known in the army to be denied the promotion. That left only Cushing's old position as second in command, and in filling it Dearborn and Jefferson decided to buck the tradition of promotion according to seniority. (John Adams had done so successfully on a few occasions, but only in the midst of the turmoil created by the disbanding of Hamilton's army.) Samuel Hammond of St. Louis was the administration's candidate. Hammond was a Virginian and a Revolutionary War veteran who had recently been made a civil commandant in the new territory of Upper Louisiana. There he had repeatedly clashed with Wilkinson, the Governor.

Hammond's appointment would both dilute the Federalist character of the most senior officers in the infantry regiments, and provide a new rallying point for Wilkinson's opponents. Hammond's nomination as a lieutenant colonel—and second in command of the 2d Infantry Regiment—was forwarded by the President to Congress in February 1806. But, that effort was too transparent for even the Republican Senate. William Plumer noted two objections that were raised against him—Hammond was not next in line for promotion, and he had been associated with the Frenchman Genet.[81] The Senate rejected the administration move nineteen to twelve, when Republican backers of Wilkinson, like Samuel Smith, joined ranks with the Federalists.

The rejection of the nomination by Congress was applauded by many in the army. For Colonel Henry Burbeck, the chief of artillery, it was an action "for which in my opinion, [those Senators] deserve great credit." They had stopped the movement "to the destruction of the promotion of the Army."[82] The younger Pike was more blunt:

But what would my *father* and all old, and indeed I may say young officers have said in case [Hammond's] Nomination had succeeded? What is not striking at the very root of ambition, & stifling in the bud every noble sentiment?

For who is the poor miserable wretch who would be so despicable as to retain his commission and daily to see citizens called in to fill vacancies over his head.[83]

Jefferson and Dearborn, however, were slow to accept defeat. For a time they refused to fill the vacancy. In 1807 they tried again; they nominated Lieutenant William Clark, who had accompanied Meriwether Lewis. But once more the Senate rejected the effort. With this, the administration gave up the scheme and promoted the next senior officer, Richard Sparks, another Wilkinson man. The failure to overcome the traditional system meant that opposition to Wilkinson within the army had no patron. That situation continued until the dramatic expansion of the army the next year and the appointment of Wade Hampton—but that is the subject of a later chapter.[84]

The loyalty of the army was a continuing concern to the administration; subsequent events show that clearly. Despite efforts at reform, the sentiments of significant segments of the officer corps—the more senior officers in particular—continued to be suspect. Whatever benefit might have accrued as a result of the rivalry between Butler and Wilkinson had been lost.

The army was now led exclusively by men on whom Wilkinson could count for support, and men whose loyalties to the administration were untested. The General had further enhanced his control by moving the army's new Adjutant General, Major A. Y. Nicoli (who replaced Cushing), out of Washington and to his headquarters in St. Louis. There, he was ensconced with a concentration of troops second only to that in New Orleans.[85] Despite the administration's machinations, General Wilkinson was more firmly in control of the army than ever.

CHAPTER 6

General Wilkinson's Army

The events of 1805 had seemingly conspired against further reformation of the military establishment. Circumstances, in fact, made the army appear more ominous than usual. The death of Colonel Thomas Butler, who had been the focal point for anti-Wilkinson sentiment in the army, had left the general in undiluted control. Moreover, the strategic necessity of concentrating forces at New Orleans and St. Louis put a growing number of troops at Wilkinson's disposal. Alone, those circumstances might have caused only modest concern, but two added factors magnified their importance. First, Spanish moves in the Southwest had made it increasingly likely that Wilkinson would have to be put at the head of the army in the field—where he could create real mischief. And, second, there was a growing concern about Aaron Burr's intentions, and about the role Wilkinson and the army might play in association with him.

The administration was in a particularly difficult position; they had no attractive options. The occupation and defense of the new territories necessitated the concentration of forces that was taking place. And, in the short run, there was nothing more that could be done to assure the political loyalty of the army. When the army was put to the test, the administration would have no alternative but simply to wait and watch.

I

When James Monroe broke off the futile negotiations with Spain in May 1805, the Spanish concluded that the ambitious demands of the United States would ultimately lead to war in the provinces. In Washington the administration watched the situation with concern. Dearborn warned Wilkinson that affairs with Spain were "cloudy" and that "the officers on the Lower Miss[iss]ippi & Mobile should be on the alert." Then, in a reference to plans Wilkinson had drawn up to invade Mexico from the north if war should break out, Dearborn wrote, "I am not sure that a project of that kind may not become necessary." [1]

In October 1805, in what can best be characterized as defensive preparations, the Spanish established two outposts of ten to twenty men each, east of the Sabine River in territory claimed by both nations. Reports of the Spanish move reached Washington the next month. Under instructions from Jefferson, Dearborn ordered Major Moses Porter, commandant at Natchitoches, to expel the Spanish and to extend his patrols to the Sabine to insure that there would be no further incursions. [2] At the same time, Dearborn ordered Wilkinson to begin reconnaissance and intelligence collection throughout the region. He suggested that "individuals in the character of hunters or traders may probably be employed with success." [3]

The President sounded a public warning in his annual message in December. "Inroads," he pointed out, had been made by "the regular officers and soldiers of [the Spanish] Government." He then revealed that he had given "orders to our troops on that frontier to be in readiness to protect our citizens, and to repel by arms any similar aggressions in future." In consideration of this and of difficulties with both England and France, the President called upon Congress to give the nation's defense needs a high priority. [4]

Porter's orders arrived January 24, 1806, and he dispatched Lieutenant William Piatt to Nacogdoches, the Spanish garrison and headquarters, to demand that the Spanish observe the Sabine boundary. The Spanish commander replied that, though Spain intended no aggression, he could give no such assurances. On February 1 Major Porter ordered Captain Edward D. Turner and a company of about

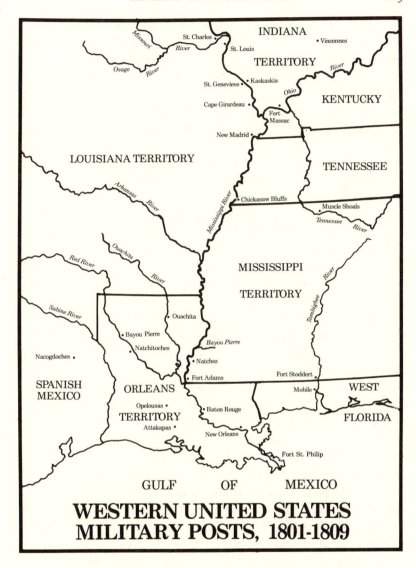

WESTERN UNITED STATES
MILITARY POSTS, 1801-1809

sixty men to march toward Bayou Pierre—one of the Spanish outposts. The Spanish commander protested, but the action had the desired result; the Spanish agreed to withdraw beyond the Sabine.[5]

That withdrawal of the Spanish was not the end of the affair, however; their government had no intention of permanently abandoning the disputed territory. War fever built up throughout the winter and spring of 1806. On the Spanish side, a number of officials, some still in New Orleans, urged war in the belief that many of the residents of Louisiana would join their cause. Meanwhile, in the United States, Western newspapers kept up a steady barrage of stories that promoted war against the Spanish. "On the Fourth of July," reported one paper, "there were not a thousand persons in the United States who did not think war with Spain inevitable, impending, begun!"[6]

In March, as a precaution, Dearborn ordered that all available troops be moved nearer the Sabine frontier. Colonel Thomas Cushing was instructed to send three companies of infantry and two field pieces from Fort Adams to Natchitoches. At the same time, Lieutenant Colonel Jacob Kingsbury was instructed to take the forces from St. Louis to Fort Adams—leaving only a single artillery company at the former. Lieutenant Colonel Constance Freeman, at New Orleans, whose command had already been denuded, was told that he would have to make do with the troops left to him, including the local militia and the five gunboats stationed there at the time.[7] In Washington, the war fever had not reached the same critical point as in the West. Though the administration did make some quiet preparations for war, they declined, for the moment, to seek any increase in the size of the army.[8] Congress, which had been toying with its own schemes concerning the force, now also dropped the matter.[9]

Still, when spring brought no sign of a Spanish stand down, Dearborn ordered General Wilkinson to the scene "with as little delay as practicable," to take command of the troops there.[10] Upon receipt of the letter the general wrote Dearborn that he would have left immediately except that conditions along the Sabine and Mobile had cooled a bit and he felt secure in tarrying to arrange the civil affairs and to provide detailed instructions to the territorial secretary who would be left in charge. He said nothing of his wife's serious illness, but her very delicate condition was another reason for delay. He promised Dearborn, nonetheless, to be on the way by late July, and expressed appreciation for the "testimony of the President's confidence" which the Secretary of War's letter had contained. His letter to Samuel Smith the next day, however, complained that the order was nothing more

James Wilkinson by Charles Willson Peale.
INDEPENDENCE NATIONAL HISTORICAL PARK COLLECTION.

Brigadier General James Wilkinson commanded the army under Presidents Adams and Jefferson. Long, but incorrectly, considered a coconspirator with Aaron Burr, he was nonetheless a scoundrel of significant proportions. His longtime association with the Spanish—often in their pay—was widely rumored, though (at the time) unproven. Still, his fidelity in resisting the Burr conspiracy earned him the trust and approbation of Jefferson and Dearborn.

than a means of getting him out of the way—making room for Samuel Hammond.[11]

Again and again Wilkinson delayed his departure. July came and went and the general continued on in St. Louis. His wife had rallied briefly in late June, but by mid-July was again dangerously ill. Wilkinson waited day-by-day in the hopes that she would improve. Finally, in late August, unable to delay longer, he departed. Mrs. Wilkinson, though still gravely ill, followed him a few months later. The general said nothing in his official correspondence about his wife's condition, but it weighed heavily on his mind. Mrs. Wilkinson died in New Orleans, early the next year.

General Wilkinson arrived at Fort Adams from St. Louis early in September, but while he had delayed his departure the Spanish had acted. In July they had once again crossed the Sabine and briefly garrisoned Bayou Pierre. News of the event spread quickly and rekindled fears of war. Claiborne, in Orleans Territory, ordered the territorial militia put on a campaign footing. Cowles Meade, the acting Governor of the Mississippi Territory, did likewise. At Natchitoches, however, Colonel Cushing, acting on Wilkinson's orders, prevented Claiborne from moving against the Spanish.

Wilkinson, now en route, wrote Dearborn from Fort Adams that he intended to discourage any offensive by the militia until he ascertained the real situation on the Sabine. He did, however, urge Meade to get his troops prepared. In early September Spanish patrols pushed east once more and again occupied Bayou Pierre. But, whatever the temper elsewhere, those at the scene did not crave conflict. The two sides maintained their positions and restrained further provocative action.[12]

General Wilkinson arrived at Natchitoches on September 22, and two days later opened communications with Governor Cordero of Texas at Nacogdoches. The Spanish had already agreed not to establish any further posts, but this did not satisfy the instructions Wilkinson carried. His letter informed the Texas Governor that the country east of the Sabine was considered "as fully within the limits . . . of the United States" and that on instructions of the President he must "sustain the jurisdiction of the United States . . . against any force." The Spanish forces would have to be withdrawn beyond the Sabine or fight. The border issue, Wilkinson suggested, should be settled through the negotiations then under way. He urged the Governor to withdraw his forces.[13]

On September 27 Wilkinson wrote Dearborn of the situation at Natchitoches and outlined the actions he had taken. He had ordered forward as many regulars as could be spared from the posts in the region, and was expecting 250 militia from Mississippi and another 450 from Orleans. "With this Force I have no doubt of success in the outset and think I shall be able to drive our opponents before me and take Nacogdoches." He was not, however, sanguine of sustaining such a drive or of even holding what he might gain, and indicated that he had no means of equipping the militia for any extended campaign.[14] With the troops and provisions he had he could neither push into the interior of Texas, nor resist the forces that the Spanish could ultimately bring to bear.

Wilkinson wrote John Smith, the Ohio senator, in even more blunt terms concerning the situation and the forces he would need if a major campaign was ordered. If he was to draw the sword, Wilkinson insisted, the nation must be prepared to accept the consequences.

If, therefore, this business should not be speedily terminated by negotiations you must speedily send me a force to support our pretensions, or we must yield them up, together with the Territory of Orleans. Five thousand mounted infantry to operate as dragoons, or fight on foot, may suffice to carry us forward as far as the [Rio Grande]."[15]

Even more troops would be needed if they were to push beyond the Rio Grande, Wilkinson warned. The nation, he argued, must not attack into Spanish territory unless it was prepared for a full-scale war.

He wrote in a similar vain to John Adair, but played on the Kentuckian's long-nourished imperialistic dreams.[16]

The time long looked for by many and wished for by more, has now arrived for subverting the Spanish government in Mexico. Be you ready to join me; we will want little more than light-armed troops with a few [dragoons]. More will be done by marching than fighting; 5,000 men will give us the Rio [Grande]; 10,000 to [Monterey]; we must here divide our army into three parts and will then require 30,000 men to conquer the whole of the province of Mexico. We cannot fail of success.[17]

Despite his concerns about the potential hazard that the use of force entailed, he kept his men prepared for combat. He ordered target practice and offered an extra pint of whiskey to the best shots. The officers were instructed to procure uniforms "as nearly similar to that of the troops as possible." The midnight revelry that usually marked the first days in the field was proscribed; lights were ordered out at tattoo. "In a moment like the present," Wilkinson chided, "every man and every officer, should hold himself in readiness to march, to fight, and to die at a minute's warning; Repose is indispensable to such a state of preparations and readiness."[18]

As usual, supplies and equipage for the campaign were a problem. There were shortages of horses, mules, wagons, and tentage, and no amount of badgering produced the desired effect. These shortages plagued and worried the general throughout.

Just as preparations were being completed, and as the militia began to arrive, Colonel Herrera, who had taken command the Spanish troops at the front, withdrew his exposed outposts to the west bank of the Sabine. This tactical move was taken without superior orders, but was not without strategic effect. The withdrawal and a more concil-iatory tone in Spanish messages—answering Wilkinson's own temper-ate words—were enough to defuse the tense situation. Wilkinson re-acted immediately by dismissing the militia who had arrived (except for a small contingent of volunteer mounted riflemen) and counter-manding the march orders of those preparing to come.[19] The next day he reported these events to Dearborn, but pointed out that Spanish troops still occupied the west bank of the Sabine and remained a threat to American interests. Wilkinson assured the Secretary that he would continue his preparations for action with the regulars in his command, but added that he was taking care not to provoke the Spanish unne-cessarily. The same day he wrote Governor Cordero and advised him that the Americans would be moving forward to the Sabine, but that the move was not meant to be hostile. He was writing, he said, "to prevent the misinterpretation of my motives."[20]

Wilkinson was content to let negotiations solve the issues. He wrote Samuel Smith, his old friend in the Senate, that he anticipated that his regulars and the mounted riflemen he had retained would be suf-ficient force unless the boundary negotiations "blow up." But, if that was expected, he wrote, "you should immediately put a competent character, at the Head of the War Department and prepare to reinforce me with from three to five thousand more [troops]." He berated Dearborn to Smith as "utterly unqualified for his place." He blamed the army's lack of preparedness on the Secretary and advised Smith to "say to the President that it is my [Wilkinson's] opinion that we are approaching a crisis."[21]

II

When he wrote Smith, Wilkinson did not realize either how close a crisis really was, or the nature it was to take—but he was to learn the very next day. On the sixth of October, Samuel Swartwout arrived at Natchitoches with two letters for the general. One was from Aaron Burr and a second from Jonathan Dayton, a long-time Burr associate. Both letters had been written in late July and Burr's was in a cipher that he and the general had worked out years before.[22]

Wilkinson was appalled by what unfolded before him. Dearborn's letter of the preceding fall advising him against any association with Burr had prompted the general to write Robert Smith, Secretary of the Navy, and warn against the former Vice-President's activities. Dearborn's letter implied that the administration was prepared to nip this affair in the bud. Now, it seemed, that effort had yielded nothing. Moreover, his own attempts to dissuade Burr or disassociate himself had been too oblique.

"Are you ready?," Dayton's letter asked. "Are your numerous associates ready?" Clearly Dayton assumed that many of the officers under Wilkinson were already engaged, or would willingly follow the general's lead. "Wealth and glory! Louisiana and Mexico!" he offered. But Wilkinson had long since cast his die.[23]

The full extent of Burr's mature plan emerged slowly as Wilkinson worked late into the night to decipher the letter. This was no longer a fantasy, described only in vague terms. "Detachments will rendezvous on the Ohio first of November," the deciphered text read. "Naval protection of England is secured . . . [and] a navy of the United States, are ready to join. . . . Wilkinson shall be second to Burr only," read the message, and "Wilkinson shall dictate the rank and promo-

Aaron Burr by John Vanderlyn.
COURTESY OF THE NEW-YORK HISTORICAL SOCIETY, NEW YORK CITY.

Burr's biographers have often portrayed the former vice-president as the *victim* of General Wilkinson—who they insist "betrayed" him. In fact, Wilkinson had deserted the Burr scheme a year earlier, but his subsequent, quite indirect efforts to discourage Burr's adventure failed. In the end, the general did his duty.

tion of his officers." Burr then spelled out his plan of operation. He would "move down rapidly from the Falls [on the Ohio], on the fifteenth of November, with the first five hundred or a thousand men, in light boats . . . ; to be at Natchez between the fifth and fifteenth of December, there to meet you. . . . On receipt of this send Burr an answer."[24] Despite his efforts, this letter directly implicated him in the scheme, and he now sought to extricate himself.

Wilkinson has been counted a co-conspirator of Burr's by many in his own time, and by historians generally. His unconscionable dealings with the Spanish seemed to confirm his guilt—by implication. Yet, the evidence now suggests otherwise. The Dearborn letter—and Wilkinson's response to Robert Smith—cast his subsequent actions in a different light. And in that light, the circumstances argue for his exoneration. Co-conspirators? There was a remarkable and unexplainable asymmetry in the efforts of the two men. Burr and all the others involved in the plan—even Andrew Jackson—labored diligently in planning and promoting, and in arranging supplies, equipment and men for the expedition. Wilkinson, from all evidence, did nothing. There is no suggestion of any plans or preparations to support Burr's activities. He did not recruit among his officers; their personal correspondence contains not even a hint of it. Wilkinson's enemies in and out of the service could have been counted upon to make much of such stories.[25] The public rumors of his involvement originated in the extensive association of the two men in 1805—and were fed by Burr's repeated assurances to potential supporters of the general's affiliation. Still, Burr's believing that Wilkinson was with him did not make it so.

It was widely assumed that Burr's scheme could not succeed without war with Spain. Yet Wilkinson did everything in his power to avoid such a conflict. If the general had been in league with Burr this conduct would indeed be difficult to explain. He had numerous opportunities, ample excuse, and sufficient authority to initiate hostilities. Instead, from the beginning, he exercised restraint, limited the buildup of forces, and actively sought peace. Upon Swartwout's arrival he redoubled the effort to forestall a clash.

If Wilkinson had ever been involved with Burr's plan, he had abandoned that connection long before he set out for the Sabine. The

evidence clearly indicates that he had no further involvement following the latter's visit to St. Louis in September 1805, or more precisely, subsequent to Dearborn's warning about Burr that had followed immediately thereafter. The evidence is less clear concerning
the extent of his previous connection with Burr's scheme. The rapid-
ity with which he backed away suggests that he understood his unique
situation as commanding general of the army. At the worst, he was
no more culpable than the many others whom the affable New Yorker
cultivated unsuccessfully.

Wilkinson sat through the night, pondering his situation. Despite
efforts to disassociate himself, he was now irretrievably identified with
the project, and each denial would cause him new embarrassment.
When he excluded references to himself from the Burr documents that
he sent Jefferson, he only traded a short-term advantage for long-run
difficulties. This action resulted in charges of perjury when he appeared before the grand jury hearing the evidence against Burr, and
those charges plagued him the rest of his life.

The next morning he pulled Cushing aside, told him of the letters,
and briefly laid out the plan he was formulating.[26] In the next ten
days or so he worked out the details of that plan and then set it in
motion. On October 17 he wrote Dearborn that he now had an elite
force of about one hundred men posted just east of the Sabine, and
that he and the remainder of the force would move up as soon as
transport was available. He did not yet reveal the conspiracy, but the
unusual activity that that would have entailed (the extraordinary reports and secrecy) might have triggered speculation that could have
alerted Burr's agent who was still in camp. Wilkinson could not afford
to precipitate any action on the part of Burr's supporters—particularly
in exposed New Orleans—while his army was tied down facing the
Spanish.

One of the problems Wilkinson had to solve was how to disengage
himself from the Spanish so that he could be in position to intercept
Burr's force. He laid the groundwork for his solution in his letter to
Dearborn. If he was forced to fight he would push forward and seize
Nacogdoches, but then would offer to withdraw to previous positions
in exchange for a truce.[27] Having worked out his course, the general

dismissed Swartwout, who had been awaiting his reply. Burr's messenger departed on the eighteenth without a response.

With his plans now taking final shape, and with Burr's agent out of camp, Wilkinson undertook a flurry of activities. He began by carefully drafting three documents for Jefferson. The first was a letter in which he protested the assault on him being conducted by a Frankfort, Kentucky paper, the *Western World;* he assured the President that neither wealth nor power could "for a moment divert my course from the path of Honor."[28] He enclosed a second document—which he said had fallen into his hands, but which he clearly had authored—describing in general terms an expedition which was forming on the western rivers for an assault on Veracruz. That party of eight to ten thousand men was, he reported, to rendezvous in New Orleans in December. Their intentions concerning the Territory of Orleans, he said, were unknown.[29] The third document, also dated (like the first) October 21, contained Wilkinson's comments on the unsigned enclosure. "The magnitude of the Enterprise staggers my belief," he reported. The leadership of this enterprise remained unknown to him, he insisted. He told of rumors that the expedition enjoyed the support of the administration—but professed not to believe them. He then built a case for his own plan.

I have no doubt the revolt of this Territory, will be made an auxiliary step to the main design of attacking Mexico, to give it a New Master in place of the promised liberty; could the fact be ascertained to me, I believe I should hazard my discretion, make the best compromise with Salcedo in my Power and throw myself with my little Band into New Orleans, to be ready to defend that capital against usurpation and violence.[30]

Wilkinson again wrote Dearborn saying that he would advance immediately to the east bank of the Sabine, but that he also intended to propose to the Spanish a mutual withdrawal "to points of occupancy at the Period of Secession of the Province to the United States."[31] On October 22, four days after the departure of Swartwout, Lieutenant Thomas A. Smith was dispatched to Washington with these important communications. The next day Wilkinson wrote Freeman, in New Orleans, of a threat "too highly confidential to be whispered" and ordered defensive preparations accelerated.[32] Later in the day he began the sixty-mile march to the Sabine. His camp was raised on that river in early November.[33]

On October 29, still some miles from the Sabine, he had sent Walter Burling, a volunteer aide and Mississippi planter, with a letter to Governor Cordero at Nacogdoches.[34] As Wilkinson had outlined to Dearborn, the letter proposed a mutual withdrawal. He suggested that,

without yielding a Pretension, ceding a right, or interfering with the discussion which belongs to our superiors, to restore the 'status quo' at the delivery of the provinces of Louisiana to the United States, by the withdrawal of our troops from the points they at present occupy, to the posts of Nacogdoches and Natchitoches respectively.[35]

Wilkinson further promised that his troops would not cross the Arroyo Hondo (the boundary the Spanish claimed) so long as the Spanish respected the Sabine.

Though Governor Cordero insisted that he had no such authority, Colonel Herrera took it upon himself to accept Wilkinson's offer and defuse the situation.[36] The agreement was finalized the next day, November 5. Wilkinson immediately ordered the troops to break camp and then, with a small party, departed for Natchitoches. Riding hard, he arrived the next day and immediately ordered the troops still there to begin the march to New Orleans. Colonel Cushing, who commanded the elements being withdrawn from the Sabine, was instructed to follow "with the utmost dispatch," and to leave only a small detachment at Natchitoches.[37]

Confident that he had stabilized the situation along that frontier, Wilkinson moved rapidly to put the balance of his plan into action. Freeman, in New Orleans, was already putting that city into a posture of defense—but in a quiet way. Wilkinson had warned him against revealing his true aims. "Your silence must be profound; and while you pursue the operation most industriously, you must show no anxiety." Wilkinson had instructed him to repair the forts in and below the city. They were "to be completed by the 20th of December; and in those works have all your artillery, arms, and military stores, and utensils secured."[38] Wilkinson's greatest concern was that Burr truly had the broad-based support he claimed. He prepared for the worst.

After a day and a half at Natchitoches he proceeded to Fort Adams at Natchez, arriving on the eleventh of November. That garrison, he decided, could not stand up against the numbers that he believed would soon be on their way. He ordered the fort dismantled, and removed the troops, weapons, and military stores to New Orleans.

The day after his arrival at Fort Adams, he wrote the President that his doubts had ceased, the explosion was coming! Again without mentioning Burr, he posited that there was afoot,

a deep, dark, and wide-spread conspiracy, embracing the young and the old, the democrat and the federalist, the native and the foreigner, the patriot of '76 and the exotic of yesterday, the opulent and needy, the ins and the outs; and I fear it will receive strong support in New Orleans.[39]

Martial law, he concluded, would be essential in the city to defend the nation's interests. "To insure the triumph of government over its enemies," he told the President, "I am obliged to resort to political finesse and military stratagem." That may have been less reassuring to Jefferson than the general intended, and the President might have been even more concerned had he seen Wilkinson's letter of two days later to Samuel Smith. Army officers, the general wrote, "are universally disgusted with the service." Still, he anticipated the defection of only a few; most, he thought, would stick by him.[40]

With the President's letter went one to Dearborn which outlined his plan to defeat the insurgents. He had ordered all the small posts evacuated; the troops, except a company to garrison Natchitoches, were to move to New Orleans. He would defend at that point. The enemy, he reported, was expected to arrive in December.[41] Likewise, on November 12, he wrote Governor Claiborne a warning. "You are surrounded by dangers of which you dream not." Still, he did not provide any details, but only warned that defensive preparations must be made quietly. His first concern was that Burr's sympathizers would act before they could be resisted effectively. That sympathy, he believed, was widespread. "I have little confidence in your militia, yet I trust we may find a few patriotic spirits among them."[42]

As Wilkinson penned his advice to Claiborne, others were warning the governor against the general. "You have enemies within your own city, that may try to subvert your Government and try to separate it from the Union," wrote Andrew Jackson. "Keep a watchful eye upon our General," he warned.[43]

Despite Wilkinson's various efforts to extricate himself, Burr remained convinced—and in conversations with potential supporters, repeatedly indicated—that the general would play a key role. Burr believed what he wished to believe, but in the process made believers of others. The conviction that Wilkinson was deeply involved was widespread. Cowles Meade, whom the general had just visited (but apparently failed to reassure) also wrote Claiborne a warning. "It is here believed that General Wilkinson is the soul of conspiracy." Noting that the general had just been to Natchez and had requested that Mississippi militia be sent to New Orleans, Meade wondered whether or not the general was acting *against* the city.[44]

III

Speculation concerning Burr's activities became widespread in the midsummer of 1805—in the midst of the latter's western reconnaissance. A set of "Queries" on the subject had first appeared in the Philadelphia *Gazette of the United States* and had suggested a number of illicit activities that might account for Burr's tour. These included the disunion of the western territories and the conquest of Mexico. Though William Duane, editor of the Republican *Aurora*, had treated these speculations more as farce—good political theater—than as fact, the reports persisted. The President received a number of anonymous reports warning against Burr's designs, but tended to ignore them, as he did most unsigned accusations or charges that seemed little more than politically motivated gossip.

Rumors of the general's involvement had circulated from the beginning. By the summer of 1806 they were open items of conjecture in papers across the Union. To be certain, Wilkinson had admirers as well as detractors, and he had both in the nation's capital. Jefferson, at the moment, was ambivalent. The general had proven useful and accommodating when it came to administration reforms, and in return had enjoyed a measure of patronage. Still, neither Dearborn nor Jefferson could have missed the gossip that linked their commanding general to Burr and his alleged scheming. When, in January 1806, Joseph H. Davies, the United States Attorney in Kentucky, wrote the President warning him explicitly against General Wilkinson, the administration was finally moved to action. Though the charges were the old ones—that he was once in the pay of the Spanish—they could not be dismissed out of hand.[45]

If the administration could shrug off the speculation about Burr and his designs, they could hardly ignore reports that linked Wilkinson to him. The tinkering and pipe dreaming of an unemployed, former Vice-President was one thing. The dabbling in this kind of enterprise by the army's commanding general was quite another. Where Wilkinson led, his officers and men were likely to follow.[46]

Jefferson immediately queried various members of the Cabinet concerning the general. They gave Davies's specific charge little credibility. Gallatin replied that he had "no very exalted opinion" of Wilkinson, and thought that he might use his official position to aid his speculation, but did not believe he would betray the country to a foreign power. Nonetheless, he added, in light of recent information "if anything can be done which may lead to discoveries either in respect to him or others, it would seem proper; but how to proceed I do not know."[47]

As spring wore on, Jefferson became increasingly convinced that Wilkinson was a problem with which he would have to deal. Dearborn had already admonished Wilkinson to keep Burr at arm's length, and the evidence reveals that Wilkinson had taken that advice to heart. Still, a chorus of reports suggesting otherwise had had their effect in Washington, and Jefferson and Dearborn decided to remove the general from his post as Governor of the Louisiana Territory. Senator Samuel Smith, a staunch Wilkinson supporter, must have sensed the change, for he queried Jefferson on the subject. Jefferson's reply was evasive at best. "Not a single fact," he said, has raised any "doubt that I could have made a fitter appointment than General Wilkinson." Nothing, he indicated, was planned, with respect to the general at that time.[48] The very same day, however, he wrote Monroe that if he were in Washington rather than London he would have his "choice of

Samuel Smith by Gilbert Stuart.
NATIONAL PORTRAIT GALLERY, SMITHSONIAN INSTITUTION, WASHINGTON, D.C.

Senator Samuel Smith often served General Wilkinson as a conduit to Jefferson, providing an informal means of access to the President. Smith was one of several prominent men who championed James Wilkinson's cause in Washington. Wilkinson, who commanded wide but not unversal admiration in the army, seems to have left few men—in or out of the service—ambivalent about his character. They either admired or loathed the general—and among civilians the proportions in each camp seems to have been roughly equal.

the two governments of Orleans and Louisiana."[49] Two days later he instructed Dearborn to order Wilkinson to proceed as quickly as practicable to the Sabine and assume command of the forces there. In October, while the general engaged the Spanish on the Sabine, the governorship of Louisiana was offered to John Graham, then secretary to the Orleans Territory.[50]

Despite his assurances to Senator Smith, Jefferson had made a decision of sorts concerning Wilkinson, though it would appear a rather desperate choice; the administration chose simply to disassociate itself from the general. Correspondence from Washington came to an abrupt halt when Wilkinson was ordered to the Sabine.[51] The general, who had been accustomed to a regular flow of correspondence from the President and Secretary, heard no more from either quarter. He was hurt and confused by this turn of events, and complained to the administration and to friends about the lack of communication.[52] The five month silence was not broken until November 8, and then only out of the administration's near desperation. It was not until somewhat later that month—with the arrival in Washington of Lieutenant Smith and the messages he carried, and with the subsequent arrival of Wilkinson's letters of November 12 that outlined his plans for the defense of New Orleans *against Burr*—that the attitude of Dearborn and Jefferson changed.[53]

This hiatus in communication suggests that the administration had no better idea of how to proceed against Wilkinson than to simply allow him to draw out rope with which to hang himself—if he would. One suspects that the President and his close advisors, like the Secretary of the Treasury, had found it hard to believe Wilkinson would betray the country outright. But, as the Burr threat grew more real in their eyes, they had had second thoughts.

Under the circumstances the more direct alternatives were even less appealing than inaction. Colonel Butler's death in September 1805 had removed the most powerful figure of the anti-Wilkinson faction of the army. His replacement by Cushing, a strong pro-Wilkinson man (and the administration's inability to temper this by installing an anti-Wilkinson man, such as Hammond, in some key role) had left the general in a strong position. That strength was particularly evident in the army in the West, among the officers with whom the general had served longest and closest. Winfield Scott, who was commissioned in 1808, believed that "nearly all" of the officers commissioned prior to that time were Wilkinson men—a perception that attests to the impact of losing Butler.[54] Wilkinson men controlled the army.

Direct action—such as removing the general—was fraught with dangerous consequences. Wilkinson's dismissal, just at the moment the nation was threatened by a secessionist movement, might drive him and his army into the plotter's nest. National allegiance was not yet so firmly fixed in the lexicon of American virtues as it would be in years to come. "Honor" was more vital, and its roots were not necessarily sunk in the current regime or even the young Constitution. Moreover, there was word in Washington of a general disaffection among army officers. Major James Bruff, a strong Republican who had recently had a run-in with Wilkinson in St. Louis, claimed that, "the present doctrine openly [expressed] among our officers is that republican Governments are ungrateful to the military—its *very* principles being hostile to an army—of whom it is always jealous." Bruff argued that the army needed to be further "regenerated." He posed the rhetorical question, "What does this lead to?"[55]

Wilkinson's dismissal from command without apparent cause could, if discontent was widespread among the officers, invite precisely the disaster the administration was trying to avoid. Until the general made some overt move that would justify action, or until his authority could be diluted, the President was stuck with him. In any case, the Federalist alternatives to the general in the army's senior ranks promised no certain relief—and the Senate had already demonstrated its reluctance to allow promotion from without.

In September of 1806, more than a year after the first stories implicated Burr in some untoward Western adventure, Jefferson began to give the issue serious attention. He had ignored the rumors and unsigned accusations—as was his habit—but newly received allegations were more substantial. The President asked for more specifics. He was particularly interested in knowing who would and who would not be receptive to Burr's appeal. In October, word came that Burr was recruiting men of talent and enterprise, and that he had expressed a particular interest in militia and military men.[56]

It was Burr's approach to William Eaton, however, that convinced the President that some immediate action was necessary. Eaton then enjoyed a certain notoriety for his recent military exploits in North Africa. His story came to Jefferson third-hand from Gideon Granger, the Postmaster General. It alleged that Burr had offered to make Eaton second in command under Wilkinson in an expedition that would sever the West from the Atlantic states.[57]

Eaton's revelations reached Jefferson on October 20, and two days later he called together the Cabinet to discuss the related issues of Burr, Wilkinson, and the Spanish. The Spanish threat proved the most amendable to solution, and the Cabinet approved a comprehensive set of actions: the Mississippi and Orleans militia were to provide forces to the commanding officer of the regulars; the troops from Fort Adams and New Orleans would move to Natchitoches; marines were to be sent to garrison New Orleans to release the army; and the gunboats for the defense of the city were placed at the disposition of the commander on the ground.[58]

The President then outlined the allegations against Burr. The assemblage agreed that Burr should be "strictly watched," and that "on his committing any overt act unequivocally," should be arrested and tried.[59] The remaining item of the agenda—the issue of General Wilkinson—was more difficult. The army was the most responsive and available means of defeating an insurrection—if that was what Burr was about. But could they depend on the army and its general? Inaction no longer seemed the appropriate course.

General Wilkinson being expressly declared by Burr to Eaton to be engaged with him in this design as his Lieutenant or first in command, and suspicions of infidelity in Wilkinson being now become very general, a question is proposed what is proper to be done as to him?[60]

In the absence of other evidence, the only overt act with which he could be charged was his failure to repair with dispatch to New Orleans and Natchitoches the summer before. Acting on that basis alone was too transparent. At this, and at two subsequent meetings on October 24 and 25, the problem was discussed without resolution. It admitted no obvious, easy course of action. Jefferson's notes of these meetings suggest that the Cabinet wrestled hard with proposals that might allow them to somehow negate Wilkinson's power. The issue seemed to call for action, but upon reflection each proposed action evidenced some fatal flaw.

On October 24, it was decided to send two navy Captains, Preble and Decatur, to New Orleans "to take command of the forces on the water." The record sheds little light on what the Cabinet expected them to do, although it is obvious that the small flotilla there would not have required two such senior navy officers. Jefferson only hints at the answer when he noted that the staunchly Republican Preble "shall, on consultation with Governor Claiborne have great discretionary powers."[61] The orders to these officers, both of whom were out of Washington at the time, instructed them to report to the capitol immediately and to "come prepared for any service upon which you may be sent." Secrecy was vital, their orders indicated. They were instructed to "disclose this order to no person whatever." Even the fact that they were going to Washington was to be concealed.[62] Was it contemplated to place Preble in command at New Orleans? Were they to act against Wilkinson, or in support of him—if he were engaged on the Sabine? We will likely never know. Whatever the notion, it was short-lived.

The next day, October 25, that plan was abandoned. Robert Smith, the Secretary of the Navy, wrote a terse recension: "Information has been received which renders it unnecessary for you to come."[63] The Cabinet then decided that, in lieu of writing to the Governors or other loyal officials of the middle states, an official should be sent in pursuit of Burr. John Graham, who had recently arrived in Washington from New Orleans, was chosen. He carried confidential authority to put the local officials on their guard, to inquire into Burr's movements, and to arrest the errant New Yorker if that became necessary (or possible). Letters of warning were sent to Claiborne in New Orleans, and Meade at Natchez.

Two days after that meeting Dearborn wrote a very guarded letter to Lieutenant Colonel Constance Freeman, the artillerist, who in the absence of Wilkinson and Cushing commanded the forces at New Orleans. There was no mention of Burr, and only veiled hints of possible trouble. Be on guard and "pay some attention to the movement and the conduct of suspicious characters, either citizens, foreigners, or strangers," he was told. He could "communicate freely," the Secretary added, with Governor Claiborne and with Wilkinson.[64] The latter instruction may have been intended as an indirect method of reminding the general of administration concerns—and of his duty. At worst, such communication might reveal to Freeman some illicit scheme that he would resist.

Over the next ten days Jefferson and Dearborn studied their options and drew up new plans. On November 8, the President again summoned the Cabinet. The President and Secretary of War had decided that hostilities on the Sabine must be avoided or, if already begun, must cease. It was a calculated risk, but if Wilkinson was loyal— if the rumors were no more than that—then the army should be freed to deal with Burr. If Wilkinson was with Burr such instructions could do little to further exacerbate the situation. Moreover, it would remove any pretext Wilkinson might have for action in support of Burr that was dependent on hostilities.

Dearborn issued the orders the same day. Regardless of what had already transpired, he informed Wilkinson, "you are immediately instructed to propose to the Spanish commandant, a written convention" that called for a withdrawal to posts previously held, but that allowed the Spanish to garrison Bayou Pierre.[65] (There was no way for those in Washington to know that the general had already negotiated a "neutral-ground" agreement on even more favorable terms.) In a separate letter, the same day, the Secretary informed the general that arrangements had been made to provide him the militia he had requested but pointedly noted that the general should make no "innovations in the organization especially as to the rank of field grade officers." This foreclosed the possibility that Wilkinson might appoint senior officers of his own choosing. At the same time, Dearborn wrote Captain Thomas Swaine, who commanded the post on the Mobile opposite the Floridas, and ordered him to disregard any instruction he had or might receive from Wilkinson that called for offensive action. If any action was under way he was told to suspend it "and remain at your Post, prepared only to act on the defensive."[66]

The tension that was building is evident in a brief but bitter letter

Dearborn penned to Wilkinson on November 15. The subject was a newspaper article reprinting the contents of one of the general's letters—possibly criticism of Dearborn himself. "Would any commander with the smallest share of prudence," he wrote, "put his own reputation as well as the honor and safety of his troops and the interest of his Country at stake by such a communication?"[67] Dearborn's pique was born of frustration, but was to be short-lived. News was on its way to the capitol that would allay the administration's most serious concern—the question of Wilkinson's fidelity.

The arrival in Washington of Lieutenant Smith on November 25 with Wilkinson's first reports concerning the conspiracy and his plans to oppose it, brought relief and then action. Smith was ushered into Jefferson's presence where he removed the letters from their hiding place between the soles of a slipper. The President read the messages and then questioned Smith closely. This young officer, whom Jefferson had appointed just three years earlier, could fill many of the gaps in Wilkinson's oblique communication. He told of Swartwout's visit, of the letter from Burr, and of the latter's offer to allow the general to name the rank of his officers if the army would join him. He must also have relayed an observation Wilkinson had made to him when instructing him on the delivery of the message. "Of all traitors," the general had told him, "a military one was the greatest, and that there was but one course for him to pursue, which was to oppose [Burr] with all his force."[68]

Wilkinson's letters, and the interrogation of Lieutenant Smith, were followed almost immediately by receipt of the general's report to Dearborn outlining his efforts to seek a mutual withdrawal from the Sabine and the details of his plans to oppose Burr. All this reassured a nervous government of the continued loyalty of its distant army commander. That cleared the way for strong action against Burr and his associates.

Jefferson and his Cabinet, now reassured of the allegiance of the general and his officers, immediately hammered out a new and more aggressive policy. The President would issue a proclamation exposing the conspiracy and calling for the detention of those involved. Orders would be issued, the Cabinet agreed, to army detachments at Pittsburgh, Fort Massac, Chickasaw Bluffs, and Fort Adams, to be "vigilant in order to discover whether there are any preparations making . . . [for] a military enterprise . . ., and to stop all bodies of armed men . . . believed to have such an enterprise in view."[69] Over the next two days Dearborn personally issued these orders. He then instructed Wilkinson to take charge of the gunboats at New Orleans and to incorporate them into the defense, and to use his own judgment as to the disposition of forces. The coolness in the Secretary's tone disappeared and the occasional jocularity returned. "If the inspector can find sufficient leisure once in two or three years," he chided the general good-naturedly in a postscript, he would appreciate a report on the status of the troops. The administration's anxious moments were not over, but they could now face them with more confidence.[70]

Milton Lomask, a modern Burr biographer, has puzzled over Jefferson's sudden call to action. Why, after ignoring letters and alarms for fifteen months, he wondered, did the President spring into action to crush the expedition "in a matter of hours" after receiving Wilkinson's messages?[71] The answer is now clear. Jefferson was not waiting for confirmation of Burr's treachery—he had all the information he needed on that subject. He had, instead, been waiting to confirm Wilkinson's fidelity. Now, assured of the loyalty of the general and his army, the President could and did move boldly to stop Burr.

Meanwhile, on the Ohio, Burr had set up a headquarters of sorts on Harmon Blennerhasset's island a few miles below Marietta. Blennerhasset, an eccentric, but wealthy Irishman, had been an early and tireless supporter, and a financial mainstay of the Burr effort. Throughout September and October, Burr had moved back and forth between Cincinnati and Nashville in an effort to build support for an enterprise which, though widely boasted of, frequently had to be denied.[72] In part because of the latter situation, recruits and money came slowly, particularly so after Jefferson's November proclamation. He was investigated in Kentucky but no indictment was obtained. In the meantime, supplies and recruits were assembled in the Pittsburgh area. Recruiting was carried on throughout the Northeast and West, though it is not known just how many men were enlisted. One modern calculation based on the quantity of supplies contracted for and the number of boats built, estimates that a total force of at least 1,500 was contemplated.[73]

John Graham, whom Jefferson had put on Burr's trail in November, proved particularly effective at both penetrating the scheme and at precipitating counteraction. In a series of interviews in Pennsylvania and Ohio—posting alternately in support and opposition to the enterprise—he concluded that Burr intended to seize New Orleans. There he would take possession of the deposits at the bank and treasury, seize the military stores, and erect a government which, by its position at the mouth of the Mississippi, could induce the Western country to join it.

On December 1, Graham traveled to Chillicothe—the frontier capital of Ohio—and persuaded Governor Edward Tiffin to seek legislative authorization to seize the boats, stores, and agents of Burr's force. A bill to that effect was passed by the legislature on December 5, and Tiffin immediately dispatched forces to implement it. On December 9, one force seized eleven finished and four unfinished boats along with some 200 barrels of provisions. Blennerhasset, Comfort Tyler, and a few others escaped down the river in boats Tyler had brought from Pittsburgh. Several such small parties ultimately joined forces, but the Ohio raid had fatally damaged the prospects of the expedition.

In the meantime, Burr called again on Andrew Jackson in Nashville. Jackson, who had been sympathetic during earlier visits, was now suspicious of Burr's intentions and could not be fully convinced. Burr left Nashville without the support he had hoped for and joined the flotilla—now only ten or eleven craft, with a complement of no more than a hundred men. This force alone posed no serious threat, but Burr expected to attract further supporters along the way and in New Orleans. On December 29, they stopped at Fort Massac where Burr visited with the commander, Captain Daniel Bissell. He did the same at Chickasaw Bluffs—always a few days ahead of the warning against his enterprise. At the last stop, however, Burr won over the young lieutenant, Jacob Jackson, who commanded the small detachment that garrisoned the post. Jackson refused to join the expedition directly but did agree to resign his commission and to return home to raise a volunteer company for the battles Burr spoke of with the Spanish.[74] As the group proceeded down the Mississippi, Burr drilled his small force in the manual of arms. His actions suggest that he still expected aid from Wilkinson, though by now he knew that the general was in New Orleans and not on the Sabine.

The bubble burst on January 10, 1807, upon reaching Bayou Pierre, above Natchez.[75] Here he learned that Wilkinson had not followed his lead, and that the President had condemned the expedition. The effort was now hopeless. Burr also learned that his arrest had been ordered, and after some negotiations, surrendered on January 17. He handed himself over to the civil authority of the Mississippi Territory on the understanding that he would be tried there. Burr lounged in the Natchez area until his appearance on February 2 before the Territorial Superior Court. After several days of hearings he was absolved—though the United States Attorney had refused to seek an indictment, claiming that this court was not competent to hear the case.

Despite his exoneration by the territorial court, the federal government still sought him, and Burr went into hiding, narrowly escaping capture by agents Wilkinson had dispatched from New Orleans. The hopelessness of his situation was evident; there was nothing left but surrender or flight. He chose the latter. On February 13 he made a farewell speech to his men at the boats and departed.[76]

A few months earlier, before leaving Natchez for New Orleans, Wilkinson had played a familiar game with the Spanish. Walter Burling, who had been his emissary just a few weeks earlier during the "neutral ground" negotiations, was now sent to Mexico. He was ostensibly to sell some excess mules, but the true purpose was to ask a reward for "the risk of . . . life, fame, and future" that the general had taken in saving Spanish Mexico from Burr.

It was a significant flaw in Wilkinson's character that allowed him to treat such dealings in ethical isolation. His honor was deeply and easily wounded by slights and insults, yet he never acknowledged (and seemingly did not understand) the dishonorable nature of these affairs. The Spanish had paid Wilkinson $12,000 in 1804 for his "Reflections" on their situation along the new boundaries with the United States. Earlier, for a period of about five years during the late 1780s and early 1790s, he had been the recipient of a Spanish pension of about $2,000 annually.[77] Now, even as he denied accusations of involvement with Burr—some of which repeated rumors of the earlier Spanish intrigues—he was seeking a small fortune from the Dons. He would be "crowned Emperor of Mexico, in place of Burr," he wrote Samuel Smith, alluding to the handsome reward he was anticipating.[78] The Spanish were unimpressed, however, and Burling left with nothing more for Wilkinson than a note thanking him for his efforts and wishing him well.[79]

Wilkinson arrived in New Orleans on November 25, just as Jefferson, in Washington, received the first of his letters concerning Burr's adventure. The general immediately took charge of the defensive preparations begun by Constance Freeman the month before. Some in Washington favored a defense above the city, but Wilkinson knew nothing of that. Three factors convinced him to make his defense in New Orleans: the size of force he believed Burr to have in hand—1,000 to 1,500; the possibility of naval support—and an attack up the river from the South; and the internal threat. With 800–1,000 regulars, two bomb ketches, and four gunboats, he was more than a match for the small force Burr ultimately marshalled, but Wilkinson had no way of knowing that Burr's plans and force would be crippled by Graham in Ohio only days later. Nor could he afford to ignore the possibility that Burr had secured some form of naval support. "We knew here," wrote Jefferson some years after the fact, "that there never was danger of a British fleet from below, and that Burr's band was crushed before it reached the Mississippi. But General Wilkinson's information was very different, and he could act on no other." In any case Wilkinson was concerned about discontent among various elements of the Louisiana population—most of which was concentrated in New Orleans. Even the loyalty of the local militia was suspect. He had only recently been warned that their attachment to the United States was not yet firm.[80] They had been quite ready to join him against the Spanish, but now it was Burr who held out that promise. The city, with its defenses, was a prize he did not wish to abandon.

In New Orleans it was the internal threat that most concerned the general. The "Mexican Association" in that city had long aimed at driving Spain from the neighboring province. Many of these men were now supporters of Burr. Even before leaving the Sabine, Wilkinson had written the President that "to give effect to military arrangements, it is absolutely indispensable, New Orleans and its environs should be placed under martial law."[81] The administration's responses—which began to arrive toward year's end—did not advise him otherwise, though the President did caution against sending east any but the most important of the suspects.[82] Wilkinson attempted to work through Claiborne. He repeatedly urged him to suspend the writ of habeas corpus and to declare martial law, but the Governor just as often refused. Finally, on December 14, the general took matters into his own hands and ordered the arrest of suspected conspirators. His methods raised heckles locally and among the administration's political opponents in Washington. But circumstances suggested that to err on the side of moderation was to court disaster. The men against whom he believed himself pitted were among the most powerful in the city. Furthermore, his actions seemed largely appropriate to the administration whose first concern was with holding the Union together. Though his actions were possibly extralegal, and at least inconvenient, or disruptive, they were also, for the times, quite humane. That fact was not lost on everyone; "in any other country", wrote Duane in the *Aurora*, men suspected of plotting against the regime under such circumstances "would be decapitated."[83]

Erich Bollman, a Burr envoy who had delivered a second copy of the ciphered letter, was jailed, as was Samuel Swartwout. When local authorities threatened to intervene, Wilkinson put the two men on a vessel under military guard, and shipped them to Baltimore. Likewise James Alexander, Peter V. Ogden, and John Adair were arrested and sent east. When Judge James Workman (a key member of the Mexican Association) attempted to obtain their release, he was also jailed for a time.

When Swartwout and Bollman arrived on the East Coast, Jefferson wrote his general that sending them "and adding to them Burr, Blennerhasset, and Tyler" would be "supported by the public opinion." He cautioned, however, that, "I hope . . . you will not extend this deportation to persons against whom there is only suspicion, or shades of offense not strongly marked."[84]

In the East, however, the arraignment of Burr's associates produced ill omens. Adair, Ogden, Bollman, and Swartwout, were released in

Baltimore, as was Alexander in the District of Columbia, on the grounds that they had committed no crime in those jurisdictions. Bollman and Swartwout, meanwhile, sought fuller exoneration and went before Chief Justice John Marshall at the Supreme Court of the United States asking for a writ of habeas corpus. Marshall found in their favor, ruling that there was not sufficient evidence to warrant their arraignment on charges of treason.

Burr was finally captured late in February near Fort Stoddert, Georgia, and was sent under guard to Richmond. There he was brought before a grand jury. For reasons that have long been misunderstood—but which we shall explore forthwith—the enmity of this body became focused more on Wilkinson than Burr. From the moment the general appeared in the courtroom he was as much the accused as was the defendant himself.

IV

In the end it was Wilkinson and not the conspirators who came under the most violent attacks, though he retained the support of the President. "On great occasions," Jefferson offered, "every good officer must be ready to risk himself in going beyond the strict line of law, when the public preservation requires it."[85] The President's support, however, was not enough to quiet the censors. Wilkinson was convinced he had acted to save the nation, but this only made the criticism more hurtful.

In May, the general headed east. His stay in New Orleans had proven a time of very real tragedy. In the midst of all else that had transpired, his wife—a constant companion who had willingly shared the hardships of army life—died of the tuberculosis that had plagued her for several years. "Oh God," he wrote Jonathan Williams, "how heavy have been my afflictions."[86]

Wilkinson had had broad support in the Capitol in the early days of the affair, but as time went on that had faded. "There has been a great alarm [about Burr]," wrote Samuel Taggart, "but . . . now as many people are alarmed at the illegal arbitrary proceedings of Wilkinson."[87] Senator William Plumer had anticipated this shift.

"When the danger of this rebellion is past—when feelings, our bitter feelings subside—when time has rendered the transactions less important—Wilkinson himself will probably fall a victim."[88]

Plumer proved correct; the general's detractors soon assumed the upper hand and would maintain it. Wilkinson would spend the balance of his life defending himself.

His chief critic and tormentor was John Randolph, whose lasting antipathy toward the general grew largely out of the affair in New Orleans. But Randolph's extraordinary rancor drew on something beyond Wilkinson's conduct. It was the special, very personal context in which he viewed and understood those events which stirred him to anger.

The issue grew out of the hapless juxtaposition, in early 1807, of Randolph's (uncharacteristic) support for an enlargement of the regular military establishment, and Wilkinson's action against Burr's supporters in New Orleans. In January, with the Spanish still on the Sabine, and with Burr still at large, the administration had signaled an intention to enlarge the army.[89] "*I know* that this additional army-force is what the *President wishes*," Samuel Smith told William Plumer in January 1807, after he had introduced legislation which would add an infantry regiment and a cavalry battalion—increasing the strength of the army by nearly fifty percent.[90]

In the debates on the issue in the House, Randolph found himself in a peculiar position vis-à-vis the regular establishment; given the Spanish threat, such an army now seemed essential. The year before he had recommended strong action against the Spanish. He had objected to the administration's tactic of negotiating about boundaries, and had proposed raising a force and seizing what was claimed. If the Congress and the administration had acted then, he now chided, they wouldn't be facing this problem.

It is now conceded that had we taken an imposing attitude towards Spain, last winter, we should not only have avoided the enormous expense of Wilkinson's late campaign, and of the measures which he feels himself obliged to take in defense of New Orleans, (at least equal to that of raising and maintaining, for one year the troops proposed to be levied) but that Burr's projects would, thereby, have been crushed in embryo. It is now ascertained that, even since the peace of 1783, Spain has unceasingly labored to detach the western country from the Union. That propositions to leading characters in Kentucky were made by her to that effect [no one can doubt]. . . . And no man, in his senses, can doubt that the schemes of Burr are . . . in concert with the cabinet of Madrid.[91]

While Spain "was treating with one hand," he said, "she was preparing to stab us in the dark with the other." The United States had paid "fifteen millions for the Mississippi and its delta," he noted, then added, "shall we be so penurious not to defend this important post—this key to our strong box."[92]

The difficulty now, Randolph said, was that *he* did not "believe the militia adequate to defend New Orleans." That city was simply too far from the mass of the nation's population. "I have no disposition to raise regular forces for the defense on New York, or Baltimore, or of my native State—there is sufficient population for their defense. . . . But in the country I have spoken of, there is no militia." There, he believed, a regular force was necessary, though he would have liked "to get rid of the present inefficient one."[93]

However he might qualify it, Randolph found himself supporting an enlargement of the regular establishment. For the first time he had betrayed the principles of 1798—the old republican line that regulars, in any form, were an evil.

That decision began to haunt him just six days later, on January 22, 1807, when the President released the first official information about Wilkinson's actions in New Orleans. Jefferson laid out the whole sequence of events, as he then knew them. He told of Wilkinson's letters of October 21, which had informed the administration of Burr's designs, and the general's letters of December 14 and 18 which had just been received telling of the arrest and shipment of prisoners to Washington. In Randolph's view the regular establishment that he had just voted to enlarge—personified by their general, James Wilkinson—had turned on the people. "This business of seizing the person of the citizen with the strong hand of military power . . . strikes me with consternation," he wrote Joseph Nicholson in early February.[94]

For Randolph, however, consternation turned to indignation when he was required to explain his retreat from principle. It was, to him, a public humiliation. "In advocating an increase of the public force," he proclaimed, "my object was to chastise an insolent foe [Spain], not to employ it against our citizens and to substitute it in lieu of the civil authority. My dread of standing armies has been more than a hundred times increased in consequence of the services to which our present little force has been put." Indignation then turned to vindictiveness. "I would teach the military that they are to be subordinate to the civil power," he stormed, "and that if they undertake to violate the civil institutions of their country they should pay the penalty of their lives." Turning to his colleagues he said, "If you do not guard the people from such an excess of military power the time will come when you will be kicked out . . . at the point of a bayonet."[95]

With that, however, Randolph's own words were turned against him. James Sloan, a long-time nemesis, reviewed Randolph's statements of just a month before and invited the members to contrast them with his remarks in the current debate. Randolph's words about the *necessity* for a regular force in New Orleans were juxtaposed with his more recent assertion that such a "trifling intrigue . . . might have been suppressed by the militia of a county." Now, Sloan asserted, Randolph would have the members to believe that he had known for some time that Wilkinson had been concerned in a treasonable combination.

Randolph was livid. The attack, he charged, was motivated by the administration and designed to intimidate him. Wilkinson became the focal point of all his rage. To the Virginia congressman the general had become a villain and tyrant on a grand scale. Randolph held Wilkinson personally responsible for the embarrassment he suffered on this issue—one so fundamental to his political creed. That was the unforgivable.[96]

Randolph's opportunity to extract revenge was not long in coming. He sat as the foreman of the grand jury at Richmond that was empaneled to hear evidence against Burr. Wilkinson came before them and was sworn on June 15. He arrived in the courtroom resplendent in full uniform with his sword at his side. Randolph wasted not a moment. The general had no more than entered the room when Randolph, as foreman, demanded that he surrender the weapon he wore. "Take that man out and disarm him," he shrilled. "I will allow no attempt to intimidate the jury."[97]

Randolph kept the general on the witness stand for four days. Wilk-inson was forced to admit to a series of misrepresentations and even perjured statements relative to Burr's recent adventure: his version of Burr's cipher letter had omitted the passages which tended to impli-cate him; and the cipher, which he originally said was devised in 1804, actually dated from some years earlier. A motion to indict him for misprision of treason failed by only two votes. "The mammoth of iniquity escaped," wrote Randolph. He was "from the bark to the very core a villain," and worse, he stood "on the very summit and pinnacle of executive favor."[98] Wilkinson, Randolph insisted, was "the most finished scoundrel that ever lived."[99]

Burr was ultimately arraigned on charges of treason, but the trial was anticlimactic. It ended with a three-hour charge to the jury by Mar-shall, a twenty-five minute deliberation, and a verdict that Burr was not proved to be guilty by the evidence submitted. With that the cases against the co-conspirators also collapsed. Burr was again brought to trial in September for organizing an expedition against a friendly na-tion—Spain—but was soon acquitted on this charge also.

The administration's actions had proved futile—even embarrassing, in light of the verdicts. What's more, the animosity that had grown between Wilkinson and Randolph would erupt at year's end and com-plicate the final act of the administration's reform of the military es-tablishment.

These events provided an acid test of the army, and of Wilkinson. The central issue was loyalty, and the litmus was Burr. The circum-stances lent credibility to rumors that Wilkinson and Burr were scheming to establish a new dominion in the West. The threat of a conflict with Spain along the Sabine frontier seemed to serve that end. And with Wilkinson at the head of the army in the field, concern heightened just as Burr seemed prepared to launch his adventure. Still, Dearborn and Jefferson found themselves unable to do more than sim-ply wait and watch. General Wilkinson's army would follow where he led.

But, Wilkinson proved loyal. The general's link to Burr (whatever its earlier nature) had been effectively dissolved the year before by the simple expedient of warning him away—although the administration surely doubted the efficacy of that alone. "There had been a time when General Wilkinson did not stand well with the Executive," reported one administration official, "but his energetic measures at New Orleans had regained him [Jefferson's] confidence.[100]

CHAPTER 7

Mr. Jefferson's Army

The administration's concern about the loyalty of the commanding general were no sooner resolved, than concern arose about the loyalty of the officers of the army in general. The strongly Republican *Aurora*—often a harbinger of administration thinking—charged, in January 1807, that army officers in Pittsburgh had been sympathetic to the conspirators and had made no attempt to block their preparations until they had received explicit orders to do so.[1] Rumors were rampant about officer disaffection and complicity in the Burr affair. Even among the officer corps it was a matter of speculation. "Several officers are said to be among the Conspirators," wrote one to another.[2]

Wilkinson soon confirmed the rumors. "Let [Ensign William C.] Meade and [Lieutenant George Washington] Sevier be arrested," he ordered, for "they are deeply involved in the military part of the conspiracy."[3] As early as the spring of 1806, the Mexican Association in New Orleans, which had links to Burr, had attempted to recruit supporters from among the officers of the army. One group of four young officers, including Meade, were hosted by Judge Workman and told that the intention was to seize the shipping and banks of New Orleans in order to support and finance the attack on the Spanish. Though apparently not all these officers had agreed to join the intrigue (and one had since died), the affair confirmed the suspicions the administration had held about the loyalty of the army.[4]

The administration immediately undertook a quiet investigation aimed at learning the extent of the danger. Wilkinson took depositions in New Orleans and Dearborn interrogated officers passing through Washington. The Secretary shared the findings with the President. The reports, one after another, indicated a problem of substantial proportion.

Various methods were considered and rejected for dealing with the problem. Dearborn at first favored dismissal but the President demurred. "Many officers of the army" were involved, he noted, and "some line must . . . be drawn to separate the more from the less guilty." He believed that many had thought "the enterprise was with the approbations of the government, open or secret." These, he insisted, should be retained. Those who had "meant to proceed in defiance of the government" should be cashiered, he agreed, but "to remove the whole without trial . . . would be a proceeding of unusual severity."[5]

A purge was out of the question. Wholly aside from the issue of severity or justice, this simply was not a propitious moment to either alienate or denude the army. Napoleon's victories on the Continent threatened to change the power structure of Europe, and Jefferson understood the consequences for America. If the British Navy were somehow removed, the United States, and especially New Orleans, would lay exposed to both French and Spanish whims. Of course, the British were a threat in their own right. Moreover, the continuing economic warfare between England and France—the Orders of Council and the Berlin Decrees it spawned—so endangered American shipping that it seemed only a matter of time before the nation would be drawn into the conflict.

In the spring of 1807, as the dimensions of the loyalty problem became more apparent—and as the lists of the unfaithful grew—Jefferson and Dearborn weighed their alternatives. They balanced the difficulty of drawing "strong lines of distinction" between degress of guilt, and the risk of either action or inaction. In the end they concluded that it was simply "inexpedient" to take action against any of the officers.[6]

Inaction, of course, did not make the problem go away. It only meant, as the administration well understood, that the army would continue to contain a sizable number of officers whose fidelity was suspect. Much of the army was not beholden to the administration.

Jefferson was only too well aware that the Federalist stain that had marked the army just a few years ago had not been wholly eradicated. Dismissals and new appointments had made inroads, but progress had been slow. The senior ranks in particular had not yet yielded to Republicanization. Until they did, the army would not truly belong to Jefferson.

A solution to this quandary emerged unexpectedly in June 1807, in the wake of an unfortunate naval incident off the coast at Norfolk, where the British ship *Leopard* mauled the nearly defenseless American frigate *Chesapeake*. Jefferson, who realized that the nation was unprepared for a major war, was determined to avoid a conflict. Still, the rising national sentiment for war offered an intriguing possibility. If the army were expanded, the present officer corps could be submerged in a larger establishment. The residual influence and power of the old Federalist establishment could be diluted by an influx of staunch Republicans *in every grade*. Here at last was a way to overcome the previous difficulty that stemmed from the rule of promotion by seniority. To date, even the deliberate infusion of Republican officers had altered the complexion of only the most junior elements of the army.

Enlarging the army was a disarmingly simple solution, but it was not an easy decision and one not reached in haste. Enlarging the army seemed a most unrepublican answer. Yet, as Jefferson would demonstrate, it could be made palatable—even to many Republicans who were usually inclined to oppose *any* expansion. A larger army promised security when war threatened. Yet, even peace yielded up a substantial rationale for expansion. The new boundaries of the nation and the need to station sizable numbers at New Orleans indicated a larger force. Clearly, more troops could profitably be employed in either peace or war. To the administration, of course, this solution held out the additional benefit of an army beholden to the regime—and one that was Republican throughout.

I

The USS *Chesapeake*, a frigate with more than 370 men aboard—including a small number who had deserted from the British Navy—

weighed anchor at Norfolk and made sail on Monday, June 22, bound for the Mediterranean. Shortly after midday they sighted a British man-of-war, the HMS *Leopard*. When hailed, the American captain, James Barron, ordered his ship to heave to. The British insisted that they be allowed to search for some of their seamen who had deserted in Norfolk. When Barron refused, the *Leopard* opened fire, heavily damaging the American vessel. The *Chesapeake*, which had been wholly unprepared for action, struck its colors without firing a shot. The British then took off four deserters. Barron got the crippled ship under way again late in the evening, and made Hampton Roads about noon the next day. Three seamen had been killed and eighteen more were wounded, including the captain. It was one of the most humiliating episodes in the American naval experience.

Word of the event reached Washington on June 25. The capital, which had had its attention riveted on the trial in Richmond, now focused on the new crisis. Jefferson ordered all British ships out of American ports, and undertook some precautionary measures, including a study of the defenses of the new federal city.[7] News of the affair traveled fast. Resentment in America quickly turned to war fever. "The only subject at present is War—War—War. We are no federalists—no democrats but the cry of every heart is defend our rites and avenge the wrongs we suffered."[8]

Dearborn was away and Jefferson urged him to complete his business and return as soon as possible. "I begin to fear we shall not be justified in separating this autumn, and that even an earlier meeting of Congress than we had contemplated may be required."[9] He set the process of government in motion.

Wilkinson was quick to respond and proposed a comprehensive but essentially defensive plan. The general laid out five steps: reconvene the Congress; proclaim an embargo on goods going to Britain; prepare to defend the nation's more critical and vulnerable points; expel any remaining armed British ships; and make general offensive and defensive preparations.[10] Jefferson reacted cautiously. "We shall avoid . . . every act which would precipitate general hostilities," he wrote Samuel Smith.[11] Still, the next day he called on the Congress to assemble in special session.

The President worked actively with Dearborn, giving careful thought to the preparations that would be necessary if war came. "Should we have war with England, regular troops will be necessary," he noted, but when Dearborn suggested increasing the regular force immediately to 15,000 he hesitated.[12] He was not yet ready. For the moment he preferred the idea of volunteers—but not militia. He complained to Dearborn of problems at Norfolk where the militia had been in charge. "More bungling conduct [is] to be expected when the command should devolve on a militia Major."[13]

The *Leopard-Chesapeake* affair not only ignited American passions, but also sparked a heated debate about the militia and the kind of defense the nation should have. William Duane argued that the country needed only to adopt a correct organization and discipline for the militia; that it need not rely on regulars. He proposed a militia of cavalry, artillery, and infantry, but put the emphasis on the light elements of these, particularly the flying artillery, light infantry, and riflemen.[14]

Jefferson recognized that an effective militia would vastly multiply the nations strength; still, he had no desire to struggle with a militia force unless that institution was reformed. And that, he realized, was unlikely. Moreover, Jefferson was less concerned than Duane over the danger of regulars. General Wilkinson and his army had stood fast in the face of recent temptation and had acted to preserve the union. The meaning was not lost on Jefferson. Still, he held back his request to enlarge the regular establishment until the issue of militia reform had been addressed by the Congress.[15]

Militia reform was a perennial issue, one pursued by every succeeding administration. Each had offered some scheme of classing the militia by age, usually requiring only the younger to be prepared for immediate service. Jefferson had made several such calls for reform—it was a staple of his annual messages—but with little effect. In 1806, prompted by renewed tensions with Spain in the Southwest, he did manage to get the issue of classing introduced in the Congress, but it was rejected handily. Even Republican House leader Joseph Varnum, who usually championed the administration's military measures, opposed the idea. Such proposals, it was repeatedly demonstrated, had no chance of passing.[16] In a sense the legislators were victims of the rhetoric—

the myth of the militia—that had been spawned in the years immediately after the Revolution. As an institution it was inviolate.

Congress was willing to arm the existing militia forces, but Jefferson resisted. That, he believed, was a waste and more; it would do little to improve effectiveness and would relieve what pressure there was for substantive reform. Though he continued to seek militia reform, it was obvious to all who cared to see that such reform was impossible. Without reform he saw very limited potential in the militia.

Jefferson's growing ambivalence toward the militia, however, reflected more than simple concern about their effectiveness. The militia, too, was bound up in partisan politics. Militia officers wore their political stripes as visibly as their rank. Worse, too frequently the militia was dominated by Federalists even in Republican counties. Jefferson's concern was revealed in an observation he made just a few years later. He cited the example of one Virginia county with a militia of 1,500 men of which only sixty were Federalists. But, with the county leadership disproportionately Federalist—twenty of thirty members of the court were Federalists—"the militia [was] as disproportionately under federal officers."[17] It was this political nature as much as the inefficiency of the militia that prompted Jefferson to seek volunteers in their stead.

As he had suggested to Dearborn, Jefferson concluded that it was essential to call a special session of Congress to deal with the crisis created by the *Leopard-Chesapeake* affair. But, at the beginning of that session he indicated that the administration was still considering what measure it should take. "Whether a regular army is to be raised, and to what extent, must depend on the information so shortly expected."[18] Delay was seemingly a tactic; time—or the increased demand for action that time brought—would be made to work on the side of the administration.

With no recommendation from the administration on the expansion of the regular establishment, however, the Congress busied itself with other issues—port and harbor defense, gunboats, and the militia. Dearborn furnished the reports that the Congress requested but went little further.[19] For four months the issue was held in suspense. This delay was calculated, some concluded. There was in this, Federalist

James Elliott of Vermont claimed, the invisible hand of the administration. "We all know that this business has long been cut and dried by the Executive", he insisted. The President was operating, he said, "in a secret side-way manner."[20]

Rumors, however, pervaded the government, predicting an expansion of the regular force. "An augmentation of the Army is very confidently spoken of," reported one officer to another. "Wilkinson," he added, "is to be a Major General."[21]

II

Such rumors may have pleased some, but not John Randolph. But, if Randolph was disturbed by the prospect of a larger force, he was apoplectic when it came to Wilkinson—the more so at the thought of his promotion. To Randolph, by 1807, the general had become the *personification* of all that was evil in the military establishment. On him, he focused his abhorrence both of the standing army and of Jefferson's plan to enlarge it. All the indignities, slights, and discomforts he had suffered, all the frustration and pain associated with seeing his principles trampled on—all at the expense of a standing army—coalesced in a white-hot hatred of Wilkinson.

On December 31, Randolph attacked Wilkinson on the floor of the House—calling for a presidential inquiry into the general's conduct, and saying that he had evidence revealing that "while in the service of the United States, [Wilkinson had] corruptly received money from the Government of Spain or its agents." This call for an investigation, he said, was "a duty which he owed not only to himself, but to [his constituents], and to the country at large."[22] Randolph claimed to have learned of evidence against Wilkinson on December 24. That evidence—relating to allegations that Wilkinson had been in the Spanish pay in 1796—had been delivered to him, he said, on December 30.[23] That may have been, but the real reason for this sudden attack had little or nothing to do with the charges alleged—charges that had been bandied about for years.

The issue that had once again brought Randolph to attack the general was not some new revelation of Wilkinson's misdeeds, but rather a letter from the general delivered on December 24 challenging him to a duel.

John Randolph (of Roanoke) by John Wesley Jarvis.
NATIONAL PORTRAIT GALLERY, SMITHSONIAN INSTITUTION, WASHINGTON, D.C.

Randolph, who internalized and personalized issues in the extreme, came to focus all his hatred of the regular military on General Wilkinson. Randolph's personal and vicious attacks against the general were unrepresentative of other critics—though they have often been used by historians to characterize Wilkinson. Randolph's charges concerning the general's involvement some years earlier with the Spanish proved correct later, but the balance of his accusations were little more than malicious slander.

I understand several expressions have escaped you, in their nature personal, and highly injurious to my reputation . . . that you have avowed the opinion I was a rogue—that you have ascribed to me the infernal disposition to commit murder, to prevent the exposition of my sinister designs, and through me have stigmatized [the army]. . . . Under these impressions, I can have no hesitation to appeal to your justice, your magnanimity and your gallantry, to prescribe the manner and the measure of redress.[24]

Randolph refused the challenge but did not give an inch. "Several months ago," he wrote,

I was informed of your having said, that you were acquainted with what had passed in the grand-jury-room at Richmond, last spring, and that you had declared a determination to challenge me. . . . Whatever may have been the expressions used by me, in relation to your character, they were the result of deliberate opinion, founded upon the most authentic evidence. . . . In you, sir, I can recognize no right to hold me accountable for my public or private opinion of your character. . . . I cannot descend to your level. This is my *final* answer.[25]

When Randolph refused to duel, Wilkinson denounced him publicly "as a prevaricating, base, calumniating scoundrel, poltroon and coward."[26] The general was heaping the fuel high, and would suffer the consequences.

The debate on Randolph's motion to investigate Wilkinson went on for hours but did not produce the results desired by the angry Virginian. Many, like James Sloan of New Jersey, considered the charges and insinuations nothing more than petty malice. Nathaniel Macon, a Randolph confederate, insisted however, that these charges—added to already widely held suspicions—necessitated some inquiry. Without it, he insisted, the people could not have the proper confidence in the general. Some members were persuaded, but more preferred to simply turn the evidence over to the President to do with as he would.[27]

But Randolph was not easily put off; he raised the issue again during debates on the army bill. That provoked another long session and more criticism of his motives. Randolph simply "calculated to injure the officer," charged James Holland of North Carolina.[28]

As the debates continued, Randolph broadened his attack—now including the whole army. "Within the year," he said, there had been a project, through the instrumentality of the Army . . . , to dismember the Union; and he had no hesitation in saying . . . that the Army . . . was

James Wilkinson by John Wesley Jarvis.
THE FILSON CLUB, LOUISVILLE, KENTUCKY.

General Wilkinson's arrest and deportation of Burr's coadjutors, as he prepared to defend against the conspirator's anticipated assault, made him as
much a target of attack as the central culprit himself—particularly after the
danger of the situation subsided. Though his loyalty earned him the backing
of Jefferson, and though he continued to serve until 1814, he was never able
to put that incident, nor charges that he had been involved with Burr, behind
him.

tainted with the disease; and that . . . the moment it was found that the courage of that Army had failed, the project was abandoned by those who had undertaken it, because the agency of the Army was the whole pivot on which that plot turned.

"These conspirators," he argued, "were caressed at the different posts" as they made their way down the river, and were given public arms. "[Am I] not justified in the belief that the whole army . . . was connected in the project," he asked?[29]

Still, Randolph found little support. John Smilie of Pennsylvania objected to his effort to "denounce the Army as corrupt throughout." The army "had tried . . . their officers and found them trusty," he noted. And then he added, "To hold them up as unworthy of trust at this time, in a crisis like the present, was impolitic and unjust."[30] Others also rose to the defense of the army and its general. John Taylor of South Carolina noted that the general was

charged with being a Spanish pensioner in 1796—again, on the river Sabine— a conspirator with Burr—a perjured man—[and] a conspirator against the liberties of the citizens whom he had arrested as traitors and coadjutors with Burr.

These charges, Taylor said, were leveled with "eloquence, [then] mixed . . . and animadverted upon" by some of the best talents in the nation. But the denunciations, he pointed out, were supported by only one document. "If he were a demon," Taylor objected, "I would not use him thus unfairly."[31]

Randolph's motives and target were too obvious. "The high sounding words 'Commander-in-Chief of the Army of the United States,' and the republican jealousy against standing armies, were weapons which these gentlemen had managed with great adroitness and dexterity," Taylor complained. But, these were false issues, he insisted, that "had been made use of as a bugbear to get at a particular character."[32]

Randolph, vocal as he was, had come to represent only a small segment of the Republican party. Few now shared either the bitterness of his animosity toward Wilkinson, or his inordinate concern over regular troops.

III

At the end of February, the administration finally revealed its proposals for an enlarged military establishment. Jefferson reminded the Congress that he had earlier communicated "the dangers to our country arising from the contests of other nations and the urgency of making preparations." Now, he said,

To secure ourselves by due precautions an augmentation of our military force, as well regular as of volunteer militia, seems to be expedient. The precise extent of that augmentation cannot as yet be satisfactorily suggested . . . [but he recommended] a commencement of this precautionary work by a present provision for raising and organizing some additional forces.[33]

If the President seemed tentative, the Secretary of War was not. Enclosed with Jefferson's message was a proposal from Dearborn that called for five added infantry regiments, and new regiments of riflemen, light artillery, and cavalry—a new complement of about 6,000 men, bringing the total force to over 9,000.[34]

Both houses moved quickly to consider the administration's proposal. The debates showed clearly that the majority of Republicans no longer subscribed to what Randolph had called "the old Republican maximum"—never to "consent to increase our standing military force by one man, until . . . the enemy against whom we are to contend [can be seen]." John Clopton insisted that the nation not place its sole reliance on regular troops. "The militia," he argued, "ought always to constitute the bulwark of defense, [and] in no situation whatsoever ought regulars to he embodied to such an amount as to form a force superior or nearly equal to that of this body of militia." Still, he supported the enlargement of the army. For many duties, he indicated "regular troops . . . appear to be best adapted."[35] In this manner Clopton and others accommodated the old rhetoric to the new realities.

John Taylor put the issue into perspective.

A great deal has been said of the danger of standing armies; if I could believe that there was the least danger to the liberties of 800,000 or one million of freemen by the forces now to be raised, I should think very little of my country. I should think it deserved not the liberty it enjoyed.[36]

On April 7, the bill passed the House 95–15. Some Republicans squarely faced the meaning of their support. Matthew Lyon "had no idea of fighting under false colors," he said. In 1798 he had been convicted of sedition by the Federalists for, among other things, his efforts to inhibit recruiting for the New Army. Now, he said, "he had voted for this motion as *standing regular force,* and he was perfectly satisfied with the bill."[37]

As the vote revealed, a substantial majority of both parties favored efforts to increase the army.[38] Nonetheless, for both the issue was also divisive. "I suppose both old parties will be divided," noted Macon the day before the vote, but the division among the Old Republicans was particularly painful to him. "I never regretted differing with [Randolph] so much in my life as I did on the bill raising troops," he confided. "He followed his judgment, I mine."[39]

The addition virtually tripled the size of the army and increased the officer strength from roughly 200 to over 500. The act, which was signed into law on April 12, was a bonanza of appointment opportunities.

The administration wasted no time in seeking qualified applicants. Two days after the bill became law, Dearborn sent letters to a number of Republican members of the House and Senate, inviting them to recommend candidates to fill these new vacancies—Republican candidates of course. The President made his position clear to Dearborn; this was not an opportunity to be lost. He was expected to screen the applicants, and to recommend Republicans. When some of those recommended by Dearborn's Massachusetts colleagues turned out to be Federalists, the Secretary fired off a reprimand to the Republican leader, William Eustis. "If I recommend any such to the President," the Secretary wrote, "it will be from the effect of deception."[40] Applications which evidenced no firm allegiance to the administration or to republicanism went unanswered—a fact that was noted on the papers when they were filed.[41]

"He is undoubtedly a firm republican[,] a friend to his country, and the present administration," read one letter of recommendation from Kentucky—defining a perfectly qualified applicant.[42] When recommendations were incomplete in their political revelations, Dearborn made further inquiries. "Your letter in favor of Mr. Clark has been received," he wrote Eustis.

I wish you had added what his political standing is. We have at present a sufficient proportion of our political opponents in the Army to render any new appointments, in the small body of additional troops, of that class, unnecessary, if not inexpedient.

Dearborn went on to inquire about some other young men—Joseph Grafton and Samuel Miller—who were seeking commissions.

I will thank you to be so obliging as to ascertain their political character and let me know what you can learn relative to them . . . I will also thank you to say something about Isaiah Doan[e].[43]

A few days later Dearborn queried another Massachusetts Republican, Speaker of the House Joseph Varnum, about Doane. Even apparently solid recommendations were double-checked.

[He] has been mentioned as a good sound republican and well qualified for a Captain. Do you know him, or will you inquire about him, his character and let me know the result?[44]

Administration officials carried on similar exchanges with Republicans from throughout the nation, insuring that the officer ranks were filled with men of proper political sentiments. As usual, there were more applicants for commissions than vacancies. "Have you obtained your commission?" friends inquired of each other. "There are so many applicants," one warned, "that unless you [applied] very early and have powerful friends, I don't think you could have succeeded."[45] But even powerful friends were not always enough. One young man who claimed that his application could be "backed by nearly the whole of the republican delegation in Congress," if necessary, was rejected.[46]

The administration worked quickly, and by the end of May had fixed on candidates for all the vacancies for captains and lieutenants. "It is possible some may decline, and open a way for new competition," wrote Jefferson, but that was the only hope he could now offer applicants.[47] The senior ranks were filled more deliberately—a few as late as the next year.

For obvious reasons the administration did nothing to encourage officers of the existing line to transfer into the new regiments; from the grade of captain up they were all holdovers from the Federalist era. "Why are not the officers, who have served a number of years in subordinate situations promoted?" asked the Federalist *Boston Gazette*.

Why are beardless boys who belch beer and democracy, and "know not the division of a battle more than a spinster," placed over their heads? Because political partisans must be provided for, without any reference to etiquette, or propriety. . . . Can a government which elevates everything naturally low, and depresses everything naturally high, render a nation prosperous, happy, or glorious? Can an army be made respectable by such a wretched and partial policy?[48]

Only Zebulon M. Pike, Robert Purdy and Elizah Strong made that move. Some may have been discouraged from applying by the fact that the new regiments were created for only five years, with no assurance that they would be continued in the line. Officers transferring to one of these regiments stood the risk of being disbanded with it, if or when that should occur.

Winfield Scott was one of those newly commissioned with the additional force. He was advanced by William B. Giles, to whom Dearborn had written seeking recommendations, but Scott attributed his success to a personal visit to the President. Still, Scott was critical of the selection process.

Many of the appointments were positively bad, and a majority of the remainder indifferent. Party spirit of that day knew no bounds, and, of course, was blind to policy. Federalists were almost entirely excluded from selection, though great numbers were eager for the field, and in the New England and some other states, there were but very few educated Republicans. Hence, the selections from those communities consisted mostly of coarse and ignorant men. In the other states, where there was no lack of educated men in the dominant party, the appointments consisted, generally, of swaggerers, dependants, decayed gentlemen, and others . . . *utterly unfit for any military purpose whatsoever.*[49]

Federalists were not totally excluded, but that fact owed more to error than administration policy. "It appears that being a Federalist is an advantage to a candidate at which I am much surprised," complained one partisan observer when it appeared the administration had erred. "I cannot suppose that intentionally you prefer Federalists to Republicans, but that you are deceived by those who apply and those on whom you depend for information respecting the character of applicants."[50] Jefferson passed the letter on to his Secretary of War with the terse note: "on federal app[oint]m'ts." A few days later, now clearly with an eye to the matter, Dearborn wrote Varnum that he had noted "with some surprise, the undue proportion of Federalists recommended for commissions from Massachusetts." It was, he lamented, "a subject of deep regret, to find a large proportion of such characters recommended by our best friends, or by those who rank high in the republican Corps."[51]

The Republicans, like the Federalists before them, made a conscious effort to fill the newly created vacancies with the politically faithful. In 1801 only a dozen Republican officers could be identified in the Federalist dominated army, and only one had risen above the rank of captain. In the years since, Dearborn and Jefferson had kept close watch over the process of Republicanizing the force. The first substantial opportunities had come as a result of the Military Peace Establishment Act of 1802, and toward the end of that year, Dearborn reported the progress to the President. Though still in the minority, the party had more than tripled their numbers in the army. The officer ranks of the army, he noted, now contained 38 Republicans and 140 Federalists.[52] In another three years, officers appointed by Jefferson outnumbered those of the old army.

During Jefferson's two terms, more than three-quarters of the 267 officers of the 1801 army resigned, died, or were discharged. (See figure 7.1.) Those vacancies were filled with Republicans whose "bona fides" were checked with care. By the end of 1807 Jefferson had appointed over sixty percent of the officers of the army—though it was, of course, the junior sixty percent. Few of these Republicans had yet risen even to the rank of captain. The exceptions were among the engineers, who the President had been able to appoint without regard to seniority or service. Now, in 1808, when the size of the military establishment was almost tripled, Republican appointees truly came to dominate the army. (See figure 7.2.) They now made up a majority in virtually every rank from ensign to brigadier general.[53] (See table 7.1.)

Numbers, however, do not tell the whole story. The administration

FIGURE 7.1: *Officer Strength, 1801–9*

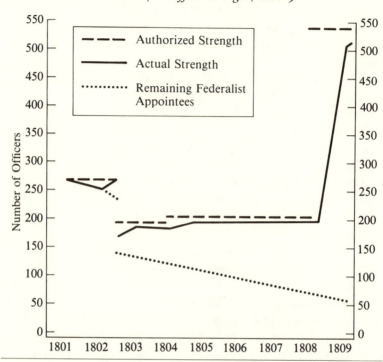

Sources: Strength figures—Thomas H. S. Hamersly, *Complete Regular Army Register of the United States* (Washington, D.C.: T. H. S. Hamersly, 1880), pp. 49–62; *American State Papers, Military Affairs,* 1:155, 175–77, 222–23, 250–55.

Data on individuals—Hamersly, *Army Register;* Heitman, *Historical Register.*

Note: The officer strength figures illustrated above do not always correspond to those given in Series Y906, *Historical Statistics of the United States, Colonial Times to 1970* (Washington, D.C.: Government Printing Office, 1975) but rather are drawn from the contemporary sources (noted above) which reflect more closely the trends indicated in records of appointment and discharge. These sources reveal that officer strength grew slowly through 1804 and then leveled off at around 195 until the army was enlarged in 1808.

had been trying, since the death of Colonel Thomas Butler, to provide an alternative to General Wilkinson around whom disaffected officers might rally. They found their man in Wade Hampton, who was appointed one of the new brigadier generals.

Reports were soon heard from Wilkinson partisans of "a deplorable picture of the state of discipline and barbarous insubordination which prevails too generally throughout the military establishment."[54] The

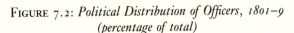

FIGURE 7.2: *Political Distribution of Officers, 1801–9*
(percentage of total)

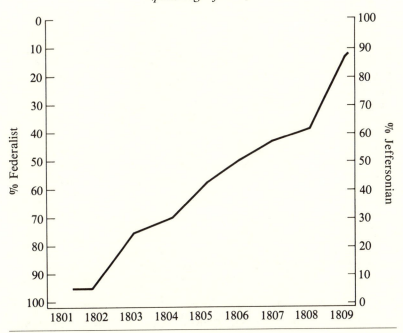

Sources: Strength figures—Hamersly, *Army Register,* pp. 49–62; *American State Papers, Military Affairs,* 1:155, 175–77, 222–23, 250–55.

Data on individuals—Hamersly, *Army Register;* Heitman, *Historical Register.*

officers of the army were divided into factions, reported Winfield Scott. "Nearly all in commission, and a majority of the appointments of 1808, were partisans of Brigadier-General Wilkinson. . . . The remainder were the supporters . . . of Brigadier-General Hampton."[55]

In just two years, Hampton himself was complaining that "intrigue" and "bitterness of party" had "grown to so great a height, in the army and out of it," that he needed assurances of support from the Secretary of War—by then William Eustis. "Nothing but the highest confidence of support of government can sustain the officer to whom the command of the army is confided," he wrote, alluding to a conflict that had continued to grow between himself and General Wilkinson.[56]

The seeds of rivalry that Jefferson and Dearborn planted bore bitter

TABLE 7.1: *Jeffersonian Appointments in the Army*
(percentage by rank)

	Jun 1802	Jan 1805	Jan 1808	Apr 1809 (1)*	(2)
Brigadier General	0	0	0	0	67
Colonel	0	0	0	0	60
Lieutenant Colonel	0	0	0	20	55
Major	0	0	14	13	38
Captain	0	2	6	9	66
First Lieutenant	2	7	77	92	97
Second Lieutenant	11	88	100	100	100
Ensign/Cornet	100	100	100	100	100
Surgeon	50	93	96	100	100
Surgeon's Mate	75			100	100

Source: Hamersly, *Army Register*, pp. 49–62; *American State Papers, Military Affairs*, 1:115, 175–77, 250–55.

*This column is displayed for purposes of comparison only. It excludes the officers appointed in the expansion of 1808. A comparison of 1809 columns (1) and (2) indicates the dramatic impact that expansion had in Republicanizing the army's senior ranks—an area previously untouched.

fruit in the years that followed. Many, though not nearly all, of the difficulties that the army experienced in the War of 1812 stemmed from this division. The direct result was a repeated failure of these two commanders to adequately cooperate. More indirectly it produced a general inefficiency—with the two camps pitted against each other in everything from the correct form of drill to the proper cut of uniforms.[57]

IV

The Embargo proved yet another test of the army's political loyalty. Exceedingly unpopular in the Federalist Northeast, from its inception in December 1807, the Embargo was a partisan issue, and one in which the army was soon involved. While Federalists warned that Jefferson planned to use the army to enforce the unpopular act, some Republicans were still concerned that the army might not support the administration.[58] Flagrant violations of the Embargo at some Massachusetts ports required the specific attention of the administration.

The collector at Bedford—near Boston— was dismissed as an example to others, but action did not stop there.[59] Captain Joseph Swift was sent to Boston to discuss, "a plan to enforce the embargo law." He assured the Republicans with whom he conferred, "There would be no difficulty in planting a battery that would ensure an obedience to the law," and promised that "political sentiment would have no influence with any officer in the harbor."[60] The threat of an insurrection in Boston particularly concerned Jefferson. He instructed Dearborn that, "on the first symptom of any open opposition to the law by force, you will fly to the scene and aid in suppressing any commotion."[61]

It was along the Canadian border in Vermont and New York, however, that opposition to the Embargo came closest to armed insurrection. And here it was not just Federalist opposition that had to be addressed. Here, one observer noted, "the most active and interested Smugglers are generally Good Republicans.[62] Gallatin and Jefferson prevailed on the New York Governor, Daniel Tompkins, to provide militia until the regulars who were then being recruited could replace them.[63] Tompkins, who had no desire to risk his political future over this issue, finally agreed, but only halfheartedly.

"The armed resistance to the embargo laws on the Canada line," wrote Jefferson to Wilkinson,

induced us [to realize] at an early period that the new recruits of the northern States should be rendezvoused there. . . . In the meantime, we have been obliged to move several detachments of militia to points on that line. This is irksome to them, expensive, troublesome, and less efficacious. Understanding that there are three companies of new recruits filled, or nearly filled at New York, I must pray you to order these, and indeed all the recruits of the State of New York, to Sackett's Harbor, Oswegatchie, and Plattsburgh, in equal proportions to each, in order to support the collectors in the execution of their duties, and this without any avoidable delay.[64]

The troops were on their way in a short time. "With the assistance of Governor Tompkins and Gen[eral] Wilkinson," reported Gallatin, the Secretary of the Treasury, "militia and regulars have arrived or are on their march to the Lakes." Gallatin reported to the President that, "I hope by the 1st of Oct[ob]er . . . the militia [will be] relieved everywhere but in Vermont by the regulars."[65]

Jefferson pressed Wilkinson to expedite recruiting and fill the new regiments; he now needed his army. The old line units were recruiting in the usual manner, but in the new regiments each captain was expected to earn his command by enlisting his own company.[66] Wilkinson and Dearborn did what they could to encourage these efforts. By late October the Secretary reported that despite delays, he expected to complete the regiments by the end of November.[67] Events proved him overly optimistic, but the records indicate that in that time they more than doubled the total force size. To have accomplished that, while replacing normal losses, would mean that they must have recruited or reenlisted roughly 4,000 men. The expanded ranks were not wholly filled in 1808, but sufficient progress had been made that the administration could reasonably expect that active recruiting the next year would complete the new establishment.

As they were available, regulars were sent to relieve the militia enforcing the Embargo along the Canadian frontier and Atlantic coast. The Vermont militia was "expensive and sometimes disaffected," reported Gallatin. He had suggested to Wilkinson, "substituting in their place such companies of new recruits . . . as were in a state of readiness."[68] Regulars were ordered to any point where the Collectors needed assistance "in carrying the embargo laws into effect."[69] When small numbers of troops did not answer the purpose, larger numbers were sent. One New York resident noted in early October that there was a detachment of thirty regulars in his village, but that smuggling had continued to increase.[70] To answer that problem, the army sent more men—150 to that location and "two to three hundred" to the immediate vicinity. This, the local gentleman reported, had restricted the smuggling "in a much more contained channel."[71]

By late 1808, the regular army—the once odious "standing army"—was employed throughout the Northeast in the enforcement of the Embargo. Jefferson, from the summer of 1808 until he left office in March 1809, stationed elements of the army through much of New England.

When the administration, in late 1808, asked for the enlistment of 50,000 volunteers and for the authority to order them to active duty upon the call of the President, Federalists bridled. Barent Gardenier of New York chastised the Republicans and called upon them to review the events of 1798. They had then called a proposed army of 12,000 "dangerous . . . to the rights of the people." There had been, in 1798, he said,

men zealous and eager . . . who had seen horrors in this small army, which they could scarcely find words to depict. Where were these men . . . now that an army of more than four times the number was raised . . . ? Are we more safe now . . . with an army of fifty thousand under our present commanders, then we were with twelve thousand men under Washington and Hamilton?[72]

John Eppes, the President's son-in-law who had once been among the more vociferous against the army, spoke in favor of the resolution. He refused, however, to be drawn into a debate involving the events of 1798—what would clearly be an embarrassing exchange.

Federalist Benjamin Tallmadge complained that the administration, "has laid before us a plan to raise fifty thousand volunteers, but nothing appears in it to justify [such a request]." The committee which had jurisdiction, he charged, had never seen the bill until it had been printed and presented. The force, he said, "must be directed against an enemy, or it must be pointed against ourselves . . . I can see no use for which these troops can be wanted, but to enforce obedience to our laws."[73] Circumstances allowed no adequate reply. Ten years had seemingly witnessed a dramatic reversal of roles.

The expansion Congress authorized in 1808 allowed the administration to make wholesale appointments of the faithful at every level from ensign to brigadier general. The outcome was indeed a Republican army—one sufficiently attached to the administration that Jefferson could undertake a politically unpopular program like the Embargo, and enforce it. The army, whose Federalist sympathies just a few years earlier might have imperiled such an operation, had truly undergone a "chaste reformation." Most of those who, in 1798 and 1799, had uttered republican exhortations of opposition to Hamilton's establishment, now discovered that they had little to fear in Mr. Jefferson's army.

Conclusion

The army that Jefferson inherited in 1801 had a Federalist character that was largely a product of the critical and intensely partisan years of 1798 to 1800. This army seemed threatening because its loyalty to the Republican regime was problematic. It had been composed almost totally of men with Federalist sympathies, many of whom had openly expressed contempt for the political philosophy of the new administration. Jefferson, almost immediately upon assuming office, undertook a carefully considered program of political and social reform that had included patronage, incentives, coercion, and removals.

By 1809, Jefferson and Henry Dearborn, his Secretary of War, had reshaped the army in almost every sense. It had become a respectable force—a Republican force—that was steadily building toward a full strength of about 9,000 men. Far from an institution left to languish and decline, it was beginning to modernize as well as to grow: Dearborn had experimented with light artillery, proving its utility and mobility even in the interior; the nation had added modern light infantry; and the administration had encouraged and even subsidized efforts in doctrinal reform. Moreover, the new military academy was now producing trained officers for all branches of the service.

The old force—aristocratic and Federalist, if not monarchical—had been reformed. The expansion Congress authorized in 1808 made the whole even more Republican. The army whose Federalist sympathies once made it a threat, had been undergone a *chaste reformation*. Jefferson and Dearborn had molded an Army which would threaten neither the republic, nor the Republican regime. As Jefferson's second term came to an end, the success of his efforts was apparent—the army had even taken on a more Republican look.

What once seemed paradoxical—that Jefferson, long viewed as antithetical to a standing army, would create a military school or dramatically enlarge the regular establishment—is explained by a new paradigm drawn around these Republican reforms. In fact, one element of that paradox, the military academy at West Point, was a pivotal element of that crusade. There, loyal Republican sons—who otherwise might not be prepared for officership—were trained for commissioned service in Mr. Jefferson's army. With the expansion of the army in 1808, the number of cadets authorized was increased from forty-four to two hundred.[1] Still, the primary function of the school continued as it had been—a source of the rudimentary instruction for Republican youth, circumventing the Federalist monopoly of education and overcoming their monopoly of office.[2]

Mr. Jefferson's army was no longer the object of suspicion and fear that the Federalist force had been only a decade earlier. For most Republicans, fears that a standing army would subvert civil liberties dissipated as reforms took effect and as the army became more Republican. As Jefferson counseled William Duane, "raising standing armies" need not necessarily be an object of concern. "While our functionaries are wise, and honest, and vigilant," he wrote, "we have nothing to fear."[3]

Even the oft suspect leadership of the army had proven loyal to the Republican regime. James Wilkinson had originally been retained as commanding general largely because the alternatives were even less to the liking of the new administration. But he had demonstrated his loyalty in the Burr affair, and when he came under attack for measures taken then, Jefferson showed that that loyalty flowed both ways. Those who "accept great charges" may be required "to risk themselves on great occasions, when the safety of the nation . . . [is] at stake," Jefferson wrote. The good officer does what he must in defense of the nation, he continued, but acts "at his own peril." That officer can then only "throw himself on the justice of his country and the rectitude of his motives."[4]

As president, Jefferson had come to terms with his army. He and Dearborn had created a force that no Republican would have countenanced in 1798, or even 1801—yet it was a nascent establishment still dependent on the interest and energy of the executive.

As the sequel would prove, the next administration was both indifferent and inadequate to its maintenance. Neither James Madison nor his first Secretary of War, William Eustis, evidenced the inclination that had characterized their predecessors. Said General Wilkinson, "the old administration raised troops, [and] the new one will make a mark of disbanding them."[5] Though it is a separate story, it needs to be said here that in the years leading up to the War of 1812, Eustis— with the apparent support of Madison—undid much of what Jefferson and Dearborn had created. Eustis stopped the army's recruiting effort, and appointed only a handful of cadets to the academy. The numbers and morale in both institutions declined immediately.[6] When the new Secretary of War was presented with "a very copious memoir on the subject of military instruction" it was, characteristically, "read, applauded, and forgotten."[7]

When Eustis ordered Captain George Peter's artillery horses sold in New Orleans, a confederate wrote the officer: "Thus end the hopes of Light Artillery in the Service of [the] U.S. at a moment too when circumstances appear to call for their use more loudly if possible than ever."[8] He could have spoken as well for the whole establishment, and events in the upcoming conflict would have witnessed the truth of it.

Still, the political and social reformation survived. Never again would such reform be necessary in the American army. Jefferson created a Republican officer corps, and at the same time created as an axiom a middle-class officer corps drawn broadly from across the social and geographic strata of the nation. That middle-class nature was institutionalized in the military academy Jefferson created, and perpetuated by it. That middle-class nature gave the American army remarkable political stability.

The Republican faction had broader appeal than the Federalists. The officers Jefferson commissioned were drawn from a much wider segment of American society than their predecessors. Their loyalties lay with the people from which they had come—and that in effect was the enfranchised American society at large, not a small military or political or even social caste. Madison's argument in *The Federalist, No. 10,* that the republic would draw strength—and security—from the diversity of its members, also proved true for the officer corps. "Extend the sphere," he wrote,

and you take in a greater variety of parties and interests; you make it less probable that a majority of the whole will have a common motive to invade the rights of other citizens; or if such a common motive exists, it will be more difficult for all who feel it to discover their own strength, and to act in unison with each other.[9]

Under Jefferson the army—and its officer corps—passed irrevocably into the hands of the people. His was truly a Republican solution—an army with its leadership drawn from every segment of the citizenry and every corner of the nation. Jefferson, who had long prized a citizen army, ultimately created one out of the regular establishment.

ℕ𝑜𝑡𝑒𝑠

In the notes and bibliography, the following abbreviations have been used:
LC Library of Congress, Washington, D.C.
NA National Archives, Washington, D.C.

Introduction

1. Henry F. May, *The Enlightenment in America* (New York: Oxford University Press, 1976), p. 287.

2. This school of analysis includes Dumas Malone, *Jefferson and His Time*, 6 vols. (Boston: Little, Brown, 1948–81), 5:507–23; James Ripley Jacobs, *The Beginning of the U. S. Army, 1783–1812* (Princeton: Princeton University Press, 1947), pp. 244–343; Walter Millis, *Arms and Men, A Study of American Military History* (New York: New American Library, 1956), pp. 53–57; Russell F. Weigley, *History of the United States Army* (New York: Macmillan, 1967), pp. 103–11; and Leonard D. White, *The Jeffersonians: A Study in Administrative History, 1801–1829* (New York: Macmillan, 1951), pp. 211–64, particularly pp. 212–13. White, for example, devotes four chapters to the Republican administration of the military but never gets beyond this simplistic analysis of Jefferson's relationship with the army.

3. Thomas Jefferson to Elbridge Gerry, January 26, 1799, *The Writings of Thomas Jefferson*, Albert Ellery Bergh, ed., 20 vols. (Washington, D.C.: The Thomas Jefferson Memorial Association, 1907), 10:74. (Hereinafter cited as Bergh.) This same general sentiment is found in his inaugural address and his first message to Congress.

4. Russell F. Weigley, *Towards an American Army: Military Thought from Washington to Marshall* (New York: Columbia University Press, 1962), p. 28; White, *Jeffersonians*, p. 252; Malone, *Jefferson*, 5:510. Richard H. Kohn, however, found this anamalous situation troubling. "The new President's motives [in founding the military academy] have never been convincingly explained," he wrote. "Jefferson," he reasoned, "must surely have understood after a decade of debate the larger meaning of a military academy. . . ." (Richard H. Kohn, *Eagle and Sword, the Federalists and the Creation of the Military Establishment in America, 1783–1802* [New York: Free Press, 1975], p. 303.)

5. Henry Adams, *History of the United States During the Second Administration of Thomas Jefferson*, 2 vols. (New York: Charles Scribner's Sons, 1890), 2:218.

6. Mary P. Adams, "Jefferson's Military Policy with Special Reference to the Frontier, 1805–1809" (PhD dissertation, University of Virginia, 1958). Marshall Smelser, *The Democratic Republic, 1801–1815* (New York: Harper Torchbooks, 1968) p. 161n.

7. J.C.A. Stagg, *Mr. Madison's War, Politics, Diplomacy, and Warfare in the Early American Republic, 1783–1830* (Princeton: Princeton University Press, 1983), pp. 129–30.

8. Richard Ellis found the same pattern in his study of the courts. (Richard E. Ellis, *The Jeffersonian Crisis: Courts and Politics in the Young Republic* [New York: W. W. Norton, 1974; Oxford University Press, 1971].

9. See particularly: John E. Ferling, *A Wilderness of Miseries, War and Warriors in Early America* (Westport, Conn.: Greenwood Press, 1980); Fred W. Anderson, *A People's Army, Massachusetts Soldiers and Society in the Seven Year's War* (Chapel Hill: University of North Carolina Press, 1984); and James Kirby Martin and Mark Edward Lender, *A Respectable Army: The Military Origins of the Republic, 1763–1789* (Arlington Heights, Ill.: Harlan Davison, 1982).

10. Ferling, *A Wilderness of Miseries*, p. 170.

11. Lawrence Delbert Cress, *Citizens in Arms, The Army and the Militia in American Society to the War of 1812* (Chapel Hill: University of North Carolina Press, 1982), p. xii. Richard E. Ellis, in his study of courts and politics in the Jeffersonian era, found a similar pattern, "The moderate Republicans had never been opposed to a strong national government *per se*, but only to the misuse of power to which such a government could be subject." (Ellis, *Jeffersonian Crisis*, pp. 21–22.)

12. On key issues, such as defense, the rules specified that nine states must approve. Usually, no more than eleven—and often only nine—states were present. With many of these represented by two-man delegations, one man who split his delegation might stop progress and three such could almost always derail action.

13. In May and June 1784, when the issue was joined in earnest, proponents of a regular force mustered majorities—in terms of both raw votes (which did not count) and state delegations (which did)—on each of the four occasions it came to a vote. Still, they never came close to obtaining the support of the required nine delegations. On June 2, the day the army was disbanded, the delegates voted 19–8 to maintain a regular force but fell short by at least three votes (one in each of three divided delegations) of achieving the required approval of nine states. (May 24, 26, and June 2, 1784, *Journals of the Continental Congress, 1774–1789*, Worthington Chauncey Ford, ed., 34 vols. [Washington: Government Printing Office, 1904–37], 27:429, 435, 517–8, 520.)

14. It has become a commonplace that Gerry's stirring speeches charging that "standing armies in time of peace are inconsistent with the principles of republican governments, dangerous to the liberties of a free people, and generally converted into destructive engines for establishing despotism," either created or represented a consensus in the Congress. (May 25, and June 2, 1784, Ford, *Journals of the Continental Congress*, 27:430–31, 517). Typical are: Cress, *Citizens in Arms*, p. 89; Warren W. Hassler, Jr., *With Shield and Sword, American Military Affairs, Colonial Times to the Present* (Ames: Iowa State University Press, 1982), p. 49. That was simply not the case.

15. Cress, *Citizens in Arms*, p. 98. Some opponents did fear that the Federal House of Representatives would be too detached from the people, would have neither their confidence nor their willing compliance, and would then have to rely on the strength of a standing army to enforce its laws. (John D. Lewis, ed., *Anti-Federalists versus Fed-*

eralists, Selected Documents [San Francisco: Chandler, 1967], p. 20.) See: Cato [George Clinton], October 25, 1787, quoted in Lewis, *Anti-Federalists versus Federalists*, p. 192.

16. "Centinel" [Samuel Bryan], October 24, 1787, quoted in Lewis, *Anti-Federalists versus Federalists*, p. 142. On this point see also: Cress, *Citizens in Arms*, p. 133.

17. Charles Royster, *A Revolutionary People at War, The Continental Army and American Character, 1775–1783* (Chapel Hill: The University of North Carolina Press, 1979), pp. 295–368. Royster's efforts to demonstrate the influence and workings of ideology at the grass roots level—to show how a set of ideas held by followers, as well as leaders, both prompted and sustained them—is an extension of the earlier work of H. Trevor Colbourn, Bernard Bailyn, and Gordon S. Wood. (H. Trevor Colbourn, *The Lamp of Experience, Whig History and the Intellectual Origins of the American Revolution* [New York: W. W. Norton, 1965]; Bailyn, *The Ideological Origins of the American Revolution;* Gordon S. Wood, *The Creation of the American Republic, 1776–1787* [Chapel Hill: University of North Carolina Press, 1969].) For another exposition of this view see: Marcus Cunliffe, *Soldiers & Civilians, The Martial Spirit in America, 1775–1865* (Boston: Little, Brown, 1968), pp. 31–40.

18. Royster, *A Revolutionary People at War*, pp. 25–53.

19. Ibid., p. 118.

20. Ibid., pp. 116, 368.

21. James Madison, *The Federalist*, "Number 10," November 24, 1787.

22. Royster, *A Revolutionary People at War*, p. 349.

23. Stephen Higginson to Samuel Adams, May 10, 1783, quoted in Don Higginbotham, *The War of American Independence, Military Attitudes, Politics, and Practice, 1763–1789* (Boston: Northeastern University Press, 1983), p. 443.

24. On the creation of this more flexible political order and its relation to the origins of the Revolution see: James Kirby Martin, *Men in Rebellion, Higher Governmental Leaders and the Coming of the American Revolution* (New York: Free Press, 1973) pp. 152–201.

25. On the erection of new boundaries in the early 1780s see: Wood, *The Creation of the American Republic*, pp. 430–518.

26. Thomas Jefferson to George Washington, April 16, 1784, *The Papers of Thomas Jefferson*, Julian P. Boyd, et al., eds., 21 vols to date (Princeton: Princeton University Press, 1950–), 7:106–7. (Hereinafter cited as Boyd).

27. Martin and Lender, *A Respectable Army*, p. 203.

28. Royster, *A Revolutionary People at War*, p. 357.

29. Ibid., p. 349.

30. Charles Nisbet to the Earl of Buchan, January 10, 1792, quoted in Kohn, *Eagle and Sword*, p. 122.

31. Malone, *Jefferson*, 1:344.

32. Thomas Jefferson to Speaker of [Virginia] House of Delegates, March 1, 1781, Boyd, 5:34.

33. Despite being in a distinct minority, Gerry was important as a prominent New England Republican. As such, his views had to be acknowledged. In January 1799 Jefferson wrote him an appeasing "profession of my political faith." "[I am] not for a standing army in time of peace, which may overawe the public sentiment," he pledged. But as events revealed, to Jefferson that meant opposition to the enlarged army then being recruited by Hamilton, not opposition to *any* regular force. (Thomas Jefferson to Elbridge Gerry, January 26, 1799, Bergh, 10:74.)

One significant difficulty with the work of some students of this period is a failure to recognize that the Republicans did not constitute a monolithic party. Cress's *Citizens in Arms* must be faulted on that count. Most unfortunately he selected, as their spokesmen, men who often better represented the small "Old Republican" faction of the party—William Duane and John Taylor of Caroline.

Reginald C. Stuart, in his *War and American Thought* (Kent, Ohio: Kent State University Press, 1982) falls into that same difficulty, but Stuart's work is even more fundamentally flawed. His concepts of "limited-war mentality" or "half-way pacifism" are stretched across so many circumstances—war, peace, defense, aggression—that they end up with little interpretative power. For example, "The limited-war mentality of the Revolutionary generation comprised a set of cultural and moral inhibitions about the resort to force." Yet, "despite their half-way pacifism, the Republicans used force as an instrument of policy." (Stuart, *War and American Thought*, pp. 105–6.)

34. Thomas Jefferson to Thomas Mann Randolph, December 11, 1791, Jefferson Papers, Aldeman Library. In reality, blame for the defeat belonged to St. Clair whose poor generalship placed the force in jeopardy even before the militia bolted.

35. Kohn, *Eagle and Sword*, p. 126. My understanding of the military establishment from 1789 to 1797 draws heavily on Kohn. See also: Paul David Nelson, *Anthony Wayne: Soldier of the Early Republic* (Bloomington: Indiana University Press, 1985).

36. Rudolph M. Bell, *Party and Factions in American Politics, The House of Representatives, 1789–1801* (Westport, Conn.: Greenwood Press, 1973) pp. 68–94.

37. James Monroe to Thomas Jefferson, March 16, 1794, *The Writings of James Monroe*, Stanislas Murray, ed., 7 vols. (New York: G. P. Putnam's Sons, 1898–1903), 1:286–87. (Hereinafter cited as *Writings of James Monroe*.) See also James Madison to Jefferson, March 14, 1794, Madison Papers, LC; and Jefferson to Madison, April 3, 1794, Jefferson Papers, LC.

38. For internal matters Washington preferred militia to regulars—telling Hamilton that if regulars were used against the people they would say: "The cat is let out. We now see for what purpose an Army was raised." (George Washington to Alexander Hamilton, September 17, 1792, *The Papers of Alexander Hamilton*, Harold C. Syrett, ed., 26 vols. (New York: Columbia University Press, 1961–1975), 12:390. (Hereinafter cited as *Hamilton Papers*.)

39. Richard A. Erney, *The Public Life of Henry Dearborn* (New York: Arno Press, 1979); and Edwin G. Burrows, "Albert Gallatin and the Political Economy of Republicanism" (PhD dissertation, Columbia University, 1974).

40. Richard Hofstadter, *The Idea of a Party System, The Rise of Legitimate Opposition in the United States, 1780–1840* (Berkeley: University of California Press, 1969) p. 102–3. See also: Daniel Sisson, *The American Revolution of 1800* (New York: Alfred A. Knopf, 1974). Unlike other sources used, Sisson argues that party formation took place after 1800 not before, but that is a debate that need not detain us. What is important to this study is his understanding of the relationship between opposition forces in the later 1790s.

41. On the formation of these parties see: Bell, *Party and Faction in American Politics*; and, Richard Buel, Jr., *Securing the Revolution, Ideology in American Politics, 1789–1815* (Ithaca, N.Y.: Cornell University Press, 1972). These works take very different perspectives; Buel focuses on the ideas of the two parties, while Bell examines what their votes on legislative issues tell us about structure. Both approaches are useful in understanding the era.

42. For a discussion of the Federalist use of the Alien and Sedition Acts see: James Morton Smith, *Freedom's Fetters* (Ithaca, N.Y.: Cornell University Press, 1956).

43. Alexander Addison, [1798], quoted in Sisson, *Revolution of 1800*, p. 268.

44. Carl E. Prince, "The Passing of the Aristocracy: Jefferson's Removal of the Federalists, 1801–1805," *Journal of American History*, 57(December 1970):563–75; Ellis, *Jeffersonian Crisis*, particularly pp. 36–52.

1. Mr. Hamilton's Army, 1798–1800

1. The twelve new regiments were called the "New Army"—to distinguish it from the original four regiments of the "old" or "western" army. In addition, a 10,000-man "Provisional Army" was authorized in May, 1798. At the same time the federal government was authorized to accept into service selected volunteer corps and independent companies—the "Presidential army" or "Presidential militia," as Jefferson called it. Finally, in March 1799, an "Eventual Army" of over twenty-eight regiments was authorized. This mix of additional forces totaled about 40,000 men. Of these, only the New Army and volunteers were organized. Although some officers were appointed, neither the Provisional nor Eventual Armies ever recruited or organized. (Kohn, *Eagle and Sword*, p. 229; Thomas Jefferson to Edmund Pendleton, April 22, 1799, Washburn Papers, Massachusetts Historical Society.)

2. Thomas Jefferson to Elbridge Gerry, January 26, 1799, Bergh, 10:74.

3. *Centinel*, August 18, 1798, quoted in Manning J. Dauer, *The Adams Federalists* (Baltimore: Johns Hopkins University Press, 1953), p. 215. See also: George Nicholas, *A Letter from George Nicholas of Kentucky to his Friend, in Virginia . . .* (Lexington: John Bradford, 1798), p. 6.

4. George Washington to James McHenry, September 30, 1798, *The Writings of George Washington*, Worthington Chauncey Ford, ed., 14 vols. (New York: G. P. Putnam's Sons, 1931–1944), 14:104–5. (Hereinafter cited as *Writings of Washington*).

5. *Hamilton Papers*, 22: passim.

6. Alexander Hamilton to James McHenry, February 6, 1799, *Hamilton Papers*, 22:467. Hamilton did add, "We thought it well to relax the rule in favor of particular merit in a few instances especially in reference to the inferior grades. It does not seem advisable to exclude all hope to give the appointments too absolute a party feature." Hamilton, however, made this remark because others were striking out even the few he had allowed to pass. (McHenry to Hamilton, January 21, 1799, *Hamilton Papers*, 22:429). William J. Murphy, Jr., argues that John Adams also realized the political value of army appointments and utilized them to gain the support of moderates in Federalist (and, to a more limited extent in Republican) ranks. ("John Adams: The Politics of the Additional Army, 1798–1800," *The New England Quarterly*, 52 [June 1979]:234–49.)

7. [Reading, Pennsylvania] *Weekly Advertiser*, August 10, 1799.

8. James McHenry to William Drake, December 18, 1798, quoted in *The* [Richmond] *Virginia Argus*, May 10, 1799.

9. Harrison Gray Otis, June 19, 1798, *Annals*, 5th Cong., 2nd Sess., p. 1989.

10. Steven Thomas Mason, June 27, 1798, *Gazette of the United States* quoted in Alexander DeConde, *The Quasi-War, The Politics and Diplomacy of the Undeclared War with France, 1791–1801* (New York: Charles Scribner's Sons, 1966), p. 98.

11. Thomas Jefferson to Archibald Stuart, February 13, 1799, *The Writings of Thomas*

Jefferson, Paul Leicester Ford, ed., 10 vols. (New York: G. P. Putnam's Sons, 1892–1899), 7:350. (Hereinafter cited as Ford.) Thomas Jefferson to Edmund Pendleton, February 14, 1799, Washburn Papers, Massachusetts Historical Society.

12. Alexander Hamilton to Theodore Sedgwick, February 2, 1799, *Hamilton Papers*, 22:452–53.

13. Thomas Jefferson to Edmund Pendleton, February 14, 1799, Washburn Papers, Massachusetts Historical Society.

14. Quoted in William Hart Davis, *The Fries Rebellion, 1798–99.* (Doylestown, Pa.: Doylestown Publishing, 1899), p. 33. On these events cast in a broader political view, see DeConde, *The Quasi-War.*

15. Thomas Jefferson to Thomas Lomax, March 12, 1799, Bergh, 10:123–24.

16. James McHenry to Alexander Hamilton, March 13, 1799, *Hamilton Papers*, 22:531.

17. John Adams, "A Proclamation," March 12, 1799, in James D. Richardson, *A Compilation of the Messages and Papers of the Presidents*, 12 vols. (Washington: Bureau of National Literature, 1911), 1:276–77.

18. James McHenry to Alexander Hamilton, March 15, 1799, *Hamilton Papers*, 22:539–41.

19. Alexander Hamilton to James McHenry, March 18, 1799, *Hamilton Papers*, 22:552–53.

20. For an examination of some of these episodes from a very different perspective see: Thomas P. Slaughter, "The Tax Man Cometh: Ideological Opposition of Internal Taxes, 1760–1790," 3d series, *William and Mary Quarterly*, 41 (October 1984):566–91.

21. John Adams to James Lloyd, February 11, 1815, *The Works of John Adams*, Charles Francis Adams, ed., 10 vols. (Boston: Little, Brown, 1850–56), 10:118.

22. Except as otherwise indicated the description of events relating to the suppression of the rebellion is drawn from Davis, *Fries Rebellion*, particularly pp. 75–86, 102–14.

23. Anonymous, April 8, 1799, quoted in Davis, *Fries Rebellion*, pp. 102–3. This and other letters appeared contemporaneously in various Republican newspapers. It is possible that they were Republican fabrications, but their content closely parallels other news items carried frequently in Republican (and occasionally in Federalist) papers during this period. Authentic or not, however, they were given wide currency at the time.

24. The first letter by an unidentified officer in Millarstown, April 10, 1799, is quoted in Davis, *Fries Rebellion*, pp. 109–10. This letter was also carried in *The* [Frankfort, Kentucky] *Palladium*, May 23, 1799, but was dated April 5. The second letter, apparently from the same officer, dated April 11, 1799, appeared in *Aurora*, April 16, 1799. It was reprinted in *The* [New London, Connecticut] *Bee*, April 24, 1799, and in the [Boston] *Independent Chronical*, April 25, 1799.

25. *Readinger Adler*, April 9, May 21, 1799.

26. "A Friend of Truth," *Reading Eagle*, April 9, 1799. *The* [Cincinnati] *Western Spy* (June 18, 1799) reprinted the April 9 piece along with other stories relating to army excesses.

27. *Readinger Adler*, April 16, 1799.

28. *Readinger Adler*, April 23, 1799.

29. [Newark, New Jersey] *Centinel of Freedom*, April 30, 1799.

30. *Aurora*, April 30, 1799.

31. Georgetown [D.C.] *Centinel of Liberty*, May 3, 1799.

32. *The Virginia Argus*, May 10, 1799; *The Paladium*, June 12, 1799.

33. *Weekly Advertiser*, April 27, 1799.

34. John Adams to James McHenry, April 13, 1799, *Works of John Adams*, 8:631–32.

35. Thomas Jefferson to Edmund Pendleton, April 22, 1799, Washburn Papers, Massachusetts Historical Society.

36. *The Bee*, May 15, 1799. See also *Aurora*, May 10, 1799.

37. *Aurora*, May 16, 1799.

38. Republican papers across the country carried Duane's account of the incident; see, for example: *The Bee*, May 29, 1799; and *The Paladium*, June 13, 1799.

39. There appear to be no extant copies of this publication. It is referenced in George Gibbs' *Memoirs of the Administrations of Washington and John Adams, Edited from the Papers of Oliver Wolcott*, 2 vols. (New York: n.p., 1846), 2:166. It seems to have borrowed its name from a book of the same title which had been widely distributed in the area the year before. The work, Anthony Aufrer's *Cannibals Progress, or the Dreadful Horrors of French Invasion; as Displayed by the Republican Officers and Soldiers . . . toward . . . Germany*, was a catalog of the horrors perpetrated by the French army. It warned that there was, in America also, "a corrupt and wicked faction who were combined with the despots of France"—referring, of course, to the Republicans. The book had been widely distributed by the Federalists in 1798, even translated into German and issued free. (Jacob Hiltzheimer, *Extracts from the Diary of Jacob Hiltzheimer of Philadelphia, 1765–1798*, Jacob Cox Parsons, ed. [Philadelphia: William F. Fell, 1893], p. 257.)

40. James McHenry to Alexander Hamilton, March 22, 1799, *Hamilton Papers*, 22:577–78; *Aurora*, April 16, 1799.

41. Alexander Hamilton to James McHenry, May 25, 1799, *Hamilton Papers*, 23:148; James McHenry to Alexander Hamilton, May 28, 1799, *Hamilton Papers*, 23:158; Alexander Hamilton to James McHenry, June 6, 1799, *Hamilton Papers*, 23:171–72; and Alexander Hamilton to John Adlum, June 8, 1799, *Hamilton Papers*, 23:178–79.

42. *Aurora*, July 1 and 3, 1799. The facts of the transaction's conclusions are somewhat clouded. One report indicated that young Heister, in defending the printer, forced the officers "to decamp precipitously—though the whole three were armed." Another indicated that young Heister's intervention was met by a drawn sword, but that he took up a hoe, resumed the attack, and drove off the officers. These reports (drawn from Schnider's accounts, and appearing in the Republican press) offended the honor of the officers. It was, however, more than a simple matter of honor. In a farming community officers could not allow it to be broadcast that a man with a hoe could cow a sword wielding gentleman—much less three of them. Pike was obliged to reply. His letter appeared in Reading's Federalist paper, the *Weekly Advertiser*. In Pike's recounting of the story (which denied none of the substance dealing with the whipping) the officers drew their swords only after they were attacked. According to Pike, it was only the intervention of Heister's father, the congressman, who pulled his own son away, that saved that young man from a fate similar to that of the fellow to whom justice had just been administered. (Z[ebulon] M[ontgomery] Pike [to editor], *Weekly Advertiser*, June 29, 1799.)

43. Donald H. Stewart, *The Opposition Press of the Federalist Period* (Albany: State University of New York Press, 1969), pp. 83–94, 443–44.

44. *The Bee*, May 8, 1799. Despite the focus of formal charges, one wonders if Holt did not earn more trouble from the barb he flung at Hamilton in the same article: "Are our young officers and soldiers to learn virtue of General Hamilton? or like their general

are they to be found in the bed of adultery?" On the charges against him see: *The Bee*, April 2, 1800.

45. *Aurora*, May 11, 1799.

46. *The Bee*, July 3, 1799. See also: *Albany* [New York] *Register*, February 21, 1799.

47. *The Bee*, July 24, 1799. Brawling and assaults on women were two targets of particular attention in the press. See: *Centinel of Freedom*, February 18, 1800; and *The Bee*, April 2, 1800.

48. Thomas Jefferson to Edmund Pendleton, April 22, 1799, Washburn Papers, Massachusetts Historical Society.

49. Thomas Jefferson to James Madison, November 26, 1799, quoted in Adrienne Koch, *Jefferson and Madison, The Great Collaboration* (New York: Alfred A. Knopf, 1950; reprinted Gloucester, Mass.: Peter Smith, 1970), pp. 202–3.

50. January 1, 1800, *Annals*, 6th Cong., 1st Sess., pp. 227–28.

51. These debates were reported widely and in unusual detail. See *Aurora*, January 16 through February 17, 1800 (with breaks).

52. John Nicholas, January 7, 1800, *Annals*, 6th Cong., 1st Sess., p. 249.

53. James A. Bayard, January 8, 1800, *Annals*, 6th Cong., 1st Sess., p. 264.

54. Thomas Jefferson to Thomas Mann Randolph, January 13, 1800, Jefferson Papers, LC.

55. John Randolph, January 9, 1800, *Annals*, 6th Cong., 1st Sess., p. 298.

56. Thomas Jefferson to Thomas Mann Randolph, January 13, 1800, Jefferson Papers, LC.

57. John Randolph, January 10, 1800, *Annals*, 6th Cong., 1st Sess., p. 367.

58. *American State Papers*, Walter Lowrie, ed., 38 vols. (Washington: 1832–1861), *Miscellaneous*, 1:195–202.

59. John Randolph to John Adams, January 11, 1800, ibid., 1:195–96; Thomas Jefferson to Thomas Mann Randolph, January 13, 1800, Jefferson Papers, LC. It is possible that the officers hoped to provoke a duel. McKnight was not adverse to such an undertaking, though possibly he should have been—he was killed in such an affair two years later.

60. [New York] *Commercial Advertiser*, January 31, 1800. Adams did direct the secretaries of war and navy to look into the matter, but little was done. (James McHenry to John Randolph, January 31, 1800, McHenry Papers, Clements Library; and James McHenry to Benjamin Stoddert, February 7, 1800, McHenry Papers, Clements Library.)

61. Robert Dawidoff, *The Education of John Randolph* (New York: W. W. Norton, 1979), p. 166. This work is a fascinating and instructive window into the mind and manners of this unique man.

62. Thomas Jefferson to Thomas Mann Randolph, January 13, 1800, Jefferson Papers, LC.

63. Dauer, *The Adams Federalists*, p. 212.

64. January 23–24, 1800, *Annals*, 6th Cong., 1st Sess., pp. 389–401.

65. *Aurora*, January 23, 1800.

66. Thomas Jefferson to Edward Livingston, April 30, 1800, Bergh 10:164. Abraham Baldwin to Joel Barlow, March 26, 1800, Miscellaneous Manuscripts, Sterling Library.

67. Thomas Jefferson to [William Bache], February 12, 1800, Jefferson Papers, Aldeman Library.

68. The discussion of the conflict between Adams and Hamilton, and its impact on the military establishment, in this paragraph and the next, follows closely the interpretations of events in Kohn, *Eagle and Sword*, particularly pp. 262–73.

69. *Centinel of Liberty*, June 17, 1800; *The* [Lexington] *Kentucky Gazette*, July 10, 1800.

70. Tench Coxe, "To the Republican Citizens," *Aurora*, October 9, 1800, cited in Jacob E. Cooke, *Tench Coxe and the Early Republic* (Chapel Hill: University of North Carolina Press, 1978), pp. 377–78.

71. Erney, *The Public Life of Henry Dearborn*, p. 30–31.

72. Thomas Jefferson to Meriwether Lewis, February 23, 1801, Jefferson Papers, LC.

73. Thomas H. Cushing to James Wilkinson, February 26, 1801, Letters Sent by the Adjutant General, Microfilm Publication 565, National Archives.

74. [Pittsburgh] *Tree of Liberty*, December 13 and 27, 1800.

2. A Chaste Reformation

1. Thomas Jefferson to Robert Livingston, December 14, 1800, Ford, 7:464–65

2. In 1784 Jefferson had laid out for James Monroe a comprehensive plan for the defense of the frontier. He contemplated a line of forts from Oswego or Niagara, through Michillimacinac and the mouth of the Illinois river, to the head of the Mobile river. Such a plan would have required a more extensive force than was ever raised in the era of the Confederation. (Thomas Jefferson to James Monroe, May 21, 1784, Boyd, 7:280.)

3. Officers Roster, July 14, 1801, Items 19697-9, and 19705, Jefferson Papers, LC. This roster was annotated to show both the military qualifications and political sentiments for all officers for whom they could be ascertained. The annotations are in the hand of Captain Meriwether Lewis, then the President's private secretary. The annotations appear to reflect the judgment of Lewis—this was apparently some of the "information which it is interesting for the administration to acquire" that the president noted when he invited Lewis to join him. (Thomas Jefferson to Meriwether Lewis, February 23, 1801, Jefferson Papers, LC.) Internal evidence—notes of deaths and discharge subsequent to the roster's original preparation, for example—suggest that the annotations were added in early 1802. Two entries were usually made: first, military qualifications; then, political sentiment. Those unknown were most often very junior officers with little service. The nature of the annotations is revealing. Symbols were used to identify each of the following categories:

(1) "1st Class, so esteemed from a superiority of genius and military proficiency."
(2) "Second Class, respectable as officers, but not altogether entitled to the first grade."
(3) "Unworthy of the commissions they bear."
(4) "Republican."
(5) "Opposed to the administration, otherwise respectable officers."
(6) "Opposed to the administration more decisively."
(7) "Opposed most violently to the administration and still active in its vilification."
(8) "Professionally the soldier without any political creed."
(9) "Political apathy."
(10) "Officers whose political opinions are not positively ascertained."
(11) "Unknown to us."

Meriwether Lewis's role in the preparation of this document was first noted in a paper by the author ("Securing the Republic: Jefferson, Politics and the Army, 1801–1809") read at the Missouri Valley Historical Conference in 1977. See also: Donald Jackson, "Jefferson, Meriwether Lewis, and the Reduction of the United States Army," *Proceedings of the American Philosophical Society*, 124(April 1980):91–96.

4. Elbridge Gerry to Thomas Jefferson, May 4, 1801, Jefferson Papers, LC.

5. Thomas Jefferson to Nathaniel Macon, May 14, 1801, Bergh, 10:261. My emphasis.

6. Thomas H. Cushing to Constance Freeman, February 6, 1801, Letters Sent, Adjutant General, M565, NA.

7. Thomas H. Cushing to James Wilkinson, February 26, 1801, Letters Sent, Adjutant General, M565, NA.

8. Thomas H. Cushing to James Wilkinson, April 9, 1801, Letters Sent, Adjutant General, M565, NA.

9. Secretary of the Treasury Albert Gallatin recommended reducing the army, but Jefferson and Dearborn chose a different tack. (Albert Gallatin to Thomas Jefferson, March 14, 1801, *Writings of Gallatin*. Henry Adams, ed., 3 vols. [Philadelphia: J. B. Lippincott, 1879], 1:24–25.) As a rule Gallatin had little influence on military affairs. On occasion he did submit his ideas on military matters, but Jefferson almost inevitably sought out and accepted Dearborn's views. The rare exception was Gallatin's urging of the use of the army, late in Jefferson's second term, to force compliance with the Embargo—an area in which he had particular cognizance.

10. Henry Dearborn to George Barron [sic Baron], April 11, 1801, Miscellaneous Letters Sent, Secretary of War, M370, NA.

11. Thomas H. Cushing to [post commanders], May 26, 1801, Letters Sent, Adjutant General, M565, NA; Thomas H. Cushing to James Wilkinson, February 26, 1801, Letters Sent, Adjutant General, M565.

12. Henry Dearborn to Caleb Swan [paymaster], June 12, 1801, Samuel C. Vance Papers, Indiana Historical Society.

13. Russell Bissell to Daniel Bissell, July 9, 1801, Jacob Kingsbury Papers, LC.

14. Thomas Jefferson to Martha Jefferson Randolph, November 27, 1802, Jefferson Papers, Virginia State Library.

15. Jonathan Williams to James Wilkinson, August 8, 1803, Williams Papers, Lilly Library.

16. Thomas Jefferson, "First Annual Message", December 8, 1801, Richardson, *Messages*, 1:317.

17. "Estimates of posts and stations where garrisons will be expedient." December 23, 1801, Original Reports, War Department, 6th Cong. to 9th Cong., 1st Sess., Record Group 233, NA.

18. January 11, 1802, *Annals*, 7th Cong., 1st Sess., p. 417. On the administration's origination of legislation see: Noble E. Cunningham, *The Process of Government under Jefferson* (Princeton: Princeton University Press, 1978), particularly pp. 188–213.

19. January 18, 1802, *Annals*, 7th Cong., 1st Sess., pp. 427–29. Despite the lack of committee reports or detailed newspaper coverage of progress on the Military Peace Establishment bill, an analysis of congressional action is possible because an annotated copy of the original bill (indicating the House mark-up) was discovered. When compared with the reports in the *Annals* and the final draft, it reveals an outline of action on the bill. ("A Bill Fixing the Military Peace Establishment of the United States," January 11, 1802, John Cropper Papers, Virginia Historical Society.) Newspaper cov-

erage of those debates, in the Senate and the House, was virtually obliterated by reports on judicial reform. The same was true in personal correspondence. From January through March 1802, the mention of legislative activity was almost certain to center around the judicial issue, to the exclusion of all other topics.

20. January 21, 1802, *Annals*, 7th Cong., 1st Sess., pp. 430–1. [Reading, Pennsylvania] *Weekly Advertiser*, January 30, 1802. (The writer was mistaken about Randolph, who opposed the Republicans on this bill.)

21. W[illiam] North to [John Francis] Hamtramck, February 23, 1801, Hamtramck Papers, Perkins Library.

22. Linda Grant De Pauw in an article on "Women in Combat, The Revolutionary War Experience," (*Armed Forces and Society* 7 [Winter 1981]:209–25) argues, among other things, that this act was the first to place a quota on women in army units, and that these women "did not do chores [washing] for enlisted men" (pp. 212–13). She is wrong on both of these counts. It was so commonly understood that these women were to wash for the men that it was generally thought unnecessary to be explicit. William Duane made light of this imprecision. "It appears," he wrote, "that there are on the American military establishment 500 *women*. We are left in the dark as to the species of duty they are to be employed upon, whether as Amazonian cavalry or light infantry." (*Aurora*, January 8, 1800.) By chance, however, the role of these wash-women had been defined in the regulations governing the issue of straw and firewood in 1797. The same regulation established their number as a ratio of one for each seventeen enlisted men, or roughly four per company—the number authorized in 1802. ("Regulations for Straw and Firewood," December 6, 1797, John O'Hara Papers, Western Pennsylvania Historical Society.) In all likelihood this provision was in effect long before. The habit was simply to copy and continue such regulations. See, for example: "Regulations for Barracks, Fuel and Straw," April 28, 1801 (Letters Sent, Secretary of War, M6, NA) which simply repeated the provisions of the 1797 version.

23. *Annals*, 7th Cong., 1st Sess., pp. 192–98, 989–90.

24. *Annals*, 7th Cong., 1st Sess., p. 994. Jonathan Williams to James Wilkinson, August 8, 1803, Wilkinson Papers, Lilly Library.

25. John Clopton to [Virginia constituents], April 3, 1802, in Noble E. Cunningham, ed., *Circular Letters of Congressmen to their Constituents 1789–1829*, 3 vols. (Chapel Hill: University of North Carolina Press, 1978), 1:276. Similarly, Thomas Sumter of South Carolina put the savings at $450,000 (1:305).

26. John Stanley of North Carolina came closer than most in his calculations, but still overestimated the size of the reduction by a factor of three when he claimed that 880 men would be eliminated. (Cunningham, *Circular Letters*, 1:300.)

27. To get to the larger figure, the administration calculated the savings that would have accrued *if* the force had been at its authorized strength when cuts began. It was, of course, nowhere near that. (Even then the larger figure is somewhat exaggerated.) The administration did temporarily reduce expenditures by delaying work on fortifications, and did stress measures of economy in all areas. (Henry Dearborn to Louis Tousard, March 18, 1801, Letters Sent, Secretary of War, M6, NA.)

28. [Alexander Hamilton], "The Examination" (No. 28), *New York Evening Post*, April 8, 1802, in *Hamilton Papers*, 25:590.

29. Annotated officer roster. See: note 3 above.

30. Annotated officer roster. Buell, though a Republican, was considered unworthy of his commission and was dismissed in 1802. See: note 3 above.

31. Thomas Jefferson to William Duane, July 24, 1803, Ford, 8:258.

32. In this respect the repeal of the Judiciary Act of 1801 and the new Military Peace Establishment Act (which had proceeded through Congress together) served a similar purpose. Both effected the dismissal of Federalist office holders. The two bills were important elements of the administration program to place the government on a more Republican tack. For a discussion of the repeal of the Judiciary Act see: Ellis, *Jeffersonian Crisis.*

33. The new artillery companies contained sixty-four privates and artificers (semi-skilled carpenters who built and maintained the gun platforms and mounts) instead of the smaller number usually assigned (fifty-two prior to 1799 and fifty-six from that date). To create a fully manned force of similar total size within the old structure would have necessitated twenty-four companies in two regiments, in other words four additional companies and an added headquarters. The organization proposed by the administration allowed the dismissal of four instead of two senior artillerists, and thirty-six instead of twenty-four company grade officers.

34. Annotated officer roster. See: note 3 above. Noble E. Cunningham first called this annotated list to attention (*The Jeffersonian Republicans in Power: Party Operations, 1801–1809* [Chapel Hill: University of North Carolina Press, 1963], pp. 66–69), but dismissed the notion of any serious political motive in the reductions. Cunningham's failure to crosstabulate politics and military merit led him to underestimate the importance of politics as a factor in dismissal decisions.

35. Henry Dearborn to James Wilkinson, February 22, 1802, Letters Sent, Secretary of War, Indian Affairs, M15, NA. The process had obviously begun even before congressional consideration was complete and well before the act was signed into law on March 16, 1802.

36. Erney, *The Public Life of Henry Dearborn,* p. 67.

37. "A Washington Federalist," *The Philadelphia Gazette,* April 5, 1802.

38. On Jefferson's actions relating to the civil service, see: Carl E. Prince, "The Passing of the Aristocracy: Jefferson's Removal of the Federalists, 1801–1805," *Journal of American History,* 57 (December 1970): 563–75. On Jefferson's efforts at similar reforms in the judiciary, see: Ellis, *Jeffersonian Crisis.*

39. Captain Campbell Smith—the same officer who had come to John Randolph's assistance at the theater earlier in our story—was the only highly regarded Republican to be discharged. He had served as Judge Advocate since 1797 but had long been in ill health. (Alexander Hamilton to James McHenry, October 15, 1799, *Hamilton Papers,* 23:558.) When the opportunity came to be discharged with even a small bonus, he asked to be dismissed. His name was added to the list that had already been sent to the President. (Henry Dearborn to Thomas H. Cushing, April 6, 1802, Letters Sent, Secretary of War, M6, NA.) Smith retired to Maryland and died the next year. (J. B. Walbach Deposition, September 5, 1807, in James Wilkinson, *Memoirs of My Own Times,* 3 vols. [Philadelphia: Abraham Small, 1816], 2:appendix 65.)

40. Foreign-born officers were also discharged at a significantly higher rate than most officers. (See: Arthur P. Wade, "Artillerists and Engineers, The Beginnings of Seacoast Fortifications, 1794–1815" [PhD dissertation, Kansas State University, 1977], particularly pp. 113ff.) Many of these dismissals can be attributed directly to merit, but some may reflect concern that their aristocratic tendencies were improper in the new republican army. (Fifty-five percent of this group were dismissed.) New applications from

abroad were politely, but firmly rejected. See: Thomas Jefferson to Tadeusz Kosciuszko, April 2, 1802, Bergh, 10:309.

41. Joseph Gardner Swift, *The Memoirs of General Joseph Gardner Swift* (Privately published, 1890), p. 24. The exchange occurred at a small dinner party at the President's house in 1806.

42. The act of 1802 granted the new colonels the same pay and allowances that they had previously received as lieutenant colonels, but created a new pay level to accommodate the new lieutenant colonels. All gained a promotion, while the latter also enjoyed a pay raise.

43. The single exception was General Wilkinson who also received a significant pay raise, though it is doubtful that he benefited from it. Wilkinson now got a lump sum that included compensation for rations, forage, and travel. He gained little, if anything, in this bargain. This situation forced the general to often seek and rely on the beneficence of the Secretary of War, a situation that could only work to the administration's advantage.

3. The Founding of West Point

1. Henry Dearborn to Commanding Officer of West Point, April 15, 1801, Letters Sent, Secretary of War, M6, NA.

2. [Statement of Fortifications, Public Buildings, Quartermaster Department, Manufacture of Cannon, Indian Affairs, State of the Army, and Military Bounty Lands], May 12, 1801, Jefferson Papers, LC; Henry Dearborn to James Wilkinson, May 12, 1801, Letters Sent, Secretary of War, M6, NA; Henry Dearborn to Captain George Fleming, May 12, 1801, Letters Sent, Secretary of War, M6, NA; Henry Dearborn to Captain George Fleming, May 26, 1801, Letters Sent, Secretary of War, M6, NA.

3. Alexander Hamilton to Oliver Wolcott, June 5, 1798, *Hamilton Papers*, 21:486.

4. Louis Le Begue Du Portail to Alexander Hamilton, December 9, 1798, *Hamilton Papers*, 22:339.

5. John Adams to James McHenry, June 24, 1799, *Works of John Adams*, 8:660. McHenry had proposed the American-born Tory, Benjamin Thompson (Court Rumford), to superintend the new school. Adams gave guarded approval, but nothing came of the matter. James McHenry to Alexander Hamilton, July 8, 1799, *Hamilton Papers*, 23:247.

6. Alexander Hamilton to James Wilkinson, October 31, 1799, *Hamilton Papers*, 23:596. See also: Alexander Hamilton to Jonathan Dayton, [October or November] 1799, *Hamilton Papers*, 23:600–601.

7. Alexander Hamilton to James McHenry, November 23, 1799, *Hamilton Papers*, 23:69–75. "Military Academy, and Reorganization of the Army," January 14, 1800, *American State Papers: Military Affairs*, 1:133–35.

8. James McHenry to Harrison Gray Otis, February 11, 1800, McHenry Papers, Clements Library, University of Michigan.

9. Manning J. Dauer in *The Adams Federalists* (pp. 212–24) argues that the increased army and Hamilton's scheming to gain its command were among the most important things that divided Adams and Hamilton. Samuel Eliot Morison, *Harrison Gray Otis, 1765–1848, The Urbane Federalist* (Boston: Houghton Mifflin, 1969), p. 145. Morison

records that Otis departed for Boston in mid-March, but roll calls indicate his presence at Philadelphia until at least the 28th.

10. April 28, 1800, *Annals*, 6th Cong., 1st Sess., pp. 690–91.

11. Alexander Hamilton to Samuel Dexter, July 9, 1800, *Hamilton Papers*, 25:18.

12. "An Act to Augment the Army of the United States, and for Other Purposes," July 16, 1798. Wilkinson demonstrated the common understanding of the law when he asked Hamilton to send instructors and instruments to the field to train his officers. Hamilton responded that he believed a formal military academy a better solution. (James Wilkinson to Alexander Hamilton, September 6, 1799, *Hamilton Papers*, 23:391; Alexander Hamilton to James Wilkinson, October 31, 1799, *Hamilton Papers*, 23:596.)

13. John Adams to Samuel Dexter, July 25, 1800, *Works of John Adams*, 9:65–66. Dexter's letter to Adams, dated July 16, 1800, is referenced in the Adams letter (July 25), but was not located. Alexander Hamilton to Samuel Dexter, July 9, 1800, *Hamilton Papers*, 25:18. Adams's sponsorship of Barron may have stemmed from a personal acquaintance. Barron had been a Harvard classmate of John Quincy Adams. (Swift, *Memoirs*, p. 32.)

14. Wade, "Artillerists and Engineers," p. 118.

15. John Adams to Samuel Dexter, August 13, 1800, *Works of John Adams*, 9:79. Dexter's letter to Adams, dated August 4, is referenced in Adam's letter, but was not located.

16. James Wilkinson to Jonathan Williams, 28 August, 1800, Graff Collection, Newberry Library; Jonathan Williams to Henry Knox, September 5, 1800, Henry Knox Papers, Massachusetts Historical Society; Jonathan Williams to Henry Knox, September 8, 1800, Williams Papers, Lilly Library. See Samuel Dexter to Jonathan Williams, January 12, 1801, Miscellaneous Letters Sent, Secretary of War, M370, NA. According to Williams the first 500 copies of the *Elements of Fortification* were burned in the War Department fire, November 8, 1800. Another 500 copies were supposedly printed. (Jonathan Williams to Henry Dearborn, February 6, 1802, Williams Papers, Lilly Library.)

17. Samuel Dexter to Captain Ja[me]s Taylor, November 19, 1800, Letters Sent, Secretary of War, M6, NA.

18. Jonathan Williams to Samuel Dexter, February 24, 1801, Williams Papers, Lilly Library.

19. Adams is more famous, in this regard, for his last minute appointment of federal judges—the "midnight judges." But, he also filled many appointive vacancies, including all the ranks of the officer corps.

20. Bergh, 1:409.

21. On Williams' selection see: Jonathan Williams to W. W. Barrows, July 17, 1803, Williams Papers, Lilly Library. On Barons' appointment see: Henry Dearborn to George Barron [sic Baron], April 11, 1801, Miscellaneous Letters Sent, Secretary of War, M370, NA. The letter to Baron was sent to Edward Livingston who was asked to forward it. In a note to Livingston, Dearborn indicated having discussed Baron with him. This indicates that consideration of an academy must have occurred in the first days of the administration or even earlier. (Henry Dearborn to Edward Livingston, April 11, 1801, Miscellaneous Letters Sent, Secretary of War, M37, NA.) Baron's appointment has usually been attributed to John Adams. Edward C. Boynton in his *History of West Point* [(New York: D. Van Nostrand, 1864), p. 206] stated that Baron was appointed on January 6, 1801. Other writers have followed his lead. Boynton, however, did not cite

evidence to support that assertion, and none has since come to light. There is no record or indication of any correspondence between Baron and the Adams administration. Baron at first rejected Dearborn's offer, but later accepted it when the Secretary agreed to ask Congress to increase the pay. (George Baron to Henry Dearborn, May 19 and June 1, 1801, Register of Letters Received, Secretary of War, M22, NA.) Baron reported to West Point in July 1801.

22. Henry Dearborn to Commanding Officer of West Point, April 15, 1801, Letters Sent, Secretary of War, M6, NA.

23. Henry Dearborn to George Fleming, May 12, 1801, Letters Sent, Secretary of War, M6, NA; Louis Tousard to Henry Dearborn, May 18, 1801, cited in Norman B. Wilkinson, "The Forgotten 'Founder' of West Point," *Military Affairs*, 24 (Winter 1960–61): 185.

24. Henry Dearborn to George Fleming, May 26, 1801, Letters Sent, Secretary of War, M6, NA.

25. Edward Lillie Pierce, *[The Life of] Major John Lillie, 1755–1801 [and] The Lillie Family of Boston, 1663–1896* (Cambridge, Mass.: John Wilson and Son, University Press, 1896, p. 31.

26. Henry Dearborn to Thomas H. Cushing, July 2, 1801, Letters Sent, Secretary of War, M6, NA.

27. On the debates of the years before see Kohn, *Eagle and Sword*.

28. Stephen E. Ambrose, *Duty, Honor, Country, A History of West Point* (Baltimore: Johns Hopkins University Press, 1966), p. 18. Why Jefferson should think a military academy had a better chance of success, among Republicans who had always opposed it, than a civil school Ambrose does not explain. See also: Adams, *History of the United States*, 1:302; Thomas J. Fleming, *West Point, the Men and Times of the United States Military Academy* (New York: William Morrow, 1969), p. 16; and Dorothy J. S. Zuersher, "Benjamin Franklin, Jonathan Williams and the United States Military Academy" (PhD dissertation, University of North Carolina at Greensboro, 1974), pp. 90–91.

29. Malone, *Jefferson*, 5:510.

30. See Jacobs, *The Beginning of the U. S. Army*, p. 297; and Wade, "Artillerists and Engineers," p. 138. Sidney Forman ("Why the United States Military Academy was Established in 1802," *Military Affairs* 29 [Spring 1965]:16–28) suggests only that it was needed to provide the practical training not available at other schools.

31. In addition to Ambrose and Malone noted above, see: Weigley, *Towards an American Army*, p. 27; and Forest Garrett Hill, *Roads, Rails and Waterways, the Army Engineers and Early Transportation* (Norman, Okla.: University of Oklahoma Press, 1957), pp. 12–13.

32. Henry Dearborn to Jonathan Williams, March 24, 1806, Letters Sent, Secretary of War, M6, NA.

33. On these developments see: George H. Daniels, *American Science in the Age of Jackson* (New York: Columbia University Press, 1968). The United States Military Philosophical Society founded by the early faculty—once called "the first national scientific society" (Goode, "The Origin of the National Scientific and Educational Institutions", p. 68)—should be viewed more as a remnant of Enlightenment science than as a precursor of the kind of professional scientific societies that came a few decades later. Despite his formal patronage, the society received only token support from Jefferson.

34. James William Kershner, "Sylvanus Thayer: A Biography," (PhD dissertation, West Virginia University, 1976), p. 10–14. Jonathan Williams ["A report on the pro-

gress and present state of the Military Academy"], March 14, 1808 in "Military Academy," *American State Papers, Military Affairs*, 1:229–230. (Hereafter cited as "Military Academy, 1808.") See also "Statement of the examination of Cadets . . . ," 1806, Jonathan Williams Papers, United States Military Academy Library.

35. Kershner, "Sylvanus Thayer," p. 47; Williams, "Military Academy, 1808," p. 229.

36. Williams, "Military Academy, 1808," p. 229.

37. Jefferson to [Marc August] Pictet, February 5, 1803, Bergh, 10:74. On Jefferson's proposals in 1806, see: G. Brown Goode, "The Origin of the National Scientific Educational Institutions of the United States," *Annual Report of the American Historical Association for the Year 1889* (Washington: Government Printing House, 1890), pp. 74–75, 92–93. Joel Barlow had proposed in 1806 that the military academy should be attached to a central university in Washington and placed under the direction of a national scientific institution. (Goode, "The Origin of the National Scientific and Educational Institutions", p. 143.) Jefferson, who better than anyone, knew the purpose of the academy, paid the idea no heed.

38. From an 1819 report by Colonel William McRee (USMA, 1806) and Brigadier General Simon Bernard, quoted in "Military Academy at West Point," *American Quarterly Review*, 22 (September 1837):91–92. The increased emphasis on civil engineering coincides both with the arrival of Thayer (1817) and the new national interest in internal improvements; it is not certain which had the greater influence. Rufus King, an early member of the board of visitors at West Point, recommended in 1821 that the academy begin to teach civil engineering, thereby providing talents the nation then needed. The subject was introduced shortly thereafter. (Rufus King to Christopher Gore, June 22, 1821, in Charles R. King, ed., *The Life and Correspondence of Rufus King*, 6 vols. [New York: G. P. Putnam's Sons, 1900], 6:393–94.

39. Henry Dearborn to Captain George Fleming, May 12, 1801, Letters Sent, Secretary of War, M6, NA.

40. "Military Academy, 1808," pp. 229–30.

41. Thomas Jefferson to John Adams, September 12, 1821, in *The Adams-Jefferson Letters*, Lester J. Cappon, ed., 2 vols. (Chapel Hill: University of North Carolina Press, 1959), 2:575.

42. War Department, "Statement of Fortifications, Public Buildings, Military Stores, Quartermaster's Department, Manufacture of Cannon, Indian Affairs, State of the Army, and Military Bounty Lands," May 12, 1801, Jefferson Papers, LC; Thomas Jefferson to Nathaniel Macon, May 14, 1801, Bergh, 10:261.

43. Joseph Gardner Swift, memoirs manuscript, Joseph Gardner Swift Papers, United States Military Academy Library, p. 34. (This line was deleted from the published version of these memoirs often cited herein.)

44. Tradition has it that the use of blackboards in American schools began at West Point; whatever the case, they have been used for recitations from the first days of the school in 1801 to today. See also: Pierce, *Life of John Lillie*, p. 31.

45. William A. Barron to Jonathan Williams, May 7, 1806, Williams Papers, Lilly Library.

46. Swift, *Memoirs*, p. 27.

47. Ibid., pp. 27–28.

48. Academy Orders, January 18, 1802, Williams Papers, Lilly Library.

49. Jonathan Williams to William Amhurst Barron, June 9, 1802, Williams Papers, Lilly Library.

50. "An Act Fixing the Military Peace Establishment of the United States," March 16, 1802. Some misunderstanding about the role of the military academy has stemmed from a more modern meaning to the word "constitute" than contemporaries intended. Noah Webster, in his 1806 work, *A Compendious Dictionary of the English Language*, defined the word to mean "to make" or "to set up."

51. "An Act Fixing the Military Peace Establishment of the United States," March 16, 1802.

52. Henry Dearborn to Edward Livingston, April 11, 1801, Miscellaneous Letters Sent, Secretary of War, M370, NA. Joseph Gardner Swift claimed that Baron mingled "his Mathematical Instruction with notions of Politics [and the thoughts of Thomas Paine]." Swift, it should be recalled, however, is not an altogether unbiased observer where Baron is concerned. Jonathan Williams, Swift noted, substituted "moral lectures," sermons, and "conversation at his own table" for Baron's politics and Paine. (Swift, "[manuscript notes on] Jonathan Williams," [p. 3 (unnumbered)], Swift Papers, United States Military Academy Library.)

53. Louis Tousard has sometimes been credited with an important role in the founding of the military academy. (Wilkinson, "The Forgotten 'Founder' of West Point." See also: Ambrose, *Duty, Honor, Country*, p. 34; and Wade, "Artillerists and Engineers," p. 110.) Dearborn did post him to West Point as Inspector of Artillery, but his note that Tousard should instruct the artillery officers there if time allowed appears to have been merely an afterthought. There is nothing to indicate that he taught so much as a single class. Moreover, Dearborn had already begun to sketch out the future shape of the army and knew there was little place for men whose Federalist views were as strongly held as were Tousard's. Tousard had not been at West Point six months when Dearborn wrote in confidence to Williams that that artillerist was soon to be eliminated from the service. (Henry Dearborn to Jonathan Williams, February 17, 1802, Williams Papers, Lilly Library.)

54. Jonathan Williams to Thomas Jefferson, March 7, 1801, Jefferson Papers, LC; Jonathan Williams to Samuel Dexter, February 24, 1801, Williams Papers, Lilly Library: Jonathan Williams to W. W. Burrows, July 17, 1803, Williams Papers, United States Military Academy Library. Williams's political views were unknown to Meriwether Lewis who annotated Jefferson's roster of officers (see previous chapter)—an indication that he was not vocal in his attachment to Federalism.

55. Charlotte W. Dudley, "Jared Mansfield: United States Surveyor General," *Ohio History*, 85 (Summer 1976): 231–46. On Mansfield, politics, and the President, see Jared Mansfield to Thomas Jefferson, October 31, 1806 and May 9, 1807, Jefferson Papers, LC.

56. Abraham Baldwin to Thomas Jefferson, March 29, 1802, quoted in E. Millicent Sowerby, ed., *Catalogue of the Library of Thomas Jefferson*, 5 vols. (Washington: Library of Congress, 1952–59), 4:33.

57. Abraham Baldwin to Jared Mansfield, April 4, 1802, Mansfield Papers, United States Military Academy Library; Henry Dearborn to Jared Mansfield, May 4, 1802, Mansfield Papers, United States Military Academy Library.

58. Jonathan Williams to Henry Dearborn, January 19, 1802, Williams Papers, Lilly Library.

59. S. E. Tillman, "Academic History of the Military Academy," in *The Centennial of the United States Military Academy at West Point, New York,* 2 vols. (Washington: Government Printing Office, 1904; reprinted Westport, Conn.: Greenwood Press, 1969), 1:242.

60. Swift, *Memoirs,* pp. 31, 34, 42. Swift was titular superintendent of the academy from 1810 to 1815—as Chief of Engineers—but he seldom visited the school. (Ambrose, *Duty, Honor, Country,* p. 42.)

61. Jonathan Williams to Henry Dearborn, February 4, 1802, Williams Papers, Lilly Library.

62. Henry Dearborn to Jonathan Williams, May 31, 1802, Letters Sent, Secretary of War, M6, NA. See also Jonathan Williams to Henry Dearborn, February 4 & 6, 1802, Williams Papers, Lilly Library.

63. Henry Dearborn to Jonathan Williams, July 9, 1802, Letters Sent, Secretary of War, M6, NA. The list with Jefferson's note was not located. Apparently, Jefferson did not approve the purchase of Williams's text for there is no indication it was ever ordered. Williams, considering the issue closed, did not raise the question again.

64. Jonathan Williams to William A. Barron, June 9, 1802, Williams Papers, Lilly Library.

65. Jonathan Williams to Decidus Wadsworth, August 13, 1802, Williams Papers, Lilly Library; Jonathan Williams to Henry Dearborn, September 1, 1802, Williams Papers, Lilly Library.

66. William A. Barron and Jared Mansfield to Jonathan Williams, December 1, 1802, Williams Papers, Lilly Library.

67. Jonathan Williams to Henry Dearborn, September 1, 1802, Williams Papers, Lilly Library.

68. "Applicants for Military Appointments," Records Group 94, NA. This list indicates by whom applicants were recommended, and the disposition.

69. Moses Wingate to Henry Dearborn, July 18, 1806, Moses Elliott File, United States Military Academy Cadet Application Papers, 1805–66, Microfilm Publication 688, National Archives.

70. Israel Smith to Henry Dearborn, December 5, 1808, John Reed File, Cadet Application Papers, M688, NA.

71. John Willard to Henry Dearborn, January 30, 1807, Letters Received, Adjutant General, M566, NA. This letter was in reference to Huntington Minor.

72. Sylvester Roberts to Thomas Jefferson, August 5, 1807, Daniel Parker Papers, Historical Society of Pennsylvania; Sylvester Roberts to Henry Dearborn, December 8, 1807, Erastus Roberts File, Cadet Application Papers, M688, NA.

73. David W. Robson, *Educating Republicans: The College in the Era of the American Revolution, 1750–1800* (Westport, Conn.: Greenwood Press, 1985.)

74. John Adams, *A Defense of the Constitutions of Government of the United States of America,* 3d ed., 3 vols. (Philadelphia: Budd and Bartram, 1797), 1:110.

75. Sidney H. Aronson, *Status and Kinship in the Higher Civil Service* (Cambridge, Mass.: Harvard University Press, 1964), p. 9.

76. Some Republicans put considerable faith in the ability of educational institutions to reshape men. "I consider it is possible to convert men into republican machines," wrote Benjamin Rush. But Jefferson's aim for the academy was made of simpler stuff. The school was not intended to politicize; it would not, as Rush might have suggested, make republicans of army officers, but it would make army officers of Republicans.

(Rush quoted in Linda K. Kerber, *Federalists in Dissent, Imagery and Ideology in Jeffersonian America* [Ithaca, N.Y.: Cornell University Press, 1970], p. 109.) Rush's essay was first published in 1786 and reprinted in 1802.

4. A More Republican Establishment

1. William W. Burrows to Jonathan Williams, July 8, 1801, Williams Papers, Lilly Library.

2. Winfield Scott, *Memoirs of Lieut.-General Scott*, 2 vols. (New York: Sheldon, 1864), 1:34.

3. Arcadi Gluckman, *United States Muskets, Rifles and Carbines* (Buffalo, N.Y.: Otto Ulbrich, 1948), pp. 53–119; Constance McL. Green, *Eli Whitney and the Birth of American Technology* (Boston: Little, Brown, 1956), pp. 97–143.

4. Cooke, *Tench Coxe*, pp. 424–26.

5. James Wilkinson to Callander Irvine, December 20, 1808, Wilkinson Papers, University of Kentucky Library.

6. White, *Jeffersonians*, p. 224.

7. The discussion of the logistical activities in this paragraph and the two following has been informed by two excellent works: Erna Risch, *Quartermaster Support of the Army: A History of the Corps, 1775–1939* (Washington: Government Printing Office, 1962), pp. 115–33; and Cooke, *Tench Coxe*, pp. 413–31. The American army never adopted (in the nineteenth century) a logistical system that allowed it to prepare effectively for war. The French under Napoleon did better—but were almost constantly at war. The Prussian (and then German) General Staff in the last half of the century was the first really effective logistics planning organization in the modern era.

8. Gluckman, *United States Muskets, Rifles and Carbines*, pp. 193–94.

9. Alexander Wilson, "The Foresters," 1804, quoted in Berkeley R. Lewis, *Small Arms and Ammunition in the United States Service*, Smithsonian Miscellaneous Collections, vol. 129 (Washington: Smithsonian, 1959), p. 129.

10. Erney, *The Public Life of Henry Dearborn*, pp. 80–81.

11. William E. Birkhimer, *Historical Sketches of . . . The Artillery, United States Army* (Washington: James A. Chapman, 1884; reprinted Westport, Conn.: Greenwood Press, 1968), pp. 228–31; Erney, *The Public Life of Henry Dearborn*, pp. 81–83.

12. Birkhimer, *Historical Sketches of Artillery*, p. 164.

13. Ibid., pp. 258–62.

14. Henry Dearborn to George Peter, May 6, 1808, Letters Sent, Secretary of War, M6, NA.

15. George Peter to Henry Dearborn, January 9, 1809, Letters Received, Secretary of War, M221, NA.

16. Thomas H. Cushing to James Wilkinson, February 26, 1801, Letters Sent, Adjutant General, M565, NA.

17. Thomas H. Cushing to Samuel Dexter, December 24, 1800, Letters Sent, Adjutant General, M565, NA.

18. Thomas H. Cushing to James Bruff, August 1, 1801, Letters Sent, Adjutant General, M565, NA.

19. The apparent movement toward war in 1807 also prompted several other works, but most simply made minor modifications to Steuben's work, without reference to any recent improvements in tactical doctrine. Typical are Larned Lamb, *The Militia's Guide*

(Montpelier, Vt.: Samuel Goss, 1807); and Samuel J. Winston, *Military Tactics* (Richmond, Va.: S. Grantland, 1808). One writer, Edward Gillespy, sought to introduce the English modifications and improvements in tactics in his *The Military Instructor* (Boston: Joshua Cushing, 1809).

20. William Duane, *The American Military Library*, 2 vols. (Philadelphia: William Duane, 1809), 2:3–5. Duane's *Library* was first produced piecemeal, the first segments coming off the press in 1807. Part IV, from which the quote is drawn, was the first to be published. (Ibid., 1:ii.) See also: Theodore J. Crackel, "William Duane," *Dictionary of American Military Biography* (Westport, Conn.: Greenwood Press, 1985).

21. Michael Howard, *War in European History* (New York: Oxford University Press, 1976), p. 79. Howard's work, particularly the chapter, "The Wars of the Revolution," has been extremely useful in guiding my understanding of the revolution of European military thought of this era. Much of the discussion herein draws on that source.

22. Maximillian Godefroy, *Military Reflections, on Four Modes of Defense, for the United States* (Baltimore: Joseph Robinson, 1807).

23. [William Duane], "On National Defense," *Aurora*, October 30, 31, November 2, 3, 4, 5, 1807; "On a National Militia," *Aurora*, November 10, 11, 12, 14, 1807.

24. *Aurora*, October 30, 31, 1807.

25. *Aurora*, November 18, 1807.

26. Antoine Henri Jomini's *Traité des grandes opérations militaires* (1805–1810) appeared in six volumes. The first five volumes of the first edition of the *Traité* were among some 350 military titles listed in the *Catalogue of the Library of the Late Col. William Duane* (Philadelphia: n.p., 1836) when that collection went to auction.

27. Duane had Jomini's pieces "specially translated" for his *American Military Library* (*American Military Library*, 1:ii) and remarked on Jomini's "profound and able conceptions." (Ibid, 1:40.)

28. In the first edition this phrase appeared in the brief sixth volume. (The phrase appeared again in the expanded second edition—Jomini, *Traité*, 2d ed., 8 vols. [Paris: Chez Magime, 1811–1816], 8:677.) Duane clearly owned the first five volumes which had appeared by 1809, but it is uncertain whether he ever purchased the brief (fourteen-page) but important sixth part which included *l'art de la guerre, râmène' à ses véritables principes*, the basis for his early acclaim and of his later (1836–38) theoretical work. In any case, this last volume did not appear until 1810. On Jomini, see: John Shy, "Jomini," in Peter Paret, ed., *Makers of Modern Strategy, from Machiavelli to the Nuclear Age* (Princeton: Princeton University Press, 1986), pp. 143–85. See also: John I. Alger, "Antoine Henri Jomini, A Biographical Sketch," United States Military Academy Library Occasional Paper No. 3 (West Point: United States Military Academy, 1975).

29. The clearest statement of this came in the final (sixth) volume of the *Traité*, and, much later, in his 1836 *Précis de l'art de la guerre* and in an appendix added in 1838. Nonetheless, the idea appears throughout the *Traité*. On Jomini and the principles of war see: John I. Alger, *The Quest for Victory, The History of the Principles of War* (Westport, Conn.: Greenwood Press, 1982).

30. Duane, *American Military Library*, 1:114.

31. Ibid., 1:114 and 2:6.

32. For a discussion of the struggle for an effective doctrine or drill during the War of 1812, see Theodore J. Crackel, "The Battle of Queenston Heights, 13 October 1812," in Charles E. Heller and William A. Stofft, eds., *America's First Battles, 1776–1965* (Lawrence: University of Kansas Press, 1986).

33. "Rules and Articles of War," September 20, 1776. The administration had, in 1802, proposed that the law be explicit that the old Articles applied only so long as they were compatible with the new Constitution. This language was stricken, however, in the Senate.

34. "Rules and Articles for the Administration of Justice," May 31, 1786.

35. Articles 63, 87, & 92, "An Act for Establishing Rules and Articles for the Government of the Armies of the United States," April 10, 1806. Article 26, "Rules and Articles for the Administration of Justice," May 31, 1786.

36. Section II, Article 1, Articles of War, 1776. (My emphasis.)

37. Joseph Nicholson, March 15, 1804, *Annals*, 8th Cong., 1st Sess., p. 1191.

38. John Sibley to W. C. C. Claiborne, [1804 or early 1805], quoted in Jacobs, *The Beginning of the U. S. Army*, p. 314.

39. "Report of the Committee to whom was referred the Bill entitled 'An Act for Establishing Rules and Articles for the Government of the Armies of the United States,'" January 10, 1805, Senate Records, RG 46, NA.

40. Committee Report, January 10, 1805, RG 46, NA; William Plumer, *William Plumer's Memorandum of Proceedings in the United States Senate, 1803–1807* (New York: Macmillan, 1923), p. 254.

41. "Disobedience of Orders Justified on the Ground of Illegality," January 30, 1805, *American State Papers, Military Affairs*, 1:173–74.

42. Giles quoted in Plumer, *Memorandum*, p. 261.

43. "Report [by Mr. Varnum] from the Committee to whom was referred on the 13th instant the amendments proposed by the Senate to the bill entitled, 'An Act for Establishing Rules and Articles for the Government of the Armies of the United States'," March 17, 1806, House Records, RG 233, NA.

44. Henry Dearborn to James Wilkinson, June 11, 1801, Letters Sent, Secretary of War, M6, NA.

45. Henry Dearborn to Thomas H. Cushing, November 28, 1803, Letters Sent, Secretary of War, M6, NA. The old man lived on for years. He was carried on the rolls until 1815, but lived until 1834. In 1828, living in Dearborn County, Indiana, he was added to the pension rolls for his Revolutionary War service. He received $600 per year. (Secretary of War, "Indiana Pension Roll of 1835" in *Pension Establishment of the United States*, 4 vols. [Baltimore: Genealogical Publishing Company, 1968], 4:77).

46. Henry Dearborn to William Yates, May 20, 1803, Letters Sent, Secretary of War, M6, NA.

47. Henry Dearborn to Daniel Jackson, April 19, 1803, Letters Sent, Secretary of War, M6, NA.

48. Henry Dearborn to Thomas Hunt, May 6, 1803, Letters Sent, Secretary of War, M6, NA.

49. See Henry Dearborn to J. F. Hamtramck, March 9, 1803, Letters Sent, Secretary of War, M6, NA; Henry Dearborn to James Wilkinson, June 28, 1804, Letters Sent, Secretary of War, M6, NA; and Henry Dearborn to Commanding Officer, Detroit, August 5, 1805, Letters Sent, Secretary of War, M6, NA.

50. "An Act for Fixing the Military Peace Establishment on the United States," March 16, 1802.

51. Jacob Kingsbury to Thomas H. Cushing, October 4, 1805, Kingsbury Papers, Chicago Historical Society.

52. William A. Barron and Jared Mansfield to Jonathan Williams, March 16, 1803, Williams Papers, Lilly Library.

53. Henry Dearborn to John McClellan, July 11, 1803, Letters Sent, Secretary of War, M6, NA.

54. Henry Dearborn to [various post commanders], June 17, 1803, Letters Sent, Secretary of War, M6, NA.

55. Henry Dearborn to John Saunders, July 6, 1803, Letters Sent, Secretary of War, M6, NA; Henry Dearborn to Constance Freeman, July 27, 1803, Letters Sent, Secretary of War, M6, NA.

56. Henry Dearborn to [various post commanders], May 25, 1804, Letters Sent, Secretary of War, M6, NA.

57. Erna Risch, *Quartermaster Support of the Army: A History of the Corps, 1775–1939* (Washington: Government Printing Office, 1962), p. 118; "An Act in addition to 'An Act for Fixing the Military Peace Establishment of the United States'," March 26, 1804.

58. Garrison Order Book, December 5, 19, and 24, 1804, John Whipple Papers, Burton Collection, Detroit Public Library.

59. Jacob Kingsbury, Order Book, Early American Orderly Books, New-York Historical Society; John Whipple, Garrison Order Book, Whipple Papers. Burton Collection, Detroit Public Library. Henry Dearborn to Constance Freeman, April 23, 1804, Letters Sent, Secretary of War, M6, NA.

60. See: Risch, *Quartermaster Support of the Army*, pp. 120–2; James Ripley Jacobs, *Tarnished Warrior, Major General James Wilkinson* (New York: Macmillan, 1938), pp. 199–200; S. B. Holabird, "Army Clothing," *Journal of Military Service Institute of the United States*, 2 (1882):370–1; and Jacobs, *Beginnings of the U. S. Army*, pp. 261–63. It is worth noting that the new Articles of War of 1806 for the first time gave the President the power to prescribe the uniform for the army.

61. Wilkinson was quoted by Thomas Butler in a letter to Andrew Jackson and again by Jackson to the president. Based on Butler's note that the Wilkinson comment was written "a few weeks previous to the commencement of my trial [July 1, 1805]" this letter must have been written in May or June of that year. (Thomas Butler to Andrew Jackson, August 26, 1805, *Jackson Papers*, 2:71; Andrew Jackson to Thomas Jefferson, September 23, 1805, *Jackson Papers*, 2:72–73.)

62. Donald R. Hickey, "The United States Army Versus Long Hair: The Trials of Colonel Thomas Butler, 1801–1805," *The Pennsylvania Magazine of History and Biography* (October 1977): 462–74. "Disobedience of Orders Justified on the Grounds of Illegality," January 30, 1805, *American State Papers, Military Affairs*, 1:173. Swift, *Memoirs*, pp. 42–3.

63. Thomas Jefferson to Edmund Pendleton, April 22, 1799, Washburn Papers, Massachusetts Historical Society. J. Maner to Jacob Kingsbury, April 18, 1803, Kingsbury Papers, Burton Collection, Detroit Public Library.

64. Alexander Macomb to Jonathan Williams, June 24, 1803, Williams Papers, Lilly Library.

65. Henry Dearborn to G[ilbert] C[hristian] Russel, January 3, 1805, Letters Sent, Secretary of War, M6, NA.

66. Henry Dearborn to Samuel Gates, February 22, 1805, Letters Sent, Secretary of War, M6, NA.

67. Henry Dearborn to Thomas H. Cushing, December 24, 1802, Letters Sent, Secretary of War, M6, NA.

68. James Wilkinson, General Orders, June 17, 1801, Wilkinson's Order Book, M654, NA.

69. Henry Dearborn to Thomas H. Cushing, December 24, 1802, Letters Sent, Secretary of War, M6, NA. Artillery companies stationed in the coastal cities were an exception and recruited locally. See James Wilkinson to Henry Dearborn, March 25, 1805, Daniel Parker Papers, Historical Society of Pennsylvania.

70. The recruiting requirement in 1804 was particularly heavy because of losses the year before of a large number of men originally enlisted five years earlier during the expansion of the army in 1798. Henry Dearborn to Thomas H. Cushing, December 24, 1802, October 11, 1803, Letters Sent, Secretary of War, M6, NA; Henry Dearborn to James Wilkinson, March 29, 1805, Letters Sent, Secretary of War, M6, NA; Recruiting Return [R-1808], August, 1808, Unregistered Letters Received, Secretary of War, M222, NA.

71. James S. Swearingen to Henry Bedinger, April 1, 1805, Swearingen Papers, Chicago Historical Society.

72. There were, of course, losses among the Navy and Marines at sea and along the Barbary Coast.

73. James Wilkinson to Henry Dearborn, September 18, 1803, Wilkinson Papers, New-York Historical Society. In the spring, summer, and fall of 1809, the army around New Orleans was devastated by disease. Despite the real efforts of Wilkinson and the surgeons in the command, as many as 1,000 of a total of about 2,500 troops may have died of a variety of diseases that raged in the camps. See Mary C. Gillett, *The Army Medical Department, 1775–1818* (Washington: Government Printing Office, 1981), pp. 138–47.

74. W[illiam] W. Burrows to Jonathan Williams, August 4, 1802, Williams Papers, Lilly Library. See also Burrows to Williams, July 9, 1802, Williams Papers, Lilly Library.

75. Albert Gallatin to Hanna Gallatin [wife], July 7, 1802, in Henry Adams, *The Life of Albert Gallatin* (Philadelphia: J. B. Lippincott, 1879), p. 304. The citizen recovered from his wound and the marine was brought before a court-martial. He was found guilty of assault, fined twenty dollars (about four months' pay), and returned to duty.

76. Henry Dearborn to Thomas H. Cushing, March 18, 1802, Letters Sent, Secretary of War, M6, NA. See also Wade, "Artillerists and Engineers," Appendix D, pp. 313–15.

5. The Army in the Field

1. On the development of national authority and identity—and in particular on the problem of national unity in the new nation see: Seymour Martin Lipset, *The First New Nation* (New York: Basic Books, 1963), pp. 26–40; and Clinton Rossiter, *The American Quest, 1790–1860: An Emerging Nation in Search of Identity, Unity, and Modernity* (New York: Harcourt Brace Jovanovich, 1971), passim.

2. Adams, "Jefferson's Military Policy," p. iv.

3. On army road building see: White, *The Jeffersonians*, p. 260; and Hill, *Roads, Rails and Waterways*.

4. Thomas Jefferson to Robert E. Livingston, April 18, 1802, Bergh, 10:312.

5. Henry Dearborn to Thomas Butler, April 16, 1802, Letters Sent, Secretary of War, M6, NA.

6. Henry Dearborn to Thomas Butler, February 26, 1802, Miscellaneous Letters

Sent, Secretary of War, M370, NA; Henry Dearborn to James Wilkinson, February 18, 1803, Letters Sent, Secretary of War, M6, NA.

7. Thomas Jefferson to Henry Dearborn, July 12, 1803, Daniel Parker Papers, Historical Society of Pennsylvania. See also: Archibald Roane to Henry Dearborn, June 9, 1803, Governor's Official Papers, Tennessee State Library and Archives; Henry Dearborn to Archibald Roane, July 16, 1803, Miscellaneous Letters Sent, Secretary of War, M370, NA; and Henry Dearborn to Thomas H. Cushing, July 18, 1803, Letters Sent, Secretary of War, M6, NA.

8. Thomas Jefferson to Henry Dearborn, February 9, 1804, Daniel Parker Papers, Historical Society of Pennsylvania; Henry Dearborn to John Milledge, November 21, 1803, U. S. History Manuscripts, Lilly Library.

9. James Wilkinson to Jacob Kingsbury, February 27, 1803, Kingsbury Papers, Library of Congress. See also Jacob Kingsbury to Asa Spaulding, January 24, 1803, Kingsbury Letterbook, Burton Collection, Detroit Public Library; and R. Sparks to Jacob Kingsbury, February 2, 1803, Kingsbury Letterbook, Burton Collection, Detroit Public Library.

10. Henry Dearborn to James Wilkinson, March 7, 1803, Letters Sent, Secretary of War, M6, NA.

11. Henry Dearborn to Thomas H. Cushing, March 9, 1803, Letters Sent, Secretary of War, M6, NA; Henry Dearborn to Callander Irvine, March 21, 1803, Letters Sent, Secretary of War, M6, NA; Henry Dearborn to James Wilkinson, April 16, 1803, Letters Sent, Secretary of War, M6, NA.

12. James Wilkinson to Henry Dearborn, July 24, 1803, Wilkinson Papers, Boston Public Library.

13. Henry Dearborn to Decidus Wadsworth, July 18, 1803, Letters Sent, Secretary of War, M6, NA.

14. Henry Dearborn to Amos Stoddard, July 19, 1803, Letters Sent, Secretary of War, M6, NA.

15. Henry Dearborn to Daniel Bissell and Amos Stoddard, July 27, 1803, Letters Sent, Secretary of War, M6, NA. See also: Henry Dearborn to James Wilkinson, October 31, 1803, Letters Sent, Secretary of War, M6, NA.

16. Casa Irujo to James Madison, September 4, 1803, in James Alexander Robertson, *Louisiana Under Spain, France and the United States*, 2 vols. (Cleveland: Arthur H. Clark, 1911), 2:78.

17. Casa Irujo to James Madison, September 27, 1803, in Robertson, *Louisiana*, 2:81–82.

18. Thomas Jefferson to Wilson C. Nicholas, September 7, 1803, Bergh, 10:48.

19. Thomas Jefferson to Henry Dearborn, October 22, 1803, Daniel Parker Papers, Historical Society of Pennsylvania.

20. Henry Dearborn to James Wilkinson, October 31, 1803, Letters Sent, Secretary of War, M6, NA; Henry Dearborn to Andrew Jackson and James Morrison, October 31, 1803, Letters Sent, Secretary of War, M6, NA; Albert Gallatin to W. C. C. C[laiborne], October 31, 1803, Durrett Collection, University of Chicago Library. See also Casa Irujo to Casa Calvo, November 1, 1803, in Robertson, *Louisiana*, 2:94; and Thomas Jefferson to Dupont de Nemours, November 1, 1803, Bergh, 10:423.

21. Henry Dearborn to James Wilkinson, January 9, 1804, Letters Sent, Secretary of War, M6, NA.

22. Wilkinson Order Book, December 4, 9, and 10, 1803, M654, NA.

23. Ibid., December 17, 1803.

24. Henry Dearborn to James Wilkinson, January 16, 1804, Letters Sent, Secretary of War, M6, NA. This letter acknowledges receipt that day of letters of 15, 20, and 27 December.

25. For a fuller account of the transfer see: Jacobs, *Tarnished Warrior*, pp. 187–208.

26. W. C. C. Claiborne and James Wilkinson to James Madison, December 27, 1803, in Robertson, *Louisiana*, 2:289–91.

27. "Lists of Posts and Number of Companies at Each," February 3, 1804, Letters Sent, Secretary of War, M6, NA. The three artillery companies ordered to New Orleans are shown as assigned to that post, but could not have reported as of that date. In fact, they did not embark for that city until early April.

28. Henry Dearborn to James Wilkinson, February 2, 1804, Letters Sent, Secretary of War, M6, NA.

29. The Spanish Ambassador, Casa Irujo, always alert for such intelligence, noted in late February reports then circulating that 500–600 regulars were being sent to Louisiana. But these reports probably referred to the three companies (totaling roughly 200 men) of artillery that Dearborn had already promised from the East Coast. (Casa Irujo to Ceballos, February 21, 1804, in Robertson, *Louisiana*, 2:130–32.)

30. In March 1804 two additional companies of Marines were dispatched. (Henry Dearborn to Commanding Officer at New Orleans, March 15, 1804, Letters Sent, Secretary of War, M6, NA.)

31. Henry Dearborn to Tench Coxe, January 30, 1804, Letters Sent, Secretary of War, M6, NA; Henry Dearborn to Thomas H. Cushing, February 27, 1804, Letters Sent, Secretary of War, M6, NA.

32. Henry Dearborn to Thomas H. Cushing, January 31, 1804, Letters Sent, Secretary of War, M6, NA.

33. Henry Dearborn to James Wilkinson, February 2, 1804, Letters Sent, Secretary of War, M6, NA.

34. Henry Dearborn to Decidus Wadsworth, February 13, 1804, Letters Sent, Secretary of War, M6, NA.

35. Thomas Jefferson to W. C. C. Claiborne, February 20, 1804, Letters Sent, Secretary of War, M6, NA.

36. Thomas Jefferson to Henry Dearborn, February 9, 1804, Daniel Parker Papers, Historical Society of Pennsylvania; Henry Dearborn to John Milledge, November 21, 1803, U. S. History Manuscripts, Lilly Library.

37. James Wilkinson to Amos Stoddard, July 27 and November 7, 1803, Letters Sent, Secretary of War, M6, NA.

38. Thomas Jefferson to John Breckinridge, August 12, 1803, Bergh, 10:410.

39. Thomas Jefferson to Dupont De Nemours, November 1, 1803, Bergh, 10:423. The term *Marechausse* indicates a French mounted constabulary, but Jefferson seems to have intended a play on words—derived from the conjunction of the French words *marée* (tide or flood) and *chaussée* (embankment or dike), suggesting a barrier to the tide of settlers.

40. Meriwether Lewis to Thomas Jefferson, December 28, 1803, Daniel Parker Papers, Historical Society of Pennsylvania.

41. Henry Dearborn to Samuel Hammond, R. J. Meigs, Richard Kennon, and Seth Hunt, November 2, 1804, Letters Sent, Secretary of War, M6, NA.

42. Henry Dearborn to Amos Stoddard, May 16, 1804, Letters Sent, Secretary of

War, M6, NA; Henry Dearborn to Decidus Wadsworth, July 17, 1804, Letters Sent, Secretary of War, M6, NA; Henry Dearborn to James Bruff, December 14, 1804, Letters Sent, Secretary of War, M6, NA. Of the six young men who were appointed, five graduated (though one of these did not accept a commission). These were the last "Missouri" cadets to be admitted until statehood was achieved a decade and a half later.

43. Amos Stoddard to Henry Dearborn, May 7, 1804, War Department Miscellaneous Papers, Newberry Library.

44. The fact that Louis Loramier was commissioned in infantry (rather than artillery or engineers, as the others were) and made an ensign (rather than second lieutenant) suggests the possibility of bias, but nothing in the record substantiates it. He was promoted to second lieutenant after about a year (when the first vacancy occurred), and served a total of about three years. On these early Missouri cadets see: George T. Ness, Jr., "Missouri at West Point, Her Graduates Through The Civil War Years," *Missouri Historical Review*, 38 (January 1944):162–69; and Donald Chaput, "The Early Missouri Graduates of West Point, Officers or Merchants?" *Missouri Historical Review*, 72 (April 1978):262–70.

45. Among the many accounts of the expedition, I have found Donald Jackson's *Thomas Jefferson & the Stony Mountains* (Urbana: University of Illinois Press, 1981) to be particularly useful because he casts the events in an unusually wide perspective. For those seeking more detail there are, of course, the original journals and letters: Reuben Gold Thwaites, ed. *Original Journals of the Lewis and Clark Expedition, 1804–1806, Printed from the Original Manuscripts in the Library of the American Philosophical Society*, 8 vols. (New York: Dodd, Mead, 1904–5); and Donald Jackson, ed. *Letters of the Lewis and Clark Expedition, with Related Documents, 1783–1854*, 2nd ed., 2 vols. (Urbana: University of Illinois Press, 1978).

46. Jackson, *Jefferson & the Stony Mountains*; Alexander Mackenzie, *Voyages from Montreal, on the River St. Lawrence, through the Continent of North America, the Frozen and Pacific Ocean. . . .*, 2 vols. (London: 1801).

47. Thomas Jefferson to Meriwether Lewis, [June 20, 1803], Jefferson Papers, LC.

48. Jefferson's *ad interim* appointment was confirmed by the Senate in its next session, but there was some objection on the grounds that the military and civilian functions should not be mixed. Jefferson himself had earlier objected to appointing Wilkinson to the governorship in Mississippi.

49. James Wilkinson to Henry Dearborn, June 13, 1805, Wilkinson Papers, Indiana Historical Society.

50. James Wilkinson to George Peter, August 6, 1805, Peter Family Papers, Alderman Library; James Wilkinson to Z. M. Pike, July 30, 1805, in Donald Jackson, ed., *The Journals of Zebulon Montgomery Pike*, 2 vols. (Norman: University of Oklahoma Press, 1966), 1:3–4. On Jefferson's interest in such exploration see: Jackson, *Jefferson and the Stony Mountains*.

51. James Wilkinson to Henry Dearborn, September 8, 1805, Durrett Collection, University of Chicago Library; James Wilkinson to Jonathan Williams, August 11, 1805, Williams Papers, Lilly Library. See also: Thomas Jefferson to Henry Dearborn, October 27, 1818, Jefferson Papers, University of Virginia Library.

52. Jacobs, *Tarnished Warrior*, p. 223.

53. Ibid., p. 220.

54. Jackson, *Jefferson & the Stony Mountains*, pp. 250–54; Jackson, *Pike Journals*, 1:411.

55. On this connection see Milton Lomask, *Aaron Burr* 2 vols. (New York: Farrar,

Straus, Giroux, 1982), 2:43–54. Lomask's treatment of Wilkinson is one-dimensional and wholly inadequate for such a complex character. Wilkinson deserves more careful treatment, particularly when made the villain.

56. Burr and Wilkinson had all along planned such a meeting or even to travel together down the Ohio. Apparent delays on the part of Wilkinson had precluded any but this meeting near the fork of the Ohio and Mississippi. See: Aaron Burr to James Wilkinson, March 26, April 5, 10, and May 19, 1805, *Political Correspondence and Public Papers of Aaron Burr*, Mary-Jo Kline, ed., 2 vols. (Princeton: Princeton University Press, 1983), 2:925–26, 930–31, 932, 936. (Hereinafter cited as *Burr Papers*.)

57. *Burr Papers*, 2:921.

58. For example, Thomas Truxton claimed that even after insisting he "would have nothing to do with it," Burr continued his arguments and descriptions of his plans. (*Burr Papers*, 2:989–90.)

59. Daniel Clark to James Wilkinson, September 7, 1805, in Wilkinson, *Memoirs of My Own Times*, 2:appendix 33.

60. Henry Dearborn to James Wilkinson, August 24, 1805, Wilkinson Papers, Chicago Historical Society.

61. James Wilkinson to Henry Dearborn, September 8, 1805, Durrett Collection, Regenstein Library.

62. Wilkinson did send Burr a copy (or resume of the contents) of Clark's letter in November. (*Burr Papers*, 2:954. See also Lomask, *Aaron Burr*, 2:88.) Most students of this affair have suspected that, following Burr's departure, Wilkinson's ardor began to cool. They have usually attributed this to Clark's revelations and Wilkinson's fear that his role might be exposed. For example see: Herbert S. Parmet and Marie B. Hecht, *Aaron Burr: Portrait of an Ambitious Man* (New York: Macmillan, 1967), p. 242; Thomas Perkins Abernethy, *The Burr Conspiracy* (Gloucester, Mass.: Page Smith, 1968 [1954]), p. 32, 35–36; and Jonathan Daniels, *Ordeal of Ambition, Jefferson, Hamilton, Burr* (New York: Doubleday, 1970), p. 320.

63. Henry Dearborn to James Wilkinson, August 24, 1805, Wilkinson Papers, Chicago Historical Society. Historians have hitherto overlooked or ignored this letter, but it was this that caused Wilkinson to withdraw.

64. Daniel Hughes deposition, January 20, 1811, Wilkinson *Memoirs*, 2:appendix 70. Wilkinson testified at Burr's trial that he had sent this letter, but could not produce a copy. Captain Daniel Hughes testified at Wilkinson's court-martial in 1811 that he had copied the letter to Smith and vouched for its contents. (Jonathan Williams's notes on Wilkinson's 1811 court-martial, Williams Papers, Lilly Library.) Robert Smith indicated that he had received the letter, but that it was his "invariable practice to destroy all private letters." Still, he said, it was "within my recollection that in conversation here as well as by letter from St. Louis you have expressed to me and in a style of disapprobation your suspicions of the views of Burr." (Robert Smith to James Wilkinson, June 22, 1807, Durrett Collection, Regenstein Library.) This Smith letter, supporting Wilkinson's contention that he had alerted the government to Burr's activities, sheds new light on this issue, for Mary-Jo Kline has asserted that there was "no evidence that Smith had ever received such a communication." (*Burr Papers*, 2:941.)

65. Aaron Burr to James Wilkinson, January 6, 1806, *Burr Papers*, 2:853–54.

66. Aaron Burr to James Wilkinson, April 16, 1806, *Burr Papers*, 2:968–69. Burr had written in late September 1805 from Vincennes (after leaving St. Louis) (*Burr Papers*, 2:940). Wilkinson responded in November (not October as Burr later recalled) with a

copy of Clark's letter. Burr wrote again December 12, 1805, from Philadelphia before receiving the copy of Clark's note. (*Burr Papers*, 2:948.) Wilkinson's November letter (Clark's note) appears to have arrived late that month and was acknowledged in a letter from Burr on January 6, 1806 (*Burr Papers*, 2:953.). Wilkinson did not respond to either the December or January letters, and it was this silence that was noted by Burr.

67. Abernethy, *Burr Conspiracy*, p. 52; Lomask, *Aaron Burr*, 2:84.

68. This letter, written in May 1806, was referenced in Burr's July cipher letter. ([Aaron Burr] to James Wilkinson, 22–29 July, 1806, *Burr Papers*, 2:986–87.) No copy of Wilkinson's letter has been found. Burr refused, at his grand jury hearing in Richmond, to surrender it.

69. General Orders, August 2, 1801, Wilkinson's Order Book, M654, NA; General Orders, May 25, 1803, Wilkinson's Order Book, M654, NA; General Orders, February 1, 1804, Wilkinson's Order Book, M654, NA. On Butler and the haircut order see: Hickey, "Trials of Colonel Butler," pp. 462–74. General Order, April 30, 1801, Wilkinson's Order Book, M654, NA.

70. Thomas H. Cushing to Thomas Butler, May 25, 1802, Letters Sent, Adjutant General, M565, NA.

71. James Ripley Jacobs reported that a strong faction opposed to Wilkinson grew up under Major James Bruff, but he was mistaken. Bruff disliked Wilkinson immensely and was vocal about it, but had no following. He was not associated with Butler or the other anti-Wilkinson men. (Jacobs, *Tarnished Warrior*, p. 226.)

72. James Wilkinson to Jonathan Williams, June 24, 1803, Williams Papers, Lilly Library. See also James Wilkinson to Henry Dearborn, November 9, 1804, Letters Received, Secretary of War, M221, NA.

73. Andrew Jackson to Thomas Jefferson, August 7, 1803, *The Papers of Andrew Jackson*, Harold D. Moser and Sharon MacPherson, eds., 2 vols. (to date). (Knoxville: University of Tennessee Press, 1980–) 1:353–54 (Hereafter cited as *Jackson Papers*.); Thomas Jefferson to Andrew Jackson, September 19, 1803, *Jackson Papers*, 1:365. On Jackson and Butler see: Donald R. Hickey, "Andrew Jackson and the Army Haircut: Individual Rights Vs. Military Discipline," *Tennessee Historical Quarterly*, 35 (Winter 1976) 4:365–75.

74. Henry Dearborn to Thomas H. Cushing, May 17, 1804, Letters Sent, Secretary of War, M6, NA.

75. Andrew Jackson to Thomas Butler, August 25, 1804, *Jackson Papers*, 2:36–37.

76. Jacobs, *Tarnished Warrior*, p. 200. See also: James Wilkinson to Thomas Butler, November 25, December 10, 1804, and James Wilkinson to James Brown, March 25, 1805, James Brown Papers, LC.

77. Plumer, *Memorandum*, January 1805, p. 261. John Brown to James Wilkinson, July 20, 1805, Letters Received, Secretary of War, M221, NA; General Orders, September 20, 1805, Wilkinson's Order Book, M654, NA.

78. Swift, *Memoirs*, p. 43. Irving's Knickerbocker *History of New York*, with the essence of this story reframed as an episode of "knickerbocker' history, was first published in 1809. Irving, a longtime Burr supporter, satirized James Wilkinson at length in this work. That episode is but one of many which portrayed the general to disadvantage.

79. James Wilkinson to Jonathan Williams, October 22, 1805, Williams Papers, Lilly Library; Henry Burbeck to Jonathan Williams, October 20, 1805, Williams Papers, Lilly Library.

80. Henry Dearborn to James Wilkinson, November 21, 1805, Letters Sent, Secretary of War, M6, NA.

81. Plumer, *Memorandum*, April 2, 1806, p. 471. Cushing had been second in command of the regiment since 1802 but had served for a number of years as adjutant general, Wilkinson's eyes and ears in Washington.

82. Henry Burbeck to Jonathan Williams, April 9, 1806, Williams Papers, Lilly Library.

83. Zebulon M. Pike to Daniel Bissell, May 13, 1806, Bissell Papers, St. Louis Mercantile Library Association.

84. Scott, *Memoirs*, 1:36.

85. A[bimael] Y. Nicoli Memorandum, June 15, 1809, Daniel Parker Papers, Historical Society of Pennsylvania; "Return of Troops destined for St. Louis," March 1805, Wilkinson Papers, Chicago Historical Society.

6. General Wilkinson's Army

1. Henry Dearborn to James Wilkinson, October 16, 1805, Letters Sent, Secretary of War, M6, NA.

2. Thomas Jefferson to Henry Dearborn, November 20, 1805, Daniel Parker Papers, Historical Society of Pennsylvania; Henry Dearborn to [Moses Porter], November 20, 1805, Wilkinson Papers, Chicago Historical Society. Walter Flavius McCaleb, *The Aaron Burr Conspiracy* (New York: Argosy-Antiquarian Press, 1966), pp. 93–94.

3. Henry Dearborn to James Wilkinson, November 20, 1805, Letters Sent, Secretary of War, M6, NA.

4. Thomas Jefferson, Fifth Annual Message, December 3, 1805, in Richardson, *Messages*, 1:372–73.

5. McCaleb, *Burr Conspiracy*, pp. 94–95.

6. Ibid., pp. 95–97.

7. Henry Dearborn to James Wilkinson, March 18, 1806, Letters Sent, Secretary of War, M6, NA; Henry Dearborn to Constance Freeman, April 26, 1806, Letters Sent, Secretary of War, M6, NA.

8. In April, for example, Dearborn ordered that the stockpiles of such items as purified salt peter—a principal ingredient in gunpowder—be checked and augmented. (Henry Dearborn to William Linnard, April 17, 1806, Dearborn Papers, Burton Collection, Detroit Public Library).

9. "Report of the Committee on . . . Militia and Augmentation of the Army," April 18, 1806, Records of the U.S. House of Representatives, Reports of Select Committees, 9th Cong., 1st Sess., RG233, NA.

10. Henry Dearborn to James Wilkinson, May 6, 1806, Wilkinson Papers, Chicago Historical Society.

11. James Wilkinson to Henry Dearborn, June 16, 1806, Wilkinson Papers, Darlington Library, University of Pittsburgh; James Wilkinson to Samuel Smith, June 17, 1806, Wilkinson Papers, Darlington Library.

12. Abernethy, *Burr Conspiracy*, pp. 138–40; McCaleb, *Burr Conspiracy*, pp. 102–4.

13. James Wilkinson to Governor Cordero, September 24, 1806, Wilkinson Papers, Darlington Library.

14. James Wilkinson to Henry Dearborn, September 27, 1806, Letters Received, Secretary of War, M221, NA.

15. James Wilkinson to John Smith, September 26, 1806, quoted in Abernethy, *Burr Conspiracy*, p. 143.

16. Adair had once assured him that, "Mexico glitters in our Eyes—the word is all we wait for." (John Adair to James Wilkinson, December 10, 1804, Durrett Collection, University of Chicago.) Adair later showed up in New Orleans in support of Burr, and was arrested by Wilkinson.

17. James Wilkinson to John Adair, September 28, 1806, quoted in McCaleb, *Burr Conspiracy*, p. 112. Some historians have cited Wilkinson's letters to John Smith (September 26) and John Adair (September 28) as evidence of complicity in the Burr conspiracy. (See Abernethy, *Burr Conspiracy*, p. 143; and McCaleb, *Burr Conspiracy*, pp. 112–14.) But, if read as a warning of actions the nation might be forced to take in consequence of his orders—particularly the necessity of raising volunteers—rather than as a specific invitation to join some independent expedition (he had given Dearborn just such a warning) then these letters lose their conspiratorial connotation. The balance of the Smith and Adair letters then become, not a sinister plot against Mexico, but a set of options from which the nation could choose.

18. Wilkinson Order Book, September 23, 27, and October 2, 1806, M654, NA.

19. Wilkinson Order Book, October 3, 1806, M654, NA.

20. James Wilkinson to Governor Cordero, October 4, 1806, Letters Received, Secretary of War, M221, NA.

21. James Wilkinson to Samuel Smith, October 5, 1806, Wilkinson Papers, Darlington Library.

22. Mary-Jo Kline, editor of the Burr papers, argues that the cipher text was not from Burr at all, but from Jonathan Dayton and in his hand. Wilkinson's deciphered text was a hoax, she claims—"almost certainly not a reconstruction of any words that A[aron] B[urr] encoded." Rather, it was "a letter James Wilkinson wished the world to believe [Burr] had written him in July 1806." (*Burr Papers*, 2:986.) I read the evidence very differently.

All do agree that Burr had authored a cipher letter (copied by Swartwout) intended for General Wilkinson, that Swartwout had started out to deliver it, and that he had been overtaken and given a new message (the ciphered text in Dayton's hand) which he then delivered. (Dr. Erich Bollman delivered a second copy of the latter message.)

Here agreement ends. Kline argues that Dayton authored and sent the second cipher without Burr's knowledge, though she offers no explanation for such an action. She is driven to this conclusion by the necessity to explain several claims or assertions in the second cipher which—she argues—Burr knew to be untrue, and therefore would not make. (These included claims of support by Thomas Truxton and Joseph Alston, and information on matters relating to Burr's immediate family.) Why Dayton would betray the truth—when Burr would not—she does not explain. (Milton Lomax argues that Dayton added this information to the substance of Burr's earlier message in order to insure Wilkinson's continued support. [*Aaron Burr*, 2:121–22.])

A more likely version of events is that Burr, after dispatching Swartwout with the first message, decided to embellish his words. The additions—for the most part claims of further support—were intended to reassure Wilkinson, in whom Burr belatedly sensed a reluctance. In Swartwout's absence Dayton enciphered Burr's new dispatch, sent it in pursuit of Swartwout, and (to be safe) sent a second copy by Bollman on a different route. There is no persuasive reason to believe that Burr would not attempt to deceive the general to insure his support, or (it follows) to doubt Burr's authorship of the enciphered text that Wilkinson received. (Of course, Wilkinson's early public rendition of Burr's message did leave out the passages that tended to implicate him—a version he was later forced to recant.)

23. Jonathan Dayton to James Wilkinson, July 24, 1806, Burr Papers, Alderman Library.

24. Aaron Burr to James Wilkinson, July 22, 1806, *Burr Papers*, 2:986–87. The original (enciphered text) was delivered by Samuel Swartout. A duplicate of this letter, carried by Dr. Erich Bollman, was dated July 29.

25. One officer, Major James Bruff, testified at the Burr trial that Wilkinson, at St. Louis, had hinted at opportunities for fame and fortune. *In retrospect*, he interpreted that as an invitation to join the conspiracy. But Bruff was an officer whom the general believed to be both unreliable and unprofessional—and against whom (in 1806) the general had preferred charges of disrespect and disobedience. Of all the army's officers, Bruff was the most unlikely candidate for recruitment into some untoward scheme. Since the summer of 1806 Bruff had been complaining to all who would listen, of disaffection in the officer corps and of its need to be further "regenerated." (James Bruff to Joseph H. Nicholson, March 29, 1806, Nicholson Papers, LC.) Still, Bruff raised no alarm against Wilkinson then, and there is nothing in the record of other officers' personal or official correspondence to substantiate his latter day allegations. Even the officers who later admitted involvement in the conspiracy made no charge of complicity by the general.

26. Cushing Deposition, November 15, 1806, in Wilkinson, *Memoirs of My Own Time*, 2:appendix 42.

27. James Wilkinson to Henry Dearborn, October 17, 1806, Letters Received, Secretary of War, M221, NA.

28. James Wilkinson to Thomas Jefferson, October 21, 1806, Burr Manuscripts, LC. The article to which Wilkinson referred likely appeared in late July and was apparently widely reprinted—particularly in Federalist papers. (See: [Raleigh] *Register*, September 1, 1806.)

29. [James Wilkinson] unsigned [intended for Thomas Jefferson], October 20, 1806, Burr Manuscripts, LC.

30. James Wilkinson to Thomas Jefferson, October 21, 1806, Burr Manuscripts, LC.

31. James Wilkinson to Henry Dearborn, October 21, 1806, Letters Received, Secretary of War, M221, NA.

32. James Wilkinson to Constance Freeman, October 23, 1806, Wilkinson, *Memoirs of My Own Times*, 2:appendix 101.

33. James Wilkinson to Henry Dearborn, November 4, 1806, Letters Received, Secretary of War, M221, NA.

34. Abernethy, *Burr Conspiracy*, p. 154.

35. James Wilkinson to Governor Cordero, October 29, 1806, Letters Received, Secretary of War, M221, NA.

36. Herrera, who was acting in flagrant disregard of his instructions, received a commendation rather than punishment. (Jackson, *Pike Journals*, 1:437–42.)

37. General Orders, November 5 and 6, 1806, Wilkinson's Order Book, M654, NA.

38. James Wilkinson to Constance Freeman, October 23, 1806, Wilkinson, *Memoirs of My Own Times*, 2:appendix 101.

39. James Wilkinson to Thomas Jefferson, November 14, 1806, Wilkinson, *Memoirs of My Own Times*, 2:appendix 100.

40. James Wilkinson to Thomas Jefferson, November 14, 1806, Wilkinson, *Memoirs of My Own Times*, 2:appendix 100; James Wilkinson to Samuel Smith, November 14, 1806, Wilkinson Papers, Darlington Library.

41. James Wilkinson to Henry Dearborn, November 12, 1806, Letters Received, Secretary of War, M221, NA.

42. James Wilkinson to W. C. C. Claiborne, November 12, 1806, Wilkinson, *Memoirs of My Own Times*, 2:328–29.

43. Andrew Jackson to Governor Claiborne, November 12, 1806, *Jackson Papers*, 2:116–17. Mary-Jo Kline questioned Wilkinson's decision to defend at New Orleans rather than further up river. He did so, she argued, to protect himself. Wilkinson, she wrote, "knew that his own safety required firm action in New Orleans, where he must silence the men who would disclose his association with Burr's plans." Kline ignores the internal threat in New Orleans that even Jackson warned of, and the naval threat (which Wilkinson feared) from below. Her theory also begs the question of why he would send these men to the seat of government with their knowledge—if he were trying to prevent their testimony.

44. Cowles Meade to W. C. C. Claiborne, [mid-November] 1806, quoted in McCaleb, *Burr Conspiracy*, pp. 172–73.

45. On Davies and a fuller discussion of warnings received by Jefferson see: Malone, *Jefferson*, 5:233–51.

46. Rumors of army units defecting—based, seemingly, on no more than the suspicion of Wilkinson's participation—were "toled [sic] as a fact" as Burr proceeded toward New Orleans. The plotters counted on "the aid of the Federal troops, and the Gen[era]l at their head," it was reported. (Andrew Jackson to George W. Campbell, January 15, 1807, *Jackson Papers*, 2:147–50.)

47. Albert Gallatin to Thomas Jefferson, February 12, 1806, *Writings of Gallatin*, 1:290.

48. Thomas Jefferson to Samuel Smith, May 4, 1806, Bergh, 11:111–13.

49. Thomas Jefferson to James Monroe, May 4, 1806, Bergh, 11:109.

50. Wilkinson believed that his orders to the field were tantamount to removal from the governorship and he proved correct. (James Wilkinson to Samuel Smith, June 17, 1806, Wilkinson Papers, Darlington Library.) On Graham see: Malone, *Jefferson*, 5:244. Graham ultimately refused the position.

51. From June 10 through November 7, 1806, only four letters over Dearborn's signature were dispatched to Wilkinson and these were routine letters such as those covering a promotion list or the new Articles of War. Jefferson sent none. Wilkinson had been accustomed to receiving nearly daily correspondence from the Secretary, and more than occasional notes from the President. No other correspondent experienced such a drastic cut in mail. In fact, even in the doldrums of summer there was little perceivable decline in the number of messages sent—except to Wilkinson.

52. Wilkinson wrote Samuel Smith that he had received no orders since May. Presumably he meant *written* since May. In terms of substantive instructions he was correct, though Dearborn had sent one perfunctory note concerning the construction of blockhouses in June. (James Wilkinson to Samuel Smith, December 10, 1806, Wilkinson Papers, Darlington Library.)

53. Dearborn reopened the correspondence on November 8, but that letter and those

written to other post commanders that day, only ordered the army to cease any oper-
ations in which it was engaged. A second letter on November 15 bitterly denounced
Wilkinson. (Henry Dearborn to James Wilkinson, November 8, 15, 1806, Letters Sent,
Secretary of War, M6, NA.)

54. Scott, *Memoirs*, 1:36. It was not until this year, 1806, that the first Military
Academy graduate was commissioned in an infantry regiment. That did not become
commonplace until after 1808. Until then the Jeffersonian entrees into these regiments
had been by direct appointment.

55. James Bruff to Joseph H. Nicholson, March 29, 1806, Nicholson Papers, LC.
On Jefferson's awareness of Bruff's sentiment see: W. A. Burwell Diary, March 29,
1806, Burwell Papers, LC.

56. Malone, *Jefferson*, 5:239–41.

57. Shortly after the Eaton story came to hand, Eaton stepped forward directly saying that he could "speak with confidence" about the "Burr insurrection." (William Eaton to Robert Smith, October 25, 1806, Burr Family Papers, Yale University Library.)

58. Bergh, 1:462. The marines themselves had recently undergone a bit of a political
reformation when their staunchly Federalist commandant, William W. Burrows, had
finally been harried out of the service. See Alfred J. Marini, "Political Perceptions of
the Marine Forces: Great Britain, 1699, 1739, and the United States, 1798, 1804,"
Military Affairs, 44 (December 1980):171–75.

59. Cabinet meeting, October 20, 1806, Bergh, 1:460–61.

60. Ibid.

61. Cabinet meeting, October 24, 1806, Bergh, 1:461–62.

62. Robert Smith to Edward Preble, October 25, 1806, Letters Sent by the Secretary of the Navy to Officers, M149, NA. This correspondence was so sensitive that it
was not even entered into the letterbooks until weeks later.

63. Robert Smith to Edward Preble, October 24, 1806, Letters Sent by the Secretary of the Navy to Officers, M149, NA. This decision was first attributed to the fact
that the most recent mail from the West had revealed nothing new about the activities
of Burr. Somewhat later the decision was attributed to budgetary considerations. Neither answer is particularly satisfactory. The more likely answer is that the President
simply changed his mind, concluding that this was not as good an idea as it had appeared at first blush.

64. Henry Dearborn to Constance Freeman, October 27, 1806, Letters Sent, Secretary of War, M6, NA.

65. Cabinet meeting, November 8, 1806, Bergh, 1:462; Henry Dearborn to James
Wilkinson, November 8, 1806, Letters Sent, Secretary of War, M6, NA.

66. Henry Dearborn to James Wilkinson, November 8, 1806, Letters Sent, Secretary of War, M6, NA; Henry Dearborn to Thomas Swaine, November 8, 1806, Letters
Sent, Secretary of War, M6, NA.

67. Henry Dearborn to James Wilkinson, November 15, 1806, Letters Sent, Secretary of War, M6, NA. The article to which Dearborn referred has not been identified
and the substance to which he objected is unknown. It may, however, have been a
criticism of the Secretary himself, such as Wilkinson had penned to Samuel Smith only
a month earlier. (James Wilkinson to Samuel Smith, October 5, 1806, Wilkinson Papers, Darlington Library.)

68. Deposition of Thomas A. Smith, undated, Wilkinson, *Memoirs of My Own Times*,
2:appendix 94.

69. Cabinet meeting, November 25, 1806, Bergh, 1:462–65.

70. Henry Dearborn to James Wilkinson, November 27 and December 8, 1806, Letters Sent, Secretary of War, M6, NA.

71. Lomask, *Aaron Burr*, 2:179.

72. As Forrest McDonald put it, "Burr's doings in the West could scarcely have attracted more attention had he hired a publicity agent." (*The Presidency of Thomas Jefferson* [Lawrence: The University of Kansas Press, 1976]).

73. Abernethy, *Burr Conspiracy*, pp. 102–3.

74. Jacob Jackson Testimony, "Burr Trial", *American State Papers, Miscellaneous*, 1:610–11.

75. This Bayou Pierre was on the river about 30 miles north of Natchez in the Mississippi Territory. The location by the same name, occupied by the Spanish and referenced above, is a different site, approximately 35 miles northwest of Natchitoches in the Orleans Territory.

76. In the foregoing discussion of Burr's exploits, I have relied extensively on Abernethy, *Burr Conspiracy*, pp. 119–221.

77. I. J. Cox, "General Wilkinson and his Later Intrigues with the Spanish," *The American Historical Review*, 19 (July 1914):795–800.

78. James Wilkinson to Samuel Smith, December 10, 1806, Wilkinson Papers, Darlington Library.

79. Jacobs, *Tarnished Warrior*, pp. 233–34. Wilkinson had calculated that he should receive $111,000 from the Spanish.

80. Thomas Jefferson to J. B. Colvin, September 20, 1810, Bergh, 12:421; C. N. Shendi[?] to James Wilkinson, October 30, 1806, Wilkinson Papers, Darlington Library.

81. James Wilkinson to Thomas Jefferson, November 12, 1806, Wilkinson, *Memoirs of My Own Times*, 2:appendix 100.

82. Thomas Jefferson to James Wilkinson, January 3, 1807, Bergh, 11:127–30; Thomas Jefferson to James Wilkinson, February 3, 1807, Bergh, 11:147–50.

83. [Philadelphia] *Aurora*, February 23, 1807. Mary-Jo Kline surmised that the general used martial law to silence the men who could disclose his association with "Burr's plans"—and to that supposed end he had arrested them and dispatched them to Washington. (*Burr Papers*, 2:980ff.) To subscribe to such an analysis would require the belief that the general was peculiarly naive. For it was in Washington that these men could do the most damage.

84. Thomas Jefferson to James Wilkinson, February 3, 1807, Bergh, 11:147–50.

85. Thomas Jefferson to W. C. C. Claiborne, February 3, 1807, Bergh, 11:150–51. This continued to be the theme of his defense of Wilkinson. See also Thomas Jefferson to J. B. Colvin, September 20, 1810, Bergh, 12:418.

86. James Wilkinson to Jonathan Williams, April 2, 1807, Williams Papers, Lilly Library.

87. Samuel Taggert to [John Taylor], February 8, 1807, Taggert Papers, American Antiquarian Society.

88. January 26, 1807, Plumer, *Memorandum*, p. 592.

89. Some historians have tied Randolph's antipathy to Wilkinson to the debate over the general's appointment to the governorship of the Louisiana Territory. (For example see: Malone, *Jefferson*, 5:225–26.) Randolph had criticized the appointment, but the episode is better characterized as an assault on eroding republican principles than as an

attack on Wilkinson. There was little of the venomous form which characterized Randolph's personal attacks. Even Wilkinson, who never passed up an opportunity to magnify an attack or slight, attributed the act as much to enmities to the President as to himself. (James Wilkinson to Samuel Smith, March 29, 1806, Jefferson Papers, LC; James Wilkinson to Thomas Jefferson, March 29, 1806, Jefferson Papers, LC.)

90. Samuel Smith, January 14, 1807, quoted in Plumer, *Memorandum*, p. 573.

91. John Randolph to George Hay, January 3, 1806 [sic 1807], Randolph Papers, Library of Congress. This letter contains none of the vituperation of Wilkinson that would soon characterize Randolph's response to the mere mention of his name. Note also Randolph's apparent conviction of Burr's intent (in league with the Spanish) to detach the western country from the nation.

92. January 16, 1807, *Annals*, 9th Cong., 2nd Sess., pp. 349–351.

93. January 16, 1807, *Annals*, 9th Cong., 2nd Sess., pp. 351, 354.

94. Thomas Jefferson, Special Message, January 22, 1807, in Richardson, *Messages*, 1:400–405; John Randolph to Joseph H. Nicholson, February 5, 1807, Nicholson Papers, LC.

95. February 18, 1807, *Annals*, 9th Cong., 2nd Sess., pp. 537, 551.

96. February 19, 1807, *Annals*, 9th Cong., 2nd Sess., pp. 576, 583–85. This debate was on a Senate passed bill to suspend the right of habeas corpus during the emergency. Sloan had led a fight a year before that seemed aimed at having Randolph expelled from the House. (Malone, *Jefferson*, 5:130.)

97. Quoted in James Alston Cabell, *The Trial of Aaron Burr* (Albany, N.Y.: Argus, 1900), p. 24.

98. John Randolph to Joseph H. Nicholson, June 25, 1807, Nicholson Papers, LC.

99. John Randolph to Joseph H. Nicholson, June 28, 1807, Nicholson Papers, LC.

100. Henry Dearborn and Levi Lincoln in conversation with James Bruff, March 1807, James Bruff testimony, "Burr Trial", *American State Papers, Miscellaneous*, 1:574.

7. Mr. Jefferson's Army

1. [Philadelphia] *Aurora*, January 8, 1807.

2. Alexander Macomb to Jonathan Williams, January 8, 1807, Williams Papers, Lilly Library.

3. James Wilkinson to Henry Dearborn, January 9, 1807, Letters Received, Secretary of War, M221, NA.

4. Lieutenant William Augustus Murray, one of the officers involved, had revealed this story to Wilkinson in January. This information was partly the cause of the Judge's arrest. (James Wilkinson to Thomas Jefferson, January 18, 1807, Wilkinson, *Memoirs of My Own Times*, 2:97.) Some officers of the Marine Corps were also rumored to be involved. (James Hillhouse to Rebecca Hillhouse, January 23, 1807, Hillhouse Family Papers, Sterling Library.) When Wilkinson learned of Lieutenant Jacob Jackson's defection at Chickasaw Bluffs, he sent an officer to find and arrest him. (Daniel Hughes Deposition, January 20, 1811, Wilkinson, *Memoirs of My Own Times*, 2:appendix 70.)

5. Henry Dearborn to Thomas Jefferson, March 24, 1807, in *New American State Papers, Military Affairs, Combat Operations*, Benjamin Franklin Cooling, ed., 19 vols. (Wilmington: Scholarly Resources, 1979), 4:14–16; Thomas Jefferson to Henry Dearborn, March 29, 1807, Bergh, 11:179–80.

6. Henry Dearborn to Henry Burbeck, March 30, 1807, Dearborn Papers, Chicago

Historical Society. See also: Thomas Jefferson to Henry Dearborn, March 29, 1807, Daniel Parker Papers, Historical Society of Pennsylvania. No consolidated list of offenders has been located. Only a handful of officers were identified specifically, but indications are that a significant number were suspected. The numerous rumors reported support those suspicions.

7. Thomas Jefferson, A Proclamation, July 2, 1807, Richardson, *Messages*, 1:410–12; Thomas Digger to Thomas Jefferson, July 29, 1807, Daniel Parker Papers, Historical Society of Pennsylvania.

8. Samuel Beaumont, Jr. to Samuel Beaumont, July 26, 1807, Beaumont Papers, U.S. Army Military History Institute.

9. Thomas Jefferson to Henry Dearborn, July 7, 1807, Daniel Parker Papers, Historical Society of Pennsylvania.

10. James Wilkinson to Samuel Smith, July 18, [18]07, Wilkinson Papers, Darlington Library.

11. Thomas Jefferson to Samuel Smith, July 30, 1807, War of 1812 Manuscripts, Lilly Library.

12. Thomas Jefferson to John Taylor, August 1, 1807, Washburn Papers, Massachusetts Historical Society.

13. Thomas Jefferson to Henry Dearborn, August 9, 1807, Daniel Parker Papers, Historical Society of Pennsylvania.

14. *Aurora*, November 14, 1807. Duane expanded on these ideas in his *American Military Library* to which he appended a translation of the French drill. For a discussion of Duane's system see: chapter 4 above.

15. Militia reform was effectively killed on February 23. (*Annals*, 10th Cong., 1st Sess., p. 1676.) Jefferson called for an increase in the size of the regular force just two days later. (February 25, 1808, Richardson, *Messages*, 1:429.)

16. December 24, 1806, *Annals*, 9th Cong., 2nd Sess., pp. 209–10; January 26, 1808, *Annals*, 10th Cong., 1st Sess., pp. 1510.

17. Thomas Jefferson to John Taylor, July 21, 1816, Washburn Papers, Massachusetts Historical Society. See also: Thomas Jefferson to Edmund Pendleton, May 26, 1816, Washburn Papers, Massachusetts Historical Society.

18. Thomas Jefferson, Seventh Annual Message, October 27, 1807, in Richardson, *Messages*, 1:416–17.

19. Henry Dearborn to John Dawson, November 20, 1807, (filed with committee report of December 2, 1807). Records of the House, RF 233, NA.

20. December 10, 1807, *Annals*, 10th Cong., 1st Sess., pp. 1118, 1120. Donald R. Hickey has argued that the Federalists pursued a consistent defense policy aimed primarily at protecting the nation's coast and commerce. Defense of the interior frontiers was secondary. See: Donald R. Hickey, "Federalist Defense Policy in the Age of Jefferson, 1801–1812," *Military Affairs*, 45 (April 1981):63–70.

21. William MacRea to Jacob Kingsbury, November 22, 1807, Kingsbury Papers, Burton Collection, Detroit Public Library. See also Clarence Mulford to Jacob Kingsbury, December 7, 1807, Kingsbury Papers, Burton Collection, Detroit Public Library.

22. December 31, 1807, *Annals*, 10th Cong., 1st Sess., pp. 1257–60.

23. January 7, 1808, *Annals*, 10th Cong., 1st Sess., p. 1345. Randolph indicated this sequence in explaining how he had come to raise this issue just at this time.

24. James Wilkinson to John Randolph, December 24, 1807, *Wilkinson-Randolph Cor-*

respondence (n.p., n.d. [ca. 1808]). This six page pamphlet also contained Randolph's reply, and some of the evidence the latter had obtained concerning Wilkinson's dealings with the Spanish. The precise circumstances of its publication are unclear. (A copy of this publication resides in the rare book collection of the Library of Congress.) Wilkinson had made one other challenge only a couple of months earlier and apparently considered another. Nothing came of either. (James Wilkinson to Jonathan Williams, October 4, 9, and 27, 1807, Williams Papers, Lilly Library.)

25. John Randolph to James Wilkinson, December 25, 1807, *Wilkinson-Randolph Correspondence*.

26. Quoted in William Cabell Bruce, *John Randolph of Roanoke*, 2 vols. (New York: G. P. Putnam's Sons, 1922; Reprinted New York: Octagon Books, 1970), 1:313–15.

27. December 31, 1807, *Annals*, 10th Cong., 1st Sess., pp. 1257–68.

28. January 5, 1808, *Annals*, 10th Cong., 1st Sess., p. 1309.

29. January 11, 1808, *Annals*, 10th Cong., 1st Sess., p. 1395.

30. January 11, 1808, *Annals*, 10th Cong., 1st Sess., pp. 1398–99.

31. January 11, 1808, *Annals*, 10th Cong., 1st Sess., p. 1408.

32. January 13, 1808, *Annals*, 10th Cong., 1st Sess., p. 1438.

33. February 25, 1808, Richardson, *Messages*, 1:429.

34. February 26, 1808, *Annals*, 10th Cong, 1st Sess., pp. 1690–92. Actually Dearborn's proposals had been revealed a few days earlier to John Dawson who chaired the House committee responsible. (Henry Dearborn to John Dawson, February 18, 1808, Daniel Parker Papers, Historical Society of Pennsylvania.)

35. April 4, 1808, *Annals*, 10th Cong., 1st Sess., pp. 1903–12.

36. April 4, 1808, *Annals*, 10th Cong., 1st Sess., p. 1931.

37. April 7, 1808, *Annals*, 10th Cong., 1st Sess., p. 2061. (My emphasis.)

38. On the Federalist position see: Hickey, "Federalist Defense Policy in the Age of Jefferson."

39. Nathaniel Macon to Joseph H. Nicholson, April 6 and 11, 1808, Nicholson Papers, LC.

40. Henry Dearborn to William Eustis, May 2, 1808, Eustis Papers, LC.

41. Most letters received relating to officer appointments are missing from the Secretary of War's files, but there is ample evidence of the importance of politics in the registers which recorded their original receipt (M22), in letters in the adjutant general's files (M566), and in letters to and from Dearborn which have survived in other collections. One can only speculate about why these ltters were so systematically withdrawn. Similar letters relating to civil appointments were collected into a separate file (M418). The military appointment letters may also have been collected together, and then lost. But, it is possible that they were intentionally destroyed; Jefferson had suggested a similar course in another case. (See: Thomas Jefferson to Albert Gallatin, October 28, 1802, Gallatin Papers, New-York Historical Society.)

Jefferson certainly had no intention of passing the personal or political contents of such letters to Congress. In a letter intended for Uriah Tracy (though possibly not sent) he noted that "the Constitution has made it my duty to nominate; and has not make it my duty to lay before [Congress] the evidence or reasons wherein my nominations are founded." (Thomas Jefferson to Uriah Tracy, January 1806, Ford, 8:412. See also, Thomas Jefferson to Albert Gallatin, February 10, 1803, Ford, 8:210–11.)

42. [Matthew] Walton to [Henry Dearborn], May 1, 1808, Letters Received, Adjutant General, M566, NA.

43. Henry Dearborn to William Eustis, May 2, 1808, Eustis Papers, LC.

44. Henry Dearborn to Joseph B. Varnum, May 10, 1808, Dearborn Papers, LC. Varnum's response was received on June 22, according to the register of letters received (M22), but like most others is missing from the actual file (M221). Doane was commissioned a captain and served one year.

45. S[amuel] F. S[mith] to William S. Hamilton, May 23, 1808, Hamilton Papers, Southern Historical Collection, Wilson Library. Hamilton did receive his commission a short time thereafter.

46. Bray Brunch to Henry Dearborn, May 19, 1808, Letters Received, Adjutant General, M566, NA.

47. Thomas Jefferson to James Madison, May 31, 1808, Bergh, 12:70–71.

48. "Army Officers," *Boston Gazette,* July 14, 1808.

49. Scott, *Memoirs,* 1:25.

50. "A Cotton Planter" to Thomas Jefferson, June 5, 1808, Daniel Parker Papers, Historical Society of Pennsylvania.

51. Henry Dearborn to Joseph B. Varnum, June 12, 1808, Dearborn Papers, LC.

52. Undated [late 1802] and unsigned memorandum in Dearborn's hand, Item 42499, Jefferson Papers, LC. Dearborn seems to have counted as Republicans only those appointed by the new administration—in reality the number of Republicans was closer to 50. The number of Federalist officers reported would indicate that the memo was written in the late summer or fall of 1802. That memo showed that less progress had been made in the navy or Marine Corps. The latter contained no Republicans whatsoever. Progress in the army towards Republicanization, though better than in the other services, was short of that attained in the civilian departments, illustrating the difficulty in achieving removals in the army.

53. The one exception was the rank of major. Three captains of the old line were promoted to major in the new regiments. They account for this single anomaly.

54. William Duane to Thomas Jefferson, February 28, 1809, Jefferson Papers, LC. Duane, in this letter, was passing along information that he claimed to have received from an army officer then in the West. On the surface, Duane seems an unlikely candidate as a Wilkinson partisan, but events in the years after 1808 propelled them together.

55. Scott, *Memoirs,* 1:36. Scott was, himself, a partisan of the Hampton camp.

56. Wade Hampton to William Eustis, June 10, 1811, Eustis Papers, LC. Eustis responded with the necessary assurances. (William Eustis to Wade Hampton, July 16, 1811, Eustis Papers, LC.)

57. On the impact of this conflict in the War of 1812, see: Theodore J. Crackel, "The Battle of Queenston Heights," in Charles E. Heller and William A. Stofft, eds., *America's First Battles, 1776–1965,* (Lawrence: University Press of Kansas, 1986).

58. On the use of the military to enforce the Embargo see: Leonard W. Levy, *Jefferson and Civil Liberties* (Cambridge, Mass.: Harvard University Press, 1963).

59. Louis Martin Sears, *Jefferson and the Embargo* (New York: Octagon Books, 1978), p. 93.

60. Swift, *Memoirs,* p. 77.

61. Thomas Jefferson to Henry Dearborn, August 9, 1808, Bergh, 12:119–20.

62. Samuel Beaumont, Jr. to Samuel Beaumont, July 30, 1808, Beaumont Papers, U.S. Army Military History Institute.

63. Albert Gallatin to Henry Dearborn, August 15, 1808, Gallatin Papers, New-York Historical Society.

64. Thomas Jefferson to James Wilkinson, August 30, 1808, Bergh, 12:154–55.

65. Albert Gallatin to Thomas Jefferson, September 14, 1808, *Writings of Gallatin*, 1:413–14.

66. William Eaton to Harrison Gray Otis, July 26, 1808, Otis Papers, Massachusetts Historical Society. Eaton quotes a Wilkinson letter to him (dated July 16, 1808) in which the general revealed Jeffersons' instructions. On enlisting the new regiments see: Robert L. Nichols, *General Henry Atkinson, A Western Military Career* (Norman: University of Oklahoma Press, 1965), p. 16.

67. Henry Dearborn to Thomas Jefferson, October 24, 1808, Daniel Parker Papers, Historical Society of Pennsylvania.

68. A[lbert] G[allatin] to [Thomas Jefferson], [Oct 1808], Daniel Parker Papers, Historical Society of Pennsylvania. Jefferson noted receipt of this item on October 5, 1808.

69. Henry Dearborn to H. A. S. Dearborn, October 31, 1808, Dearborn Papers, Maine Historical Society.

70. William Beaumont to Samuel Beaumont, October 2, 1808, Beaumont Papers, U.S. Army Military History Institute.

71. William Beaumont to Samuel Beaumont, December 11, 1808, Beaumont Papers, U.S. Army Military History Institute.

72. December 30, 1808, *Annals*, 9th Cong., 2nd Sess., pp. 946–49.

73. January 27, 1809, *Annals*, 10th Cong., 2nd Sess., pp. 1192–97.

Conclusion

1. "An act to raise, for a limited time, an additional military force," April 12, 1808. By the time the bill was passed the full complement of sixteen officers (of the original twenty engineer officers and cadets) had been appointed, leaving only four openings for cadets. These added to the forty artillery cadets authorized totaled forty-four. To this number Congress added one hundred and fifty-six—one hundred cadets of infantry, twenty each of light artillery and riflemen, and sixteen of dragoons—bringing the grand total to two hundred. On Jefferson's view of the need to expand the academy see: Thomas Jefferson, March 18, 1808, Special Message, Bergh, 3:471–72; and Thomas Jefferson to Jonathan Williams, October 24, 1808, Jefferson Papers, LC.

2. Jonathan Williams, "Military Academy, 1808." Williams had hoped to expand the curriculum and faculty and model the enlarged academy after "the Royal Military College of Great Britain." (Jonathan Williams to Albert Gallatin, September 19, 1807, Williams Papers, Lilly Library.) See also: Jonathan Williams to Thomas Jefferson, March 5, 1808, Williams Papers, Lilly Library; and Marianne Williams to Jonathan Williams (husband), March 13, 1808, Williams Papers, Lilly Library.

3. Thomas Jefferson to William Duane, March 18, 1811, Bergh, 8:30.

4. Thomas Jefferson to J. B. Colvin, September 20, 1810, Bergh, 12:421–2. Jefferson had taken this same line in the immediate aftermath of the affair, see: Thomas Jefferson to W. C. C. Claiborne, February 3, 1807, Bergh, 11:147–50.

5. James Wilkinson to Samuel H. Smith, May 2, 1809, Wilkinson Papers, Darlington Library.

6. A. Y. Nicolli to William Eustis, January 31, 1811, Daniel Parker Papers, Histor-

ical Society of Pennsylvania; "Register of Cadets . . . appointed," 1819, *American State Papers, Military Affairs,* 1:840–48.

7. William Duane to William Eustis, August 2, 1809, Letters Received, Secretary of War, M221, NA; [William Duane], "Memoir on the Progress of Military Discipline," [1814], Daniel Parker Papers, Historical Society of Pennsylvania.

8. Joseph Chandler to George Peter, September 3, 1809, Z. M. Pike Papers, University of Virginia Library.

9. James Madison, *The Federalist,* "Number 10," November 24, 1787.

Bibliography

Manuscript Collections

Each of the collections listed below yielded relevant materials. Those collections searched by library staffs for the author are indicated (#).

Adams Family Papers, Massachusetts Historical Society, Boston, Mass.
Ambler-Brown Family Papers, Perkins Library, Duke University.
John Armstrong Papers, Indiana Historical Society, Indianapolis, Ind.
William King Atkinson Papers, New Hampshire Historical Society, Concord, NH.
Baldwin Family Papers, Sterling Library, Yale University.
Abraham Baldwin Papers, Sterling Library, Yale University.
Abraham Baldwin Papers, University of Georgia Library.
Joel Barlow Papers, Miscellaneous Manuscripts, Sterling Library, Yale University.
Edward Bates Papers, Virginia Historical Society, Richmond, Va.
Frederick Bates Papers, Detroit Public Library.
Frederick Bates Papers, Virginia Historical Society, Richmond, Va.
James A. Bayard Papers, New York Public Library.
Beaumont Family Papers, U. S. Army Military History Institute, Carlisle Barracks, Pennsylvania.
Daniel Bissell Papers, St. Louis Mercantile Library Association.
Borland Family Papers, Perkins Library, Duke University.

James Breckinridge Papers, Alderman Library, University of Virginia.
Breckinridge Family Papers, LC.
Brown Family Papers, Perkins Library, Duke University.
James Brown Papers, LC.
John M. Brown Papers, Sterling Library, Yale University.
Henry Burbeck Papers, New York Public Library.
Burr Family Papers, Sterling Library, Yale University.
Aaron Burr Manuscripts, LC.
Aaron Burr Papers, Alderman Library, University of Virginia.
W. W. Burrows Papers, Alderman Library, University of Virginia.
William A. Burwell Papers, LC.
George W. Campbell Papers, LC.
Peter Carr Papers, Virginia Historical Society, Richmond, Va.
Samuel B. Clark Papers, Perkins Library, Duke University.
William Clark Papers, Missouri Historical Society, St. Louis, Mo.
John Clopton Papers, Perkins Library, Duke University.
Isaac Craine Papers, Western Pennsylvania Historical Society.
John Cropper Papers, Virginia Historical Society, Richmond, Va.
David Daggert Papers, Sterling Library, Yale University.
Davis Collection, Western Pennsylvania Historical Society, Pittsburgh, Pa.
Henry Dearborn Papers, Burton Collection, Detroit Public Library.
Henry Dearborn Papers, Chicago Historical Society.
Henry Dearborn Papers, Kentucky Historical Society, Frankfort, Ky.
Henry Dearborn Papers, Library of Congress, Washington, D. C.
Henry Dearborn Papers, Maine Historical Society, Portlane, Me.
Henry Dearborn Papers, Massachusetts Historical Society, Boston, Mass.
Henry Dearborn Papers, New York Public Library.
Henry Dearborn Papers, Tennessee State Library & Archives, Nashville, Tenn.
Denny–O'Hara Papers, Western Pennsylvania Historical Society, Pittsburgh, Pa.
Draper Collection, State Historical Society of Wisconsin, Madison, Wis.
Dreer Collection, Historical Society of Pennsylvania, Philadelphia, Pa.
Seth Drew Papers, Clements Library, University of Michigan.
Durrett Collection, Regenstein Library, University of Chicago.
Theodore Dwight Papers, Alderman Library, University of Virginia.

William Eustis Papers, LC.
Federalist Letters, Alderman Library, University of Virginia.
Fogg Collection, Maine Historical Society, Augusta, Me.
Jonathan Freeman Papers, New Hampshire Historical Society.
Gaff Collection, Newberry Library, Chicago, Ill.
Albert Gallatin Papers, LC.
Albert Gallatin Papers, New-York Historical Society.
Elbridge Gerry Papers, New York Public Library.
Nicholas Gilman Papers, Library of Congress, Washington, D. C.
Governor's Official Papers, Tennessee State Library and Archives, Nashville, Tenn.
Gratz Autograph Collection, State Historical Society of Wisconsin, Madison, Wis.
Gratz Collection, Historical Society of Pennsylvania, Philadelphia, Pa.
Gregg Collection, LC.
Roger Griswold Papers, Alderman Library, University of Virginia.
Isaac Guion Papers, Southern Historical Collection, Wilson Library, University of North Carolina.
Peter Hagner Papers, Southern Historical Collection, Wilson Library, University of North Carolina.
William Hale Papers, New Hampshire Historical Society, Concord, NH.
A. B. Hamilton Papers, Historical Society of Pennsylvania, Philadelphia, Pa.
William S. Hamilton Papers, Southern Historical Collection, Wilson Library, University of North Carolina.
John Francis Hamtramck Papers, Burton Collection, Detroit Public Library.
John Francis Hamtramck Papers, Perkins Library, Duke University.
Hardin Papers, Chicago Historical Society.
William Henry Harrison Papers, Burton Collection, Detroit Public Library.
Hillhouse Family Papers, Sterling Library, Yale University.
William Hull Papers, Burton Collection, Detroit Public Library.
John W. Hunt Papers, The Filson Club, Louisville, Ky.
Andrew Jackson Papers, LC.
John George Jackson Papers, Lilly Library, Indiana University.
William Jackson Papers, Sterling Library, Yale University.
Thomas Jefferson Papers, Alderman Library, University of Virginia.
Thomas Jefferson Papers, Boston Public Library.

Thomas Jefferson Papers, Chicago Historical Society.

\# Thomas Jefferson Papers, Huntington Library, San Marino, Calif.

Thomas Jefferson Papers, LC.

Thomas Jefferson Papers, Massachusetts Historical Society, Boston, Mass.

Thomas Jefferson Papers, Missouri Historical Society, St. Louis, Mo.

Thomas Jefferson Papers, Newberry Library, Chicago, Ill.

Thomas Jefferson Papers, Virginia State Library, Richmond, Va.

Seaborn Jones, Sr. Papers, Perkins Library, Duke University.

Jacob Kingsbury Papers, Burton Collection, Detroit Public Library.

Jacob Kingsbury Papers, Chicago Historical Society.

Jacob Kingsbury Papers, LC.

Ephriam Kirby Papers, Perkins Library, Duke University.

Henry Knox Papers, Massachusetts Historical Society, Boston, Mass.

Nicholas Lafon Papers, University of Kentucky Library.

John Landon Papers, New Hampshire Historical Society, Concord, N. H.

Lenoir Family Papers, Southern Historical Collection, Wilson Library, University of North Carolina.

John Lewis Papers, The Filson Club, Louisville, Ky.

Meriwether Lewis Papers, Missouri Historical Society, St. Louis, Mo.

Robert R. Livingston Papers, LC.

Robert R. Livingston Papers, New-York Historical Society.

McBean Collection, New-York Historical Society.

James McHenry Papers, Clements Library, University of Michigan.

Thomas McKean Papers, Historical Society of Pennsylvania, Philadelphia, Pa.

Nathaniel Macon Papers, Alderman Library, University of Virginia.

James Madison Papers, LC.

Jared Mansfield Papers, U. S. Military Academy Library, West Point.

Jeremiah Mason Papers, Sterling Library, Yale University.

John Millege Papers, Perkins Library, Duke University.

Millen Collection, Indiana Historical Society, Indianapolis, Ind.

Wilson Cary Nicholas Papers, LC.

Joseph H. Nicholson Papers, LC.

Northwest Territory Collection, Indiana Historical Society, Indianapolis, Ind.

Northwest Territory Papers, Clements Library, University of Michigan.

Harrison Gray Otis Papers, Massachusetts Historical Society, Boston, Mass.

John Overton Papers, Tennessee Historical Society, Nashville, Tenn.

Daniel Parker Papers, Historical Society of Pennsylvania, Philadelphia, Pa.

Alden Partridge Papers, Norwich University Library.

Peter Family Papers, Alderman Library, University of Virginia.

Timothy Pickering Papers, Massachusetts Historical Society, Boston, Mass.

Zebulon M. Pike Papers, American Philosophical Society, Philadelphia, Pa.

Zebulon M. Pike Papers, Chicago Historical Society.

Zebulon M. Pike Papers, Western Reserve Historical Society, Cleveland, Ohio.

David Porter Papers, Clements Library, University of Michigan

Preston Family Papers, Joyes Collection, The Filson Club, Louisville, Ky.

John Randolph Papers, LC.

Rhea Family Papers, Tennessee Historical Society, Nashville, Tenn.

James Robertson Papers, Tennessee State Library & Archives, Nashville, Tenn.

Ross-Woods Papers, Western Pennsylvania Historical Society, Pittsburgh, Pa.

John Rutledge Papers, Southern Historical Collection, Wilson Library, University of North Carolina.

Isaac Shelby Papers, The Filson Club, Louisville, Ky.

Solomon Sibley Papers, Burton Collection, Detroit Public Library.

Israel Smith Papers, Manuscript Vermont State Papers, Secretary of State, State of Vermont, Montpelier, Vt.

John Smith Papers, Cincinnati Historical Society.

Samuel Smith Papers, LC.

James S. Swearingen Papers, Chicago Historical Society.

Joseph Gardner Swift Papers, U. S. Military Academy Library, West Point.

Samuel Taggert Papers, American Anitquarian Society, Worchester, Mass.

James Taylor Papers, Burton Collection, Detroit Public Library.

John Taylor (of Caroline) Papers, Alderman Library, University of Virginia.

John Taylor (of Caroline) Papers, Perkins Library, Duke University.
Tazewell Family Papers, Virginia State Library, Richmond, Va.
Torrence Papers, Cincinnati Historical Society.
Lewis Tousard Papers, Clements Library, University of Michigan.
U. S. History Manuscripts, Lilly Library, Indiana University.
Samuel C. Vance Papers, Indiana Historical Society, Indianapolis, Ind.
Benjamin Vaughn Papers, American Philosophical Society, Philadelphia, Pa.
War Department Miscellaneous Papers, Newberry Library, Chicago, Ill.
War of 1812 Manuscripts, Lilly Library, Indiana University.
War of 1812 Papers, Clements Library, University of Michigan.
Washburn Papers, Massachusetts Historical Society, Boston, Mass.
Anthony Wayne Papers, Cincinnati Historical Society.
John Whipple Papers, Burton Collection, Detroit Public Library.
Eli Whitney Papers, Sterling Library, Yale University.
James Wilkinson Papers, Alderman Library, University of Virginia.
James Wilkinson Papers, Boston Public Library.
James Wilkinson Papers, Chicago Historical Society.
James Wilkinson Papers, Darlington Library, University of Pittsburgh.
James Wilkinson Papers, The Filson Club, Louisville, Ky.
James Wilkinson Papers, Indiana Historical Society, Indianapolis, Ind.
James Wilkinson Papers, Kentucky Historical Society, Frankfort, Ky.
James Wilkinson Papers, University of Kentucky Library.
James Wilkinson Papers, Lilly Library, Indiana University.
James Wilkinson Papers, New-York Historical Society.
Jonathan Williams Papers, Lilly Library, Indiana University.
Jonathan Williams Papers, U. S. Military Academy Library, West Point.
William Writ Papers, Alderman Library, University of Virginia.

Newspapers

Albany [New York] *Register*. American Antiquarian Society, Worchester, Mass.
[Philadelphia] *Aurora*. American Philosophical Society, Philadelphia, Pa.

The [New London, Connecticut] *Bee.* LC.

[Russell's] *Boston Gazette.* LC.

[Newark] *Centinel of Freedom.* LC.

[New York] *Commercial Advertiser.* LC.

[New Haven] *Connecticut Journal.* LC.

[Philadelphia] *Gazette of the United States* [continued after 1804 as *United States Gazette*]. LC.

Georgetown [D. C.] *Centinel of Liberty.* LC.

[Boston] *Independent Chronical.* LC.

The [Lexington] *Kentucky Gazette.* LC.

The [Frankfort, Kentucky] *Palladium.* Kentucky State Library, Frankfort, Ky.

The Philadelphia Gazette. LC.

Reading [Pennsylvania] *Eagle.* Historical Society of Berks County, Reading, Pa.

Readinger [Reading, Pennsylvania] *Adler.* Historical Society of Berks County.

[Pittsburgh] *Tree of Liberty.* Carnegie Library, Pittsburgh, Pa.

The [Richmond] *Virginia Argus.* LC.

[Reading, Pennsylvania] *Weekly Advertiser.* Historical Society of Berks County.

The [Cincinnati] *Western Spy.* LC.

Public Documents

Continental Congress. *Journals of the Continental Congress, 1774–1789.* Edited by Worthington Chauncey Ford. 34 Vols. Washington: Government Printing Office, 1904–37.

U. S. Bureau of the Census. *Historical Statistics of the United States, Colonial Times to 1970.* Washington: Government Printing Office, 1975.

U. S. Congress, House. Records of the U. S. House of Representatives. Record Group 233. NA.

U. S. Congress, Senate. Records of the U. S. Senate. Record Group 46. NA.

U. S. Congress. *Annals of Congress: The Debates and Proceedings in the Congress of the United States.* 28 Vols. Washington: Gales and Seaton, 1834–54.

U. S. Congress. *American State Papers, Documents, Legislative and Exec-*

utive, of the Congress of the United States. 38 Vols. Washington: Gales and Seaton, 1832–61.

U. S. Congress. *Circular Letters of Congressmen to their Constituents 1789–1829.* Edited by Noble E. Cunningham. 3 Vols. Chapel Hill: University of North Carolina Press, 1978.

U. S. Office of the President. *A Compilation of the Messages and Papers of the Presidents.* Edited by James D. Richardson. 12 vols. Washington: Bureau of National Literature, 1911.

U. S. Department of War. Letters Sent by the Secretary of War Relating to Military Affairs. Microfilm Publication M6. NA.

U. S. Department of War. Letters Sent by the Secretary of War Relating to Indian Affairs. Microfilm Publication M15. NA.

U. S. Department of War. Registers of Letters Received by the Secretary of War. Microfilm Publication M22. NA.

U. S. Department of War. Reports to Congress from the Secretary of War, 1803–70. Microfilm Publication M220. NA.

U. S. Department of War. Letters Received by the Secretary of War. Microfilm Publication M221. NA.

U. S. Department of War. Letters Received by the Secretary of War, Unregistered Series. Microfilm Publication M222. NA.

U. S. Department of War. Miscellaneous Letters Sent by the Secretary of War. Microfilm Publication M370. NA.

U. S. Department of War. Letters Sent by the Office of the Adjutant General. Microfilm Publication M565. NA.

U. S. Department of War. Letters Received by the Office of the Adjutant General. Microfilm Publication M566. NA.

U. S. Department of War. Returns from U. S. Military Posts. Microfilm Publication M617. NA.

U. S. Department of War. General Wilkinson's Order Book. Microfilm Publication M654. NA.

U. S. Department of War. U. S. Military Academy Cadet Application Papers, 1805–1866. Microfilm Publication M688. NA.

U. S. Department of War. Registers of Letters Received by the Office of the Adjutant General. Microfilm Publication M711. NA.

U. S. Department of War. "Statement of Fortifications, Public Buildings, Military Stores, Quartermaster's Department, Manufacture of Cannon, Indian Affairs, State of the Army, and Military Bounty Lands," May 12, 1801. Jefferson Papers. LC.

U. S. Department of Navy. Letters Sent by the Secretary of the Navy to Officers. Microfilm Publication M149. NA.

Memoirs and Published Papers

Adams, John. *The Works of John Adams*. Edited by Charles Francis Adams. 10 Vols. Boston: Little, Brown, 1850–56.

Bates, Frederick. *The Life and Papers of Frederick Bates*. Edited by Thomas Maitlan Marshall. 2 Vols. St. Louis: Missouri Historical Society, 1926.

Burr, Aaron. *Memoirs of Aaron Burr*. Edited by Matthes Davis. 2 Vols. New York: Harper & Brothers, 1836.

Burr, Aaron. *Political Correspondence and Public Papers of Aaron Burr*. Edited by Mary-Jo Kline. 2 Vols. Princeton: Princeton University Press, 1983.

Duane, William. "Letters of William Duane." Edited by Worthington C. Ford. *Proceedings of the Massachusetts Historical Society*. (May–June 1906).

Gallatin, Albert. *Writings of Gallatin*. Edited by Henry Adams. 3 Vols. Philadelphia: J. B. Lippincott, 1879.

Greenwood, Ethan Allen. Manuscript diary. American Antiquarian Society, Worchester, Mass.

Hamilton, Alexander. *The Papers of Alexander Hamilton*. Edited by Harold C. Syrett. 26 Vols. New York: Columbia University Press, 1961–1975.

Hiltzheimer, Jacob. *Extracts from the Diary of Jacob Hiltzheimer of Philadelphia, 1765–1798*. Edited by Jacob Cox Parsons. Philadelphia: William F. Fell, 1893.

Jackson, Andrew. *The Papers of Andrew Jackson*. Edited by Harold D. Moser and Sharon MacPherson. 2 Vols. (to date). Knoxville: University of Tennessee Press, 1980–.

Jefferson, Thomas. *The Papers of Thomas Jefferson*. Edited by Julian P. Boyd, et al. 21 Vols. (to date). Princeton: Princeton University Press, 1950–. (Cited as Boyd.)

——. *The Writings of Thomas Jefferson*. Edited by Albert Ellery Bergh. 20 Vols. Washington, D. C.: Thomas Jefferson Memorial Association, 1907. (Cited as Bergh.)

——. *The Writings of Thomas Jefferson*. Edited by Paul Leicester Ford. 10 Vols. New York: G. P. Putnam's Sons, 1892–1899. (Cited as Ford.)

King, Rufus. *The Life and Correspondence of Rufus Kins*. Edited by Charles R. King. 6 Vols. New York: G. P. Putnam's Sons, 1900.

Lewis, Meriwether and William Clark. *Letters of the Lewis and Clark*

Expedition, with Related Documents, 1783–1854. Edited by Donald Jackson, 2nd Edition, 2 Vols. Urbana: University of Illinois Press, 1978.

Monroe, James. *The Writings of James Monroe.* Edited by Stanislas Murray. 7 Vols. New York: G. P. Putnam's Sons, 1898–1903.

New American State Papers, Military Affairs. Edited by Benjamin Franklin Cooling. 19 Vols. Wilmington: Scholarly Resources, 1979.

Pike, Zebulon Montgomery. *The Journals of Zebulon Montgomery Pike.* Edited by Donald Jackson. 2 Vols. Norman: University of Oklahoma Press, 1966.

Plumer, William. *William Plumer's Memorandum of Proceedings in the United States Senate, 1803–1807.* New York: Macmillan, 1923.

Scott, Winfield. *Memoirs of Lieut.-General Scott.* 2 Vols. New York: Sheldon, 1864.

Swift, Joseph Gardner. Manuscript memoirs. Swift Papers. United States Military Academy Library, West Point, N. Y.

Swift, Joseph Gardner. *The Memoirs of General Joseph Gardner Swift.* Privately published, 1890.

Tompkins, Daniel D. *The Public Papers of Daniel D. Tompkins, Governor of New York, 1807–1817.* Edited by Hugh Hastings. 3 Vols. New York: State of New York, 1898–1902.

Washington, George. *The Writings of George Washington.* Edited by Worthington Chauncey Ford. 14 Vols. New York: G. P. Putnam's Sons 1931–44.

Wilkinson, James. *Memoirs of My Own Times.* 3 Vols. Philadelphia: Abraham Small, 1816.

Other Contemporary Published Sources

Adams, John. *A Defense of the Constitution of Government of the United States of America.* 3d Edition, 2 Vols. Philadelphia: Budd and Bartram, 1797.

[Auction] Catalogue of the Library of the Late Col. William Duane. Philadelphia: n.p., 1836.

Duane, William. *The American Military Library.* 2 Vols. Philadelphia: William Duane, 1809.

Gillespy, Edward. *The Military Instructor.* Boston: Joshua Cushing, 1809.

Godefroy, Maximillian. *Military Reflections, on Four Modes of Defense, for the United States.* Baltimore: Joseph Robinson, 1807.

Hamersly, Thomas, H. S. *Complete Regular Army Register of the United States*. Washington, D. C.: T. H. S. Hamersly, 1880.

Heitman, Francis B. *Historical Register of the United States Army*. Washington: Government Printing Office, 1903.

Jomini, Antoine Henri. *Traité des grandes opérations militaires*. 6 Vols. Paris: Giguet et Michaud, Magimel, 1805–10; 2nd Edition, 8 Vols. Paris: Chez Magimel, 1811–1816.

Lamb, Larned. *The Militia's Guide*. Montpelier, Vt.: Samuel Goss, 1807.

Nicholas, George. *A Letter from George Nicholas of Kentucky to his Friend, in Virginia. . . .* Lexington, Ky.: John Bradford, 1798.

Winston, Samuel J. *Military Tactics*. Richmond, Va.: S. Grantland, 1808.

Secondary Sources

Abernethy, Thomas Perkins. *The Burr Conspiracy*. New York: Oxford University Press, 1954; Reprinted Gloucester, Mass.: Page Smith, 1968.

Adams, Henry. *History of the United States During the Second Administration of Thomas Jefferson*. 2 Vols. New York: Charles Scribner's Sons, 1890.

———. *The Life of Albert Gallatin*. Philadelphia: J. B. Lippincott, 1879.

Adams, Mary P. "Jefferson's Military Policy with Special Reference to the Frontier, 1805–1809." PhD Dissertation, University of Virginia, 1958.

Alexander, Holmes. *Aaron Burr, The Proud Pretender*. New York: Harper & Brothers, 1937.

Alger, John I. "Antoine Henri Jomini, A Biographical Sketch" U. S. Military Academy Library Occasional Paper No. 3 West Point: United States Military Academy, 1975.

———. *The Quest for Victory, The History of the Principles of War*. Westport, Conn.: Greenwood Press, 1982.

Ambrose, Stephen E. *Duty, Honor, County, A History of West Point*. Baltimore: Johns Hopkins University Press, 1966.

Anderson, Fred W. *A People's Army, Massachusetts Soldiers and Society in the Seven Year's War*. Chapel Hill: University of North Carolina Press, 1984.

"Army of the United States." *North American Review*. 23 (October 1826): 245–74.

Aronson, Sidney. H. *Status and Kinship in the Higher Civil Service*, Cambridge, Mass.: Harvard University Press, 1964.

Bailyn, Bernard. *The Ideological Origins of the American Revolution*. Cambridge, Mass.: Harvard University Press, 1967.

Bell, Rudolph M. *Party and Faction in American Politics, The House of Representatives, 1789–1801*. Westport, Conn.: Greenwood Press, 1973.

Beveridge, Albert J. *The Life of John Marshal*. 4 Vols. New York: Houghton Mifflin, 1919.

Billon, Frederic L. *Annals of St. Louis in its Territorial Days, From 1804 to 1821*. St. Louis: Frederic L. Billon, 1888.

Birkhimer, William E. *Historical Sketches of . . . The Artillery, United States Army*. Washington: James A. Chapman, 1884; Reprinted Westport, Conn.: Greenwood Press, 1968.

Boynton, Edward C. *History of West Point*. New York: D. Van Nostrand, 1864.

Bruce, William Cabell. *John Randolph of Roanoke*. 2 Vols. New York: G. P. Putnam's Sons, 1922; Reprinted New York: Octagon Books, 1970.

Buel, Richard, Jr. *Securing the Revolution, Ideology in American Politics, 1789–1815*. Ithaca, N. Y.: Cornell University Press, 1972.

Burrows, Edwin G. "Albert Gallatin and the Political Economy of Republicanism." PhD Dissertation, Columbia University, 1974.

Cabell, James Alston. *The Trials of Aaron Burr*. Albany, N. Y.: Argus, 1900.

Caldwell, Norman. "Civilian Personnel at the Frontier Military Post (1790–1814)." *Mid-America*. 38(1956):101–19.

——. "The Enlisted Soldier at the Frontier Post, 1790–1814." *Mid-America*. 37(1955):195–204.

——. "The Frontier Army Officer, 1794–1814." *Mid-America*. 37(1955):101–28.

Chaput, Donald. "The Early Missouri Graduates of West Point, Officers or Merchants?" *Missouri Historical Review*. 72 (April 1978): 262–70.

Colbourn, H. Trevor. *The Lamp of Experience, Whig History and the Intellectual Origins of the American Revolution*. New York: W. W. Norton, 1965.

Cooke, Jacob E. *Tench Coxe and the Early Republic*. Chapel Hill: University of North Carolina Press, 1978.

Cox, Issac Joslin. "General Wilkinson and his Later Intrigues with the Spanish." *The American Historical Review.* 19 (July 1914):794–812.

——. "The Pan-American Policy of Jefferson and Wilkinson." *Mississippi Valley Historical Review.* 1(1914):212–339.

Crackel, Theodore J. "The Battle of Queenston Heights, 13 October 1812." In *America's First Battles, 1776–1965.* Edited by Charles E. Heller and William A. Stofft. Lawrence: University of Kansas Press, 1986.

——. "The Founding of West Point: Jefferson and the Politics of Security." *Armed Forces and Society* 7 (Summer 1981):529–543.

——. "Jefferson, Politics, and the Army: An Examination of the Military Peace Establishment Act of 1802." *Journal of the Early Republic.* 2 (April 1982):21–38.

Cress, Lawrence Delbert. *Citizens in Arms, The Army and the Militia in American Society to the War of 1812.* Chapel Hill: University of North Carolina Press, 1982.

Cunliffe, Marcus. *Soldiers & Civilians, The Martial Spirit in America, 1775–1865.* Boston: Little, Brown, 1968.

Cunningham, Noble E. *The Jeffersonian Republicans, The Formation of Party Organization, 1789–1801.* Chapel Hill: University of North Carolina Press, 1957.

——. *The Jeffersonian Republicans in Power: Party Operations, 1801–1809.* Chapel Hill: University of North Carolina Press, 1963.

——. *The Process of Government under Jefferson.* Princeton: Princeton University Press, 1978.

Daniels, George H. *American Science in the Age of Jackson* New York: Columbia University Press, 1968.

Daniels, Jonathan. *Ordeal of Ambition, Jefferson, Hamilton, Burr.* New York: Doubleday, 1970.

Dauer, Manning J. *The Adams Federalists.* Baltimore: Johns Hopkins University Press, 1953.

Davis, Mrs. Elvert M. "By Invitation of Mrs. Wilkinson: An Incident of Life at Fort Fayette." *Western Pennsylvania Historical Magazine.* 13 (July 1930):145–81.

Davis, William Hart. *The Fries Rebellion, 1798–99.* Doylestown, Pa.: Doylestown Publishing, 1899.

Dawidoff, Robert. *The Education of John Randolph.* New York: W. W. Norton, 1979.

DeConde, Alexander. *The Quasi-War, The Politics and Diplomacy of the Undeclared War with France, 1791–1801.* New York: Charles Scribner's Sons, 1966.

——. *This Affair of Louisiana.* New York: Charles Scribner's Sons, 1976.

Denton, Edgar, III. "The Formative Years of the United States Military Academy, 1775–1833." PhD Dissertation, Syracuse University, 1964.

De Pauw, Linda Grant. "Women in Combat, The Revolutionary War Experience." *Armed Forces and Society.* 7 (Winter 1981):209–25.

Driver, Carl S. *John Sevier, Pioneer of the Old Southwest.* Chapel Hill: University of North Carolina Press, 1932.

Dudley, Charlotte W. "Jared Mansfield: United States Surveyor General." *Ohio History.* 85 (Summer 1976):231–46.

Ellis, Richard E. *The Jeffersonian Crisis: Courts and Politics in the Young Republic.* New York: W. W. Norton, 1974.

Erney, Richard A. *The Public Life of Henry Dearborn.* New York: Arno Press, 1979.

Ferling, John E. *A Wilderness of Miseries, War and Warriors in Early America.* Westport, Conn.: Greenwood Press, 1980.

Fleming, Thomas J. *West Point, the Men and Times of the United States Military Academy.* New York: William Morrow, 1969.

Forman, Sidney. "The First School of Engineering." *The Military Engineer.* 44(March–April 1952):109–12.

——. "Why the United States Military Academy was Established in 1802." *Military Affairs.* 29(Spring 1965):16–28.

Gains, William H., Jr. "The Forgotten Army: Recruiting for a National Emergency (1799–1800)." *Virginia Magazine of History and Biography.* 56 (1948):267–79.

Gillett, Mary C. *The Army Medical Department, 1775–1818.* Washington: Government Printing Office, 1981.

Gluckman, Arcadi. *United States Muskets, Rifles and Carbines.* Buffalo, N. Y.: Otto Ulbrich, 1948.

Goode, G. Brown. "The Origin of the National Scientific and Educational Institutions of the United States." *Annual Report of the American Historical Association for the Year 1889.* Washington: Government Printing House, 1890.

Gordon, Martin K. " Congress and the District of Columbia: The Military Impact on Federal Control." *Capitol Studies.* 6 (Fall 1978):39–53.

Green, Constance McL. *Eli Whitney and the Birth of American Technology.* Boston: Little, Brown, 1956.

Hall, Robert H. "Early Discipline at the United States Military Academy." *Journal of the Military Service Institute of the United States.* 2 (1882):448–74.

Hassler, Warren W., Jr. *With Shield and Sword, American Military Affairs, Colonial Times to the Present.* Ames: Iowa State University Press, 1982.

Hickey, Donald R. "Andrew Jackson and the Army Haircut: Individual Rights. Vs. Military Discipline." *Tennessee Historical Quarterly.* 35 (Winter 1976):365–75.

———. "Federalist Defense Policy in the Age of Jefferson, 1801–1812." *Military Affairs.* 45 (April 1981):63–70.

———. "The United States Army Versus Long Hair: The Trials of Colonel Thomas Butler, 1801–1805." *The Pennsylvania Magazine of History and Biography.* (October 1977):462–74.

Higginbotham, Sanford W. *The Keystone in the Democratic Arch: Pennsylvania Politics, 1800–1816.* Harrisburg: Pennsylvania Historical and Museum Commission, 1952.

Hill, Forest Garrett. *Roads, Rails and Waterways, The Army Engineers and Early Transportation.* Norman: University of Oklahoma Press, 1957.

Hofstadter, Richard. *The American Political Tradition and the Men Who Made It.* New York: Alfred A. Knopf, 1948; Reprinted New York: Vintage Books, 1974.

———. *The Idea of a Party System, The Rise of Legitimate Opposition in the United States, 1780–1840.* Berkeley: University of California Press, 1969.

Holabird, S. B. "Army Clothing." *Journal of the Military Service Institute of the United States.* 2 (1882): 356–87.

Howard, Michael. *War In European History.* New York: Oxford University Press, 1976.

Hunt, Gaillard. "Office-Seeking During Jefferson's Administration." *The American Historical Review.* 3 (January 1898):270–91.

Jackson, Donald "Jefferson, Meriwether Lewis, and the Reduction of the United States Army." *Proceedings of the American Philosophical Society.* 124 (April 1980): 91–96.

———. *Thomas Jefferson & the Stony Mountains.* Urbana: University of Illinois Press, 1981.

Jacobs, James Ripley. *The Beginning of the U. S. Army, 1783–1812*. Princeton: Princeton University Press, 1947.

——. *Tarnished Warrior, Major General James Wilkinson*. New York: Macmillan, 1938.

Kerber, Linda K. *Federalists in Dissent, Imagery and Ideology in Jeffersonian America*. Ithaca, N. Y.: Cornell University Press, 1970.

Kershner, James William. "Sylvanus Thayer: A Biography." PhD Dissertation, West Virginia University, 1976.

Koch, Adrienne. *Jefferson and Madison, The Great Collaboration*. New York: Alfred A. Knopf, 1950; Reprinted Gloucester, Mass.: Peter Smith, 1970.

Kohn, Richard H. *Eagle and Sword, the Federalists and the Creation of the Military Establishment in America, 1783–1802*. New York: Free Press, 1975.

Levy, Leonard W. *Jefferson and Civil Liberties, The Darker Side*. Cambridge, Mass.: Harvard University Press, 1963; Reprinted New York: Quadrangle, 1973.

Lewis, Berkeley R. *Small Arms and Ammunition in the United States Service*. Smithsonian Miscellaneous Collections, Vol 129. Washington, D. C.: Smithsonian, 1959.

Lewis, John D., ed. *Anti-Federalists versus Federalists, Selected Documents*. San Francisco: Chandler, 1967.

Lipset, Seymour Martin. *The First New Nation*. New York: Basic Books, 1963.

Lomask, Milton. *Aaron Burr*. 2 Vols. New York: Farrar, Straus, Giroux, 1979–82.

McCaleb, Walter Flavius. *The Aaron Burr Conspiracy*. New York: Argosy-Antiquarian Press, 1966.

McDonald, Forrest. *The Presidency of Thomas Jefferson*. Lawrence: University of Kansas Press, 1976.

Mahon, John. *The American Militia: Decade of Decision, 1789–1800*. University of Florida Monographs, Social Sciences, VI. Gainsville: University of Florida Press, 1960.

Malone, Dumas. *Jefferson and His Time*. 6 Vols. Boston: Little, Brown, 1948–81.

Martin, James Kirby. *Men in Rebellion, Higher Governmental Leaders and the Coming of the American Revolution*. New York: Free Press, 1973.

Martin, James Kirby and Mark Edward Lender, *A Respectable Army: The Military Origins of the Republic, 1763–1789*. Arlington Heights, Ill.: Harlan Davison, 1982.

May, Henry F. *The Enlightenment in America*. New York: Oxford University Press, 1976.

Millis, Walter. *Arms and Men, A Study of American Military History*. New York: New American Library, 1956.

Morison, Samuel Eliot. *Harrison Gray Otis, 1765–1848, The Urbane Federalist*. Boston: Houghton Mifflin, 1969.

Murphy, William J., Jr. "John Adams: The Politics of the Additional Army, 1798–1800." *The New England Quarterly*. 52(June 1979): 234–49.

Nelson, Paul David. *Anthony Wayne: Soldier of the Early Republic*. Bloomington: Indiana University Press, 1985.

Ness, George T., Jr. "Missouri at West Point, Her Graduates Through The Civil War Years." *Missouri Historical Review*. 38(January 1944):162–69.

Nichols, Roger L. *General Henry Atkinson, A Western Military Career*. Norman: University of Oklahoma Press, 1965.

Parmet, Herbert S. and Marie B. Hecht. *Aaron Burr; Portrait of an Ambitious Man*. New York: Macmillan, 1967.

Pierce, Edward Lillie. *[The Life of] Major John Lillie, 1755–1801 [and] The Lillie Family of Boston, 1663–1896*. Cambridge, Mass.: John Wilson and Son, University Press, 1896.

Prince, Carl E. "The Passing of the Aristocracy: Jefferson's Removal of the Federalists, 1801–1805." *Journal of American History*. 57(December 1970):563–75.

Prucha, Paul *The Sword of the Republic: The U. S. Army on the Frontier, 1783–1846*. New York: Macmillan, 1969.

Riedler, A. "American Technological Schools." In *Report of the Commissioner of Education*, No. 1, Part 5, Vol. 5, [1892–93]. House Executive Documents [1893–94], 53rd Cong., 2nd Sess., Vol. 18, pp. 657–86.

Risch, Erna. *Quartermaster Support of the Army: A History of the Corps, 1775–1939*. Washington: Government Printing Office, 1962.

Risjord, Norman K. *The Old Republicans, Southern Conservatism in the Age of Jefferson*. New York: Columbia University Press, 1965.

Robertson, James Alexander. *Louisiana Under Spain, France and the United States*. 2 Vols. Cleveland: Arthur H. Clark, 1911.

Robson, David W. *Educating Republicans: The College in the Era of the American Revolution, 1750–1800*. Westport, Conn.: Greenwood Press, 1985.

Rossiter, Clinton. *The American Quest, 1790–1860: An Emerging Nation in Search of Identity, Unity, and Modernity.* New York: Harcourt Brace Jovanovich, 1971.

Royster, Charles. *A Revolutionary People at War, The Continental Army and American Character, 1775–1783.* Chapel Hill: University of North Carolina Press, 1979.

Safford, William H. *The Life of Harman Blennerhassett.* Cincinnati: Moore, Anderson, Wilstach & Keys, 1853.

Schwoerer, Lois G. *"No Standing Armies!": The Antiarmy Ideology in Seventeenth-Century England.* Baltimore: Johns Hopkins University Press, 1974.

Sears, Louis Martin. *Jefferson and the Embargo.* Durham, N. C.: Duke University Press, 1927; Reprinted New York: Octagon Books, 1978.

Shalhope, Robert E. "Republicanism and Early American Historiography." *William and Mary Quarterly,* 3d Series. 39 (April 1982):334–56.

Sheehan, Bernard W. *Seeds of Extinction: Jeffersonian Philanthropy and the American Indian.* Chapel Hill: University of North Carolina Press, 1973.

Shoemaker, Floyd C. "The Louisiana Purchase, 1803, and the Transfer of Upper Louisiana to the United States, 1804." *Missouri Historical Review.* 48(October 1953):1–22.

Shy, John. "Jomini." In *Makers of Modern Strategy from Machiavelli to the Nuclear Age.* Edited by Peter Paret. Princeton: Princeton University Press, 1986.

Sisson, Daniel. *The American Revolution of 1800.* New York: Alfred A. Knopf, 1974.

Skelton, William B. "Officers and Politicians: The Origins of Army Politics in the United States Before the Civil War." *Armed Forces and Society.* 6(Fall 1979):22–48.

Slaughter, Thomas P. "The Tax Man Cometh: Ideological Opposition of Internal Taxes, 1760–1790." *William and Mary Quarterly,* 3d Series. 41(October 1984):566–91.

Smelser, Marshall. *The Democratic Republic, 1801–1815.* New York: Harper Torchbooks, 1968.

Smith, James Morton. *Freedom's Fetters.* Ithaca, N. Y.: Cornell University Press, 1956.

Sowerby, E. Millicent. *Catalogue of the Library of Thomas Jefferson.* 5 Vols. Washington: Library of Congress, 1952–59.

Spivak, Burton. *Jefferson's English Crisis, Commerce, Embargo, and the Republican Revolution.* Charlottesville: University Press of Virginia, 1979.

Stagg, J. C. A. *Mr. Madison's War, Politics, Diplomacy, and Warfare in the Early American Republic, 1783–1830.* Princeton: Princeton University Press, 1983.

Stewart, Donald H. *The Opposition Press of the Federalist Period.* Albany: State University of New York Press, 1969.

Stuart, Reginald C. *The Half-Way Pacifist: Thomas Jefferson's View of War.* Toronto: University of Toronto Press, 1978.

———. *War and American Thought, From the Revolution to the Monroe Doctrine.* Kent, Ohio: Kent State University Press, 1982.

Tillman, S. E. "Academic History of the Military Academy." In *The Centennial of the United States Military Academy at West Point, New York.* 2 Vols. Washington: Government Printing Office, 1904; Reprinted Westport, Conn.: Greenwood Press, 1969.

Tinkcom, Harry Marlin. *The Republicans and Federalists in Pennsylvania, 1790–1801.* Harrisburg, Pa.: Pennsylvania Historical and Museum Commission, 1950.

Wade, Arthur P. "Artillerists and Engineers, The Beginnings of Seacoast Fortifications, 1794–1815." PhD Dissertation, Kansas State University, 1977.

———. "A Military Offspring of the American Philosophical Society." *Military Affairs.* 38 (September 1974):103–11.

Wandell, Samuel H. and Meade Minniegerode. *Aaron Burr.* 2 Vols. New York: G. P. Putnam's Sons, 1925.

Weigley, Russell F. *History of the United States Army.* New York: Macmillan, 1967.

———. *Towards an American Army: Military Thought from Washington to Marshall.* New York: Columbia University Press, 1962.

Wensorski, John Frederick. "A Wilkinson Conspiracy." *The Oklahoma State Historical Society Review.* 4(Spring 1983):35–44.

White, Howard. *Executive Influence in Determining Military Policy in the United States.* University of Illinois Studies in the Social Sciences, XII. Urbana: University of Illinois Press, 1924.

White, Leonard D. *The Jeffersonians: A Study in Administrative History, 1801–1829.* New York: Macmillan, 1951.

Wilkinson, Norman B. "The Forgotten Founder' of West Point." *Military Affairs.* 24(Winter 1960–61):177–88.

Wish, Harvey. "The French of Old Missouri (1804–1821): A Study in Assimilation." *Mid-America.* 23(July 1941):167–89.

Zuersher, Dorothy J. S. "Benjamin Franklin, Jonathan Williams and the United States Military Academy." PhD Dissertation, University of North Carolina at Greensboro, 1974.

Index

Abernethy, Thomas P., 115–16
Abrahams, Abraham D., 76
Adair, John, 129, 151
Adams, Henry, 2
Adams, John, 22, 23, 25, 30, 31, 32, 33,
  39, 44, 51, 58, 73, 80, 121; efforts to
  create a military academy, 56–57, 59,
  64, 69
Adams, Mary P., 2, 98–99
Adlum, John, 26
Alexander, James, 151, 152
Alien and Sedition Acts, 12
Alston, Joseph, 214n22
Ambrose, Stephen E., 59
American Military Library, 83, 85
Anti-army sentiment, among republicans,
  2, 32; extent of called into question, 2;
  in colonial era, 3; in press, 27–28; and
  Elbridge Gerry, 186
Army, Republican fears of partisan political force in 1798–1799, 13, 19, 34–35;
  used in Fries's Rebellion, 22–23; Federalist concerns of partisan political force
  in 1808–1809, 178–79; *expansion of*: in
  1798–1799, 1; under new Constitution,
  3; in 1790–1791, 4; in 1792, 9; Republican opposition to, 17, 18; Hamiltonian
  plans, 18; in 1897, 18; in 1808 as an
element in Republicanization, 15, 160,
  170–73; *reduction of*: rumors of in 1801,
  39; in 1802, 15, 43–45. *See also* Regular
  military establishment; Standing army
Army officers, opposition to Jefferson, 14;
  concern about loyalty to Jefferson's administration, 122, 123, 137, 220n6;
  complicity in Burr affair, 158–60; numbers appointed by Jefferson, 173–75
Army staff, 45–46; political reform of in
  1802, 46–48, 53
Arroyo Hondo, 136
Articles of Confederation, 4
Articles of War, Rules and, of 1776, 43,
  85, 87; efforts to revise in 1804–1806,
  85–87; of 1806, 87
Attakapas (Louisiana), 106

Baldwin, Abraham, 32, 66–67
Baron, George, 58, 63, 64, 66
Barron, William Amhurst, 56, 58, 69, 70
Bayard, James A., 29, 42
Bayou Pierre (Louisiana), 125, 145
Bayou Pierre (Mississippi), 148
Bell, Rudolph M., 188n41
Bissell, Daniel, 148
Blennerhasset, Harmon, 147, 148, 151
Bollman, Erich, 151, 152

Bouis, Pascal Vincent, 110
Breckinridge, John, 108
Browne, Joseph, 114
Bruff, James, 142, 215*n*25
Buel, Richard, Jr., 188*n*41
Buell, John H., 47
Burbeck, Henry, 79, 119
Burling, Walter, 136, 149
Burr, Aaron, 15; and James Wilkinson, 113–16; and conspiracy, 131–35, 137–38, 142–52; sympathizers in New Orleans, 134, 136, 137; trial in Richmond, 152–56; authorship of cipher text, 214*n*22
Burrows, William, 74, 95, 96, 217*n*58
Butler, Edward, 119–20
Butler, Thomas, 86, 104, 113, 120, 122, 123, 141, 142, 174; conflict with James Wilkinson, 116–20

Chesapeake, U.S.S., 83, 160, 161, 162, 163
Chickasaw Bluffs, 76, 95, 100, 102, 146, 148, 219*n*4
Chouteau, Auguste P., 109
Chouteau, Jean Pierre, 111
Citizen-soldier myth, 5, 6
Claiborne, William C. C., 103, 104, 106, 107, 128, 137, 138, 144, 145
Clark, Daniel, 114, 115
Clark, William, 110, 112, 122
Clopton, John, 169
Coastal fortifications, 11
Constitution, U.S., 9
Continental Line, 6, 8
Corps of Artillery, 42, 52, 119
Corps of Engineers, 61, 64, 69, 85
Corps of Engineers and Artillerists, 11
Coxe, Tench, 77
Cress, Lawrence Delbert, xiii, 3
Cromwell, Oliver, 18
Cushing, Thomas H., 38, 39, 46, 47, 52, 69, 80, 81, 121, 122, 126, 128, 134, 136, 141, 144

Davies, Joseph H., 139
Dayton, Jonathan, 131, 214*n*22
Dearborn, Henry, 38, 40, 47, 51, 52, 64, 69, 101, 102, 104, 106, 118; study of frontier military requirements, 11; appointed Secretary of War, 34; shaping Jefferson's Republican military establishment, 39, 43; on officer removals, 49; founding of military academy, 54, 58, 61; politics of faculty at military academy, 66–70; concern with details of affairs at military academy, 70; concern with political character of applicants for military academy, 71–73; and the administration of the War Department, 74–97; and experiments with artillery, 78–80; and the welfare of soldiers, 87–88; effort to replace whiskey with beer in liquor ration, 91; and recruiting, 93–95, 178; concerned about General Wilkinson's loyalty, 98; action to secure New Orleans, 106; and reconnaissance of routes into Mexico, 111; letter warning to Wilkinson to keep Burr at arm's length, 115, 131, 133, 134, 139; effort to commission a Republican outsider into the senior officer ranks, 120–21, 122; concern about conflict with Spain, 124, 126; learns that Wilkinson is acting against Burr conspiracy, 141; issues orders to stop Burr, 146–47; assessed extent of officer involvement with Burr, 158–60; suggests increasing regular force to 15,000 in response to Leopard-Chesapeake affair, 162; proposes enlarging army by 6,000 men, 169; seeks nomination of Republicans for commissions in enlarged army, 170–71
Decatur, Stephen, 144
De Pauw, Linda Grant, 195*n*22
De Pusy, Jean Xavier Bureaux, 56
Detroit, 100
Dexter, Samuel, 55, 56, 57, 58, 59, 64, 66
Dickinson College, 8
Doane, Isaiah, 171
Duane, William, 24, 26, 27, 138, 151, 195*n*22, 204*n*28, 222*n*54; and the study of military doctrine or discipline, 82–85, 92, 162
Du Pont de Nemours, E. J., 78
Du Portail, Louis Le Begue, 54–55

Eaton, William, 143
Elliot, James, 164
Ellis, Richard, 13, 186n11
Embargo, 176, 177, 178
Eppes, John, 179
Erney, Richard Alton, 49
Eustis, William, 85, 170, 171, 175, 182
Eventual Army, 189n1

Fallen Timbers, Battle of, 11
Federalist, The, No. 10, 6, 183
Ferling, John E., 3
Foncin, Jean, 56
Fort Adams, 76, 100, 102, 106, 126, 128, 137, 143, 146
Fort McHenry, 79
Fort Massac, 100, 113, 146, 148
Fort Ontario, 100
Fort Pickering, 95
Fort St. Philip, 106
Fort Stoddert, 100, 152
Fort Wayne, 100
Fort Wilkinson, 100
Franklin, Benjamin, 66
Freeman, Constance, 92, 107, 126, 135, 136, 144, 145, 150
French Revolution, 10, 12, 82
Fries, John, 21, 22, 25
Fries's Rebellion, 21, 23, 27, 57; use of army to suppress, 22–23

Gallatin, Albert, 11, 77, 96, 139; used army to enforce Embargo, 177–78; influence on military policy, 194n9
Gansevoort, Peter, 75, 76
Gardenier, Barent, 178
General Staff. See Army staff
Genet, Edmund, 121
Gerry, Elbridge, 4, 8–9, 18, 38, 186n14, 187n33
Giles, William Branch, 87, 119, 172
Godefroy, Maximillian, 83
Grafton, Joseph, 171
Graham, John, 141, 144, 148
Granger, Gideon, 143
Gratiot, Charles, 109

Gribeauval, Baptiste de, 79
Guion, Isaac, 47

Hamilton, Alexander, 4, 9, 19, 21, 22, 23, 26, 31, 32, 33, 45, 49, 93, 179; efforts to create a military academy, 54–55
Hammond, Samuel, 109, 121, 126, 141
Hampton, Wade, 122; anti-Wilkinson rallying point, 174–75
Harmar, Josiah, 9
Harpers Ferry, 76, 78
Heister, Joseph, 27
Herrera y Leyva, Simon de, 130
Hickey, Donald R., 220n20
Holland, James, 166
Holt, Charles, 26, 27, 28
Howard, Lewis, 26–27, 64
Hughes, Daniel, 211n64
Hunt, Seth, 109
Hunt, Thomas, 88
Hutton's, C. H., Mathematics, 60, 63, 69

Irvine, Callander, 77
Irvine, William, 77
Irving, Washington, 119

Jackson, Andrew, 113, 118, 119, 133, 138, 148
Jackson, Donald, 110, 221n45
Jackson, Jacob, 219n4
Jacobins, excesses in France, 12; influence in United States, 12, 19, 22
Jefferson, Thomas, believed in necessity of small regular establishment, 4; preferred constitutional limit to size of army, 4; objections to Society of Cincinnati, 7; on limitations of militia forces, 8, 162; view of Fries's Rebellion, 22; on raising Hamilton's New Army, 25; on disbanding Hamilton's army, 28; goal of Republican dominance in 1801, 36; concerns about loyalty of army officers, 36–37, 159–60; worked closely with Henry Dearborn on military policy, 39; State of the Union Message, 1801, 40; compares removal of officers to removal of judges, 48; quizzed officers on politics,

Jefferson, Thomas (*Continued*)
    51; founding military academy at West
    Point, 54; earlier opposition to military
    academy, 58; interests in school devoted
    to science focused on Virginia, 60; spe-
    cial relationship with Corps of Engi-
    neers, 65; politics of faculty at military
    academy, 66–70; attention to details of
    affairs at military academy, 70; concern
    for political affiliation of applicants for
    military academy, 71–73; and Republi-
    canization of the army, 73, 170–73, 180–
    81; on the importance of New Orleans,
    100; plans for an Indian territory, 108,
    109; and exploration of the West, 111,
    112; sounds alarm about Spanish actions
    in Southwest, 124; receives reports and
    warnings of Burr's activities, 138–39; is
    warned that General Wilkinson is in-
    volved with Burr, 139; considers actions
    against Burr and Wilkinson, 143–46;
    learns that Wilkinson is acting against
    Burr, 141, 146; issues proclamation ex-
    posing Burr conspiracy, 146, 147; or-
    ders British ships out of American ports
    after *Chesapeake-Leopard* affair, 161; on
    political nature of militia, 163; expected
    Dearborn to find officers of Republican
    persuasion, 170; on use of army to en-
    force Embargo, 177
Jomini, Antoine Henri, 84

Kaskaskia, 100
Kennon, Richard, 109
Kentucky and Virginia Resolves, 21
Kingsbury, Jacob, 90, 126
Kline, Mary-Jo, 113, 214*n*22, 216*n*43,
    218*n*83
Knickerbocker's *History of New York*, 119
Knox, Henry, 9
Kohn, Richard H., 185*n*4

Laussat, Pierre Clement, 106
Leopard, H.M.S., 83, 160, 161, 162, 163
Lewis, Meriwether, 108, 109, 122; made
    Jefferson's private secretary, 34; role in
    officer removals in 1802, 49, 193*n*3; and
    William Clark, expedition, 110, 112

Lilly, John, 59
Linnard, William, 76
Liquor ration, 90–91
Livingston, Robert, 36, 100, 101
Logistics, 46, 75–78, 90–91, 130, 203*n*7
Lomask, Milton, 115, 116, 146, 214*n*22
Loramier, Augustus, 109
Loramier, Louis, 110, 210*n*44
Louisiana Purchase, 100
Lyon, Matthew, 170

McHenry, James, 18, 19, 21, 26, 55, 58
McKnight, James, 30
Macomb, Alexander, 93
Macon, Nathaniel, 38, 52, 62, 166, 170
Macpherson, William, 23, 25
Madison, James, 6, 21, 182, 183
Malone, Dumas, 59
Mansfield, Jared, 66–67, 68, 70
Marines, 14, 217*n*58
Marshall, John, 152, 156
Martial law, 137
Martin, James Kirby, xiii
May, Henry F., 1
Meade, Cowles, 128, 138, 144
Meade, William C., 158
Meigs, Return, 109
Mexican Association, 150, 151, 158
Michelimacanac (Mackinac, Michigan), 100
Military Academy. *See* West Point
Military doctrine, 81–85, 96
Military Peace Establishment Act of 1802,
    38–53, 54, 65, 93, 100, 101, 173
Militia, 5, 6, 7, 8, 10, 11, 129, 138, 143,
    162, 163
Militia reform, 162–63
Militia, Uniform, Act of 1792, 10
Miller, Samuel, 171
Mobile, 76, 124
Monroe, James, 11, 101, 102, 124, 139

Nacogdoches (Texas), 124, 128, 129, 134,
    136
Napoleon Bonaparte, 32, 82, 84, 159, 203*n*7
Natchitoches (Louisiana), 106, 124, 126,
    128, 136, 137, 143
New Army, 18, 27, 44, 54, 93, 170, 189*n*1;
    disbanding in 1800, 33

New Model Army, 18
New Orleans, 79, 101; possible seizure of, 101–2; occupation after Louisiana Purchase, 102–6; security of, 106, 126; concern about Burr supporters in, 134, 136,-137
Niagara, 100
Nicholas, John, 28–29
Nicholson, Joseph, 86, 154
Nicoli, A. Y., 122
Nisbet, Charles, 8

Ogden, Peter V., 151
Old Republicans, 169, 170
Opelousas (Louisiana), 106
Otis, Harrison Gray, 19, 31, 32, 55
Ouachita (Louisiana), 106

Perkin, Joseph, 78
Peter, George, 79, 80, 111, 112, 182
Pike, Zebulon, 88, 121
Pike, Zebulon Montgomery, 26, 111, 112, 113, 121, 172
Plumer, William, 121, 152, 153
Porter, Moses, 124
Preble, Edward, 144
Presidential Army, 189n1
Prince, Carl, 13
Provisional Army, 27, 189n1
Purdy, Robert, 172

Quasi-war, 12

Rage militaire, 5, 6
Randolph, John, 30, 33, 96; ragamuffin remark, 29; his vindictiveness, 31; and James Wilkinson, 153–56, 164–68, 218n89; foreman of grand jury hearing evidence against Burr (and Wilkinson), 155–56; opposition to standing armies, 29–30, 164–70
Randolph, Martha Jefferson, 40
Recruiting, 93–95, 178, 182
Regular military establishment, inception of, 10; Federalist pressure for larger, 12; Republican fears of large, 12; social and political reformations of, 14. See also Army

Reynolds, Michael, 30
Royal Military Academy at Woolwich, 58
Royster, Charles, 5, 6, 7
Rules and Articles of War. See Articles of War
Rush, Benjamin, 202n76

Sabine river, conflict with Spain along, 124–31, 133, 145–46
St. Clair, Arthur, 9, 10, 116–17
Sedgwick, Theodore, 21
Sevier, George Washington, 158
Schaumburg, Bartholomew, 47
Scheel's, H. O. de, Treatise of Artillery, 66
Schnider, Jacob, 24, 26, 27
Scott, Winfield, 76, 142, 172
Sisson, Daniel, 188n40
Sloan, James, 155, 166
Smelser, Marshall, 2
Smilie, John, 168
Smith, Campbell, 30, 196n39
Smith, John, of Ohio, 103, 129
Smith, Robert, 115, 131, 133, 144
Smith, Samuel, 42, 119, 126, 130–31, 137, 139, 141, 153
Smith, Thomas A., 135, 141, 146
Smur, John, 34–35
Society of Cincinnati, 6, 7
Soldier's life, 89–92, 96
Southwest Point, 100, 102
Springfield Armory, 76
Standing army, opposition to, 21, 186n14
Steuben, Frederick von, 46; and his Blue Book, 81, 203n19
Stoddard, Amos, 102, 108, 109, 110, 111
Strong, Elizah, 172
Stuart, Reginald C., 188n33
Subsistence ration, 90
Sutlers, 91
Swaine, Thomas, 145
Swan, Calab, 47
Swartwout, Samuel, 131, 133, 135, 146, 151, 152
Swift, Joseph Gardner, 51, 62, 64, 69–70, 177

Taggart, Samuel, 152
Talleyrand, 17

Tallmadge, Benjamin, 179
Taylor, George, 30
Taylor, John (of South Carolina), 168, 169
Thayer, Sylvanus, 60
Tiffin, Edward, 148
Tompkins, Daniel, 177
Tousard, Lewis, 49, 58; role at West Point, 201*n*53
Traité des grandes opérations militaires, 84
Truxton, Thomas, 214*n*22
Turner, Edward D., 47, 124
Tyler, Comfort, 148, 151

Uniforms, 92, 96, 130
U.S. Army. *See* Army
U.S. Military Academy. *See* West Point

Valle, Louis, 110
Varnum, Joseph B., 40, 171, 173
Veracruz, 135
Vincennes, 76, 100

Wadsworth, Decidus, 102
War of 1812, 85, 176, 182
Washington, George, 4, 7, 18, 188*n*38; death freed Adams to act, 32
Wayne, Anthony, 10
West Point, 15, 39, 90, 109; founding of military academy at West Point, 54–73; extent of scientific curriculum, 59–60, 61
Whipple, John, 91
Whiskey Rebellion, 10, 11, 23, 57
White, Leonard D., 185*n*2
Whitney, Eli, 76
Wilkins, John, 46, 47
Wilkinson, James, 14, 15, 31, 38, 39, 40, 43, 47, 49, 55, 77, 79, 80, 92, 94, 95, 102, 103, 108, 121, 122, 123; politically acceptable to Republicans, 42; and conflict with Thomas Butler and the latter's refusal to crop his hair, 86, 116–20; and occupation of New Orleans and Louisiana, 104–6; and security of New Orleans, 106; governor of Louisiana Territory, 111; reconnaissance and expeditions into West, 110–13; and involvement with Aaron Burr, 113–16, 131–35; flaws in character, 114; and Dearborn's warning to keep Burr at arm's length, 115, 131, 133, 134, 139; sends warning of Burr's activities to Secretary of Navy Robert Smith; 115, 131, 133; and Spanish along Sabine, 126–31, 135–36; wife's death, 128, 152; complains about Secretary of War Henry Dearborn, 131; acts against the Burr conspiracy, 135–38, 150–52; prepared fictitious documents concerning Burr conspiracy to send to Jefferson, 135; in the Spanish pay, 149–50; decision to defend against Burr in New Orleans, 150; becomes the target of John Randolph's anger, 153, 164–68; conflict with Wade Hampton, 174–76
Wilkinson, James B., 95, 112–13
Williams, Jonathan, 40, 43, 59, 70, 112, 118, 152; candidate in the Adams administration to be an instructor at military academy, 56–57, 64; selected by Dearborn and Jefferson to head academy at West Point, 58, 69; as superintendent of the military academy, 60, 64–66, 70–71
Wilson, William, 64
Workman, James, 151, 158
Wright, Robert, 86

XYZ Affair, 12, 18